WORLD POPULATION

A Reference Handbook

Other Titles in ABC-CLIO's
CONTEMPORARY
WORLD ISSUES
Series

Upcoming Titles

Books in the Contemporary World Issues series address vital issues in today's society such as genetic engineering, pollution, and biodiversity. Written by professional writers, scholars, and nonacademic experts, these books are authoritative, clearly written, up-to-date, and objective. They provide a good starting point for research by high school and college students, scholars, and general readers as well as by legislators, businesspeople, activists, and others.

Each book, carefully organized and easy to use, contains an overview of the subject, a detailed chronology, biographical sketches, facts and data and/or documents and other primary-source material, a directory of organizations and agencies, annotated lists of print and nonprint resources, and an index.

Readers of books in the Contemporary World Issues series will find the information they need in order to have a better understanding of the social, political, environmental, and economic issues facing the world today.

WORLD POPULATION

A Reference Handbook

SECOND EDITION

Geoffrey Gilbert

CONTEMPORARY WORLD ISSUES

A B C ⬥ C L I O

Santa Barbara, California
Denver, Colorado
Oxford, England

Library of Congress Cataloging-in-Publication Data
World population : a reference handbook / Geoffrey Gilbert.— 2nd ed.
    p.   cm. — (Contemporary world issues)
  Includes bibliographical references and index.
    ISBN 1-85109-927-1 (hardback : alk. paper) — ISBN 1-85109-928-X (ebook)   1. Population—Handbooks, manuals, etc.   2. Population—Statistics.   3. Demography—Handbooks, manuals, etc.   I. Title.
HB871.G47 2006
304.6—dc22

                                                          2006007473
10 09 08 07 06 / 10 9 8 7 6 5 4 3 2 1

This book is also available on the World Wide Web as an eBook.
Visit abc-clio.com for details.

ABC-CLIO, Inc.
130 Cremona Drive, P.O. Box 1911
Santa Barbara, California 93116-1911

This book is printed on acid-free paper ∞.
Manufactured in the United States of America.

For Emily and Anna

Contents

ix

Preface

In the years since this handbook was first published (2001), important population trends noted but not stressed in the first edition have been confirmed beyond a doubt. World population is now growing more slowly than at any time in more than half a century, and the slowdown will continue for many years to come. Some demographers are beginning to predict the year—or at least the decade—when global numbers will reach their all-time peak before starting to decline. The United Nations says this peak will be reached around the year 2075. In addition, UN experts now see a tendency for fertility rates everywhere to move toward the level of 1.85 children per woman. This represents a significant reduction from the previous assumption of 2.1 children per woman as the global norm and bolsters the idea that an end to global population growth is now in sight.

The new emphasis on slower growth, and for some countries actual shrinkage, in population comes after decades of "population bomb" worries. For centuries it had been believed that a large and growing population was a good thing, mainly for economic reasons. Then in the 1950s and 1960s, the tide of informed opinion began running in the opposite direction: plummeting death rates and persistently high fertility rates, especially on the poorer continents, aroused deep concerns about a population "explosion." Whether it was environmentalists worried about human numbers breaching the planet's carrying capacity, economists worried about the adverse impact of rapid population increases on developing countries, or national security analysts worried about political instability arising from increased population densities, everyone shared a sense of apprehension—bordering, in some cases, on panic—about global trends in population. Right into the 1970s the doomsayers appeared to have both the facts and the weight of public opinion on their side.

By the 1980s and 1990s, however, many had come to believe that overpopulation worries were greatly exaggerated. In part, this was due to the solid arguments made by Julian Simon and other population optimists, sometimes known as *cornucopians*, who pointed to the real benefits that could result from a larger population. In part, too, it was due to the successes of the Green Revolution, which seemed to deprive the doomsayers of their most potent issue—the possibility of famine caused by too many mouths to feed. Mainly, however, it was the actual, measured, and nearly universal decline of fertility rates in the late twentieth century that shifted attention away from scenarios of population explosion to scenarios of population *implosion*. No one can yet foresee the full consequences of this development, but clearly it introduces both a new paradigm and a new set of population worries into the realm of public debate.

It seems a safe bet that population concerns will be with us for years to come and that there will therefore be a continuing need for a handbook like this one, designed to serve as a convenient one-volume reference for those who want to know more about various global population problems and issues. The simplest questions about population can be answered with data, graphs, and facts, all of which are included here. When issues are more complex, we usually need a guide to reliable sources of information. This book will provide such guidance. It can be a starting point for research on a variety of population topics, whether they be historical, environmental, or policy-oriented. One of its primary aims is to give the reader an appreciation of the *controversial* aspects of population. From the publication of Malthus's classic 1798 population essay to the more recent battles between the doomsayers, led by Paul Ehrlich, and the cornucopians, led by Julian Simon, population has been discussed in raised voices, if not shouts. That of course makes it a far livelier subject to study than if it were entirely a matter of actuarial tables and scholarly monographs!

The best way to use this book is to start with the overview of world population offered in the first chapter. This chapter defines a number of important terms and explains the basic demographic processes. Chapter 2, Problems and Controversies, examines some of the critical debates that have arisen over population and some of the current policy issues we face regarding population density, environmental impacts, depopulation, and aging. Chapter 3, Special U.S. Issues, looks into the pressures that are building on Social Security, Medicare, and Medicaid as the U.S. population gets "grayer"; asks whether the United States (and other Western countries) may lose influence in the future as the developing nations claim an ever-growing share of world population; and examines the politicization of U.S. policy on international family planning. Chapter 4, Chronology, presents some highlights of the history of world population: first census counts, plagues, famines, key breakthroughs in disease control and birth control, major commissions and publications in the field of population, conferences, landmark judicial decisions, and billion-people milestones dating back to the first billion in 1804. Chapter 5, Biographical Sketches, presents short biographies of twenty-five individuals—most still living—who have worked to advance our understanding of population, to expand the world's food supplies, or to shape population policy.

The statistical heart of the book is Chapter 6, Statistics and Graphs, which gives tables of data on world population, broken down in a variety of ways. The reader can go there for answers to factual questions such as: what is the current population of Indonesia, the birth rate in Mali, the AIDS prevalence rate in sub-Saharan Africa, the ranking of the largest cities in the world, and the projected world population in 2050? Chapter 7, Documents, presents eleven key documents relating to world population (most in the form of excerpts). These include the first two chapters of Malthus's *Essay on Population,* warnings about population trends from top scientific organizations, the program of action from the world population conference in 1994, international statements of principles on aging, and a fundamental document underpinning U.S. foreign policy regarding population.

Chapter 8, Directory of Organizations, lists important organizations that gather and publish demographic data, advocate policy in this area, or simply study certain aspects of population. The data-gathering and information-dispensing services rendered by the U.S. Census Bureau in Washington, D.C., make it a population resource second to none. Another organization in the nation's capital, the Population Reference Bureau, also merits special mention for its longstanding commitment to objective, timely research on population matters. Chapter 9, Selected Print and Nonprint Resources, offers a list of recently published or classic (and still in print) works on various aspects of population.

These are mainly monographs, but several population hand-books are also listed. The reader should be aware that the hand-books or yearbooks are periodically revised, sometimes annually. The chapter also provides reviews of over twenty videos dealing with population, all of them suitable for classroom use (though for different ages, as noted). Another key nonprint resource, one that grows in importance all the time, is the Internet; therefore, an up-to-date listing of valuable websites for the study of population rounds out the chapter. The volume as a whole is completed by a glossary of technical terms and an index of subjects and names.

I am pleased to acknowledge the support and encourage-ment of my editors at ABC-CLIO, Mildred Vasan and Dayle Dermatis. Special thanks go, as well, to the students in two courses I regularly teach at Hobart and William Smith, "Popula-tion and Society" and "Seminar on Population Issues," for the many things I have learned from them over the years, in class-room discussions, office conversations, and a steady flow of re-search papers.

Geoffrey Gilbert

1

World Population: An Overview

On October 12, 1999, history of a symbolic kind was made in the maternity ward of Sarajevo's University Clinical Center. At his birth just after midnight, a Bosnian baby was officially declared Earth's six billionth inhabitant. Much fanfare marked the occasion, including a ceremonial visit by the secretary-general of the United Nations, Kofi Annan, who smiled broadly for the cameras as he held the baby in his arms. Of course, no one could say that this particular newborn was truly No. 6 billion or that precisely the right day of the week or even the right month of the year had been picked for the momentous event. Most demographers were confident, however, that 1999 was indeed "Y6B"—the year when *Homo sapiens* solidified its standing as one of the world's most impressive biological success stories by reaching the 6 billion mark. Nor was this the end of the story. World population kept right on climbing by about 75 million per year, equivalent to the combined populations of Australia, Chile, Cambodia, Saudi Arabia, and Honduras.

Did Y6B deserve to be celebrated, like the Millennium ("Y2K") that arrived a few months later? Or would a more cautious and sober reaction to the fact of ever-increasing human numbers have been more appropriate? To be sure, a number of commentators pointed out that natural resource and environmental concerns made the planet's population growth, at best, a mixed blessing. Some of these concerns will be examined in detail in Chapters 2 and 3.

It took most of human history for population to reach the 1 billion mark, around 1800. Further increments of a billion people came much faster: 130 years, then 30 years, then 14, 13, and most recently, 12 years. The pattern of shortening intervals might easily create the impression that global population is speeding, like a runaway train, toward some sort of demographic crash, and several well-known population theorists have suggested that possibility. Fortunately, however, current trends are taking us in a much less ominous direction. Demographers at both the U.S. Census Bureau and the UN Population Division expect it will take fourteen years to get from 6 to 7 billion and the same to get from 7 to 8 billion; after that it may be eighteen to twenty-one additional years before global population reaches 9 billion. Interestingly, some experts now believe humanity will *never* reach 10 billion. The United Nations, for example, now projects that world population will top out at 9.22 billion in the year 2075 (see World Population to 2300 in Chapter 7).

Global population trends can mask considerable variation at the local or national level. In 2005, the world's population was growing at an annual rate of about 1.15 percent, but in many countries the rate was much higher, and in other countries much lower—even negative. The fastest-growing countries tend to be among the world's poorest, and they are mainly in Africa. Women in some of these countries bear six, seven, or even eight children on average. No wonder that in parts of Africa population growth is well above *twice* the global average. By contrast, some nations, mainly in Europe and East Asia, are growing so slowly that they are headed toward depopulation, or shrinking numbers. Italy is an often-cited member of this group. Its population growth has come to a halt, and as early as 2008 Italy will be *losing* people. Italy is one of many wealthy nations exhibiting a pattern of slow growth verging on outright contraction of population. One country that does not conform to this pattern is the United States, a rich country with a population that is growing at a healthy clip and expected to continue that way through the twenty-first century.

When populations grow too rapidly or too slowly, a host of policy issues are raised. Government planners, demographers, and ordinary citizens have been confronting some of these issues in recent decades, but the challenges are serious and in many cases becoming more so with every passing year. We will lay out a number of those issues in the next two chapters. To be well equipped to tackle these matters, however, the reader must acquire some basic knowledge of demographic terms and principles.

Population Growth Rates

Populations grow and decline; they rarely stand still. In a closed system—an isolated country, for example, or the world as a whole—population will increase when births outnumber deaths and shrink when deaths outnumber births. A country of 100 million that had 3 million births and 1 million deaths during the year would record a 2 percent *increase* in population. With birth and death numbers reversed, the outcome would be a grim 2 percent *decline* in population. (Migration into or out of a country complicates things, of course. Immigrants, or those moving *into* a country on a permanent basis, add to its population; emigrants, or those moving *out* of a country, reduce it.) Continued over many years, even a low rate of growth can produce large changes in population. Demographers speak of the doubling time of a population—that is, the period of time in which the population, increasing at a constant rate, will double in size.

Consider the implications of various rates of growth. At a 2 percent growth rate, as in our example above, population would double in about thirty-five years. That is how fast population is currently growing in Nicaragua and the Philippines. (Unless otherwise noted, current demographic data presented in this chapter are taken from the highly useful *International Data Base,* or *IDB,* found at the International Programs Center of the U.S. Census Bureau website.) At a growth rate of 3 percent a year, population would double even faster, in about twenty-three years. Four African nations are currently growing at a 3 percent rate: Burkina Faso, Congo (Brazzaville), Madagascar, and Niger. When growth proceeds at a 4 percent pace, population doubles in about eighteen years. It is virtually impossible to find a nation in the world today experiencing a rate of natural increase that high. The two that come closest, at 3.5 percent, are Uganda and Yemen. If growth were to continue at that rate, Uganda and Yemen would see their populations double in twenty years.

In many parts of the world, the population growth rate has dropped below 2 percent, to 1 percent, 0.5 percent, even, in a few cases, to *negative* rates. If a population were growing 1 percent a year, as is currently the case in a number of small island nations as well as Chile, Tunisia, and Albania, it would take about seventy years for it to double. In countries that have fractional growth rates, the doubling time can rise above 100 years. Canada, for example, with a current annual growth rate of 0.3 percent, would need well over 200 years to double its population. And of course countries with negative growth rates can forget about doubling times; "halving times" are more relevant to them. Ukraine, with a growth rate of *negative* 0.6 percent, could see its population cut in half in a little over a century. The halving of population would not take much longer for Russia, Bulgaria, and Latvia, with their negative 0.5 percent rates of depopulation. Obviously, these scenarios are strictly hypothetical because we know that no country will proceed for any considerable length of time at a constant annual rate of population increase or decrease.

Fertility

The population growth rates cited above are rates of natural increase (birth rate minus death rate), uncomplicated by migration. Most countries have little immigration or emigration anyway, the United States being a major exception, as will be discussed below. The birth and death rates that determine the rate of natural increase are usually given in numbers of births/deaths per thousand and are sometimes called crude birth rate and crude death rate. The crude birth rate (CBR) for the United States has recently been 14—a relatively low number compared to other countries around the world. The CBR for the Philippines is 25, for Pakistan, 30, and for Nigeria, 41. The average CBR for sub-Saharan Africa is 39. For the world as a whole, it is 20. The only region of the world with broadly lower CBRs than the United States is Europe, where, for example, the CBR for Denmark, the United Kingdom, France, and the Netherlands is 11 or 12, and for Austria, the Czech Republic, Germany, Italy, and Latvia it is 8 or 9.

The "crude" aspect of the CBR can best be shown by considering a very simple example of two countries, A and B, with populations of 1,000 each. In Country A there are 300 women of childbearing age, and 10 percent of them have babies in a given year. Thus the CBR in this country is 30. In Country B, there are only 150 women of childbearing age, yet 20 percent of them give birth in the same year. Because there are 30 births in Country B, just as in Country A, demographers will record exactly the same CBR in both countries. Yet the underlying fertility rates of the two countries are markedly different. The women of Country B have a much higher rate of childbearing, for which there may be various social, historical, religious or other reasons, and if everything else about the two countries is the same, Country B will certainly end up more populous than Country A in the future.

More refined measures of fertility than the crude birth rate are needed if we want to make meaningful comparisons between countries or regions of the world, or between different historical periods. One useful measure is the age-specific fertility rate (ASFR). Here we look at rates of childbearing by age group, for example, women aged 20–24 or women aged 25–29. The ASFR is generally given in numbers of live births per thousand women in the specified age range, usually a five-year interval. For example, the ASFR in the United States for women in the age group 20–24 was 110 in the year 1995: for every 1,000 women in that age range, there were 110 live births in 1995. Some very interesting things can be learned from a table of ASFR data such as the one for the United States presented in Table 1.1. We see some noteworthy changes in the timing and rates of childbearing between 1955 and 1995. American women dramatically reduced their overall fertility in the second half of the twentieth century. This was true for each age group, most notably for those in their early twenties. There was also a clear shift to *later* childbearing. For example, in 1955 births to women in their early thirties were less than half as numerous as to women in their early twenties; by 1995 the proportion had climbed to three-quarters.

TABLE 1.1
Live Births per 1,000 U.S. Women Ages 20–34
by Age Group, 1955–1995

Year	Ages 20–24	Ages 25–29	Ages 30–34
1955	241.6	190.2	116.0
1975	113.0	108.2	52.3
1995	109.8	112.2	82.5

Source: Haupt and Kane 1998, 15.

One other measure of fertility is considered by demographers to be the most useful single number for projecting future levels of population. This is the total fertility rate, which is often shortened to simply fertility rate or TFR. This measure is somewhat complicated to calculate and even to explain, but it is so important that we will take a moment to lay out the basic idea. No one can say, at the present time, how men and women in coming decades will approach the vital question of family size. All we have to rely on are the data collected up to the present. But if our current data are complete enough to tell us, for a particular year, the age-specific fertility rates of women in a given country, we can compute its TFR. All we do is imagine—or "synthesize"—a "typical woman" who passes through her reproductive years bearing the same number of children in each subperiod of her life (usually five-year spans) as the women *currently* in that age range are bearing. Thus, when we say that the TFR in the small southern African nation of Malawi in the year 2005 was 6.0, we mean that as of that time the average Malawian infant girl could be expected, during her adult years, to give birth to six children on the assumption that in each subperiod of her reproductive span she would bear children with the same frequency as Malawian women in those age ranges *currently* were doing.

Needless to say, Malawi's TFR of 6.0 is extremely high—among the highest in the world. This should not, however, be taken as proof that Malawian women possess a greater capacity for childbearing than women elsewhere in the world. Demographers use the term *fecundity* to describe the actual capacity to bear children. Fecundity and fertility are often confused with each other. Fertility refers to actual childbearing, whereas fecundity indicates the ability or potential to bear children. There is no evidence that the women of Botswana, another southern African nation, where the TFR is 2.9, are only half as fecund as the women of Malawi, with their TFR of 6.0. Nor is there any reason to think that women in the nations of Europe and eastern Asia that are headed toward population decline have suffered any impairment of fecundity. Reduced fertility can be explained by many factors other than reduced fecundity, as will be discussed below.

The total fertility rate is a closely watched indicator of future population trends. In a society with low child mortality rates, a TFR of about 2.1 will keep population stable—neither growing nor shrinking. Obviously, if the average woman is producing two children who survive to adulthood, the current generation can eventually be replaced by a new generation of the same size (hence the term *replacement-level fertility*). A TFR above replacement level suggests future increases in population, and a TFR below replacement level, just the opposite. On this basis, demographers are predicting that the fastest future growth in the world will occur in Africa, since the TFRs for dozens of African nations are in the range of 5 to 7. At the other extreme, Western Europe's TFR is 1.5, while Eastern Europe's is even lower at 1.35. Europeans today are not bearing enough children to replace themselves! The United States has no such problem since its TFR is 2.1 and large additional gains to population come from immigration.

Mortality

Everyone dies eventually. But in some countries and regions of the world, people on average die younger—in some cases *much* younger—than in others. One way to see this is through data on life expectancy at birth. As with the TFR, life expectancy is a hypothetical measure: it tells us how many years the average newborn could expect to live if he or she passed through life facing the same mortality rates as people currently are experiencing in each age group. Life expectancies vary widely between continents, countries, and often among different areas of the same country. For example, the life expectancy at birth for all of Africa is 52, while for North America it is 78. For all of Europe it is 75, although Northern and Western Europe have life expectancies equal to that of North America. The highest life expectancy in the world, 82, is seen in Japan (Population Reference Bureau 2005, hereafter PRB 2005).

Differences in life expectancy correlate, statistically, with a number of factors, such as occupation, education, marital status (married folks live longer), race in those countries that are multiracial, and gender. Gender matters when it comes to life expectancy: women live longer than men almost everywhere, and sometimes by a wide margin. In the former Soviet republic of Kazakhstan, for example, female life expectancy at birth is 72, whereas male life expectancy is only 61. In Russia itself the gap is even wider, with female and male life expectancies of 72 and 59, respectively. In most countries, the gender gap is less dramatic: in the United States, five years, in Japan, seven years, in China, four years. There is no measured gap at all in Uganda or Namibia. Truly anomalous are the countries where male life expectancy actually exceeds female life expectancy. There were three such countries in 2005: Kenya, Zambia, and Lesotho (PRB 2005).

Wherever life expectancies are short, one is sure to find high rates of mortality for infants and children. Consider two countries at opposite ends of the spectrum: Mali, in western Africa, and Israel, in the Middle East. In Mali, the life expectancy is 48, and the infant mortality rate (number of infant deaths annually per thousand live births) is 133. In Israel, by contrast, the life expectancy is 80, and the infant mortality rate is 5.1. It is tempting to go a step further and explain these differences in terms of per capita gross domestic product (GDP); that is, one might argue that the grim statistics for Mali as compared with Israel are fully accounted for by the fact that Israel has a per capita GDP about twenty-four times higher than that of Mali. But this would be simplistic. Economic development helps make healthier, longer lives possible, but, as Amartya Sen has shown, even some fairly "poor" nations or regions (China, Sri Lanka, the Indian state of Kerala) have achieved much more impressive life expectancies for their citizens than some "richer" nations (Brazil, Namibia, South Africa, Gabon). The more extensive public provision of health and education in the former group, Sen argues, makes a critical difference (Sen 1999, 46–49).

As noted in the previous section, rates of natural increase are calculated from crude birth and death rates. The crude death rate (CDR) is defined as the number of deaths per thousand people in a given year. In the United States, the CDR is currently 8. It may at first appear surprising that a rich nation like the United States, with clean water, high vaccination rates, and few endemic diseases, has a higher death rate than some very poor countries. For example, the Middle Eastern nation of Syria has a remarkably low CDR of 5. Since Syria is much less economically advanced than the United States—its per capita GDP is less than one-tenth that of the United States—what could explain this difference in death rates? The answer lies in the "crudeness" of the CDR, which takes no account of national age structures. If a country has a large proportion of older people, subject to heart disease, cancer, diabetes, and other debilitating conditions, then, other things being equal, it will have a higher CDR than a country with a smaller proportion of older people. Syria is a "young" nation, with two out of every five Syrians under the age of 15. The United States is not so young, with only *one* out of every five under the age of 15. On the other hand, over 12 percent of Americans are 65 or older, whereas only 3 percent of Syrians are that old (PRB 2005). The greater youthfulness of Syria's population is the main factor accounting for its lower death rate.

World Population — Past

Anthropologists believe that our species, *Homo sapiens,* made its first appearance perhaps two or three hundred thousand years ago in Africa. The population of these hunter-gatherers could never have been growing at a rapid and sustained rate, given their primitive mode of subsistence. In fact, it appears that until the agricultural revolution began, around 8000 B.C., the worldwide population of humans languished in the range of a few million. The annual growth rate of population for many millennia before 8000 B.C. was probably under 0.01 percent, with a doubling time in the range of 6,500 to 7,500 years. With the beginnings of settled agriculture, however, this situation changed. There is no expert consensus on whether faster world population growth was the *cause* or the *effect* of the practice of agriculture, but a stepped-up rate of population growth evidently began around 10,000 years ago. From then until the start of the Christian era, the annual growth rate probably accelerated gradually from 0.01 to the much higher rate of 0.15 percent. Actual yearly additions to the global population also rose, from fewer than 400 per year in 5000 B.C. to something over 300,000 per year in the era of A.D. 1. By the latter date, world population had reached a total of 200–300 million (Cohen 1995, 34–36; Livi-Bacci 2001, 31–36; Weeks 2005, 34–36).

Over the next 2,000 years, global population growth rates varied substantially from year to year, and even century to century, owing mainly to swings in the death rate. Wars, plagues, and famines all made major dents in what would otherwise have been a steadier climb in population. Particularly notable was the bubonic plague (or "Black Death") of the fourteenth century, which reduced the populations of Europe and China by one-third. It has been estimated that Europe's population did not recover to its pre-plague levels of 1340 until the mid-1500s. Between 1650 and 1850, however, various forces combined to lift world population to permanently higher levels and faster growth rates. Among these forces were the global dissemination of New World crops such as maize (Indian corn), potatoes, and manioc; the discovery and exploitation of fossil fuels; and the introduction of better hygiene and public sanitation. The combined effect of these developments was an improved level of nutrition and reduced rates of disease for many of the world's people. Mortality rates declined, particularly in the younger age range, and life expectancies rose ever higher. By 1850, population was growing faster than 0.5 percent annually, for a net gain of 6 to 7 million people per year (Cohen 1995, 42–45; Livi-Bacci 2001, 57–62; Weeks 2005, 36–37).

The largest increase of world population in history, both in percentage terms and in absolute numbers, occurred during the twentieth century. Total population rose from 1.65 billion in 1900 to over 6 billion by 2000, with the peak annual rate of increase—around 2.2 percent—occurring in the early 1960s. The doubling time fell to as little as thirty-two years, probably the shortest we will ever experience on a global basis. The century-long expansion (or, as some have called it, "explosion") of population was, once again, largely a matter of declining mortality. Science played an ever-increasing role in this development, both directly, through improvements in the prevention and treatment of disease, and indirectly, through the improved nutrition made possible by agricultural research (chemical fertilizers, pesticides, plant and animal breeding, etc.), research that in fact was well under way by the latter part of the nineteenth century. The mechanization of agriculture first seen in America and Europe also played a significant role in raising agricultural productivity and lowering the cost of food (Evans 1998, chs. 6–7; Weeks 2005, ch. 5).

By the early twentieth century, most economically advanced nations had begun to lower their fertility rates; that is, couples in those nations had begun consciously to limit family size through the practice of contraception. This behavioral shift is fundamental to the demographic transition model featured in many population textbooks and discussions. According to this model, countries normally begin in a stage characterized by high levels of mortality and fertility. Population stays constant or fluctuates within narrow limits. In the second stage, death rates move downward (for reasons mentioned above), but since birth rates remain high, population increases rapidly. In the third stage, *birth* rates also decline as contraceptive practice becomes more widespread; population growth continues but less rapidly. In the final stage, birth rates descend to levels low enough to match death rates, bringing population growth to an end at a total population much larger than had been seen before the transition. At the risk of overgeneralizing, we can say that most developed nations entered the twentieth century already in the third stage of the model, with fertility declining, and finished the century in the final stage, at (or below) replacement levels of fertility. Poorer, less developed countries, mainly in Africa, Asia, and Latin America, started the century in the first stage, got to the second stage by mid-century, and by the last few decades were passing through the stage of declining fertility. It remains unclear how many of these nations will complete their demographic transition in the twenty-first century.

World Population—Present

As we move through the first decade of the twenty-first century, world population is mounting steadily toward 7 billion, a figure that should be reached by 2013. One assertion that is sometimes made to dramatize the enormity of our current global population is that more people are alive today than have lived and died in all previous history. This is quite startling—and also completely false! One respected demographer has calculated that over the past 200,000 years, about 60 billion humans have been born. That would indicate that only about 11 percent of all the humans who have ever lived are living today (Weeks 2005, 44).

Although our present numbers are but a fraction of the total number of humans who have ever lived, we remain an almost incomprehensibly numerous species. To appreciate just how numerous, an example may be useful. Let us assume the planet has 6.5 billion people. If we could have every man, woman, and child in the world hold hands 4 feet apart from one another along a "skyway" extending from the Earth toward the Moon, the line would easily reach the lunar surface. In fact, the human chain could be stretched to the Moon and back to the Earth ten times over.

On the regional level, certain demographic indicators are fairly well correlated with economic status, as seen in Table 1.2.

The United Nations classifies all of Europe and North America, as well as Japan, Australia, and New Zealand, as "more developed" nations; all other countries are categorized as "less developed." A survey of the two groups in terms of per capita GDP would give us ample reason to call the first group "rich" and the second "poor," at least relative to each other. As we see in Table 1.2, the total population of the rich countries today is less than a quarter that of the poor ones. Although the crude death rates of the two groups are rather similar, the birth rates are *not*. The poor nations, as noted earlier, have not brought down their fertility rates to the low levels reached by the rich. Indeed, the total fertility rates of the two groups are poles apart: for the rich countries, TFR has dropped below replacement level; for the poor countries, it remains well above that level. As a result, the future populations of poorer nations will be much larger than they are today, while the richer nations will lose people. Populations of both rich and poor regions will continue to age in the future, but already the rich countries are much older than the poor with three times the relative proportion of elderly (over age sixty-four). Life expectancy is a decade longer among the more developed nations than it is among the less developed.

TABLE 1.2
Demographic Differences between
More Developed and Less Developed Nations

	More developed nations	Less developed nations
Population (millions)	1,211	5,266
Crude birthrate	11	24
Crude death rate	10	8
Natural increase	0.1%	1.5%
Total fertility rate	1.6	3.0
Life expectancy	76	65
Under age 15	17%	32%
Over age 64	15%	5%

Source: PRB 2005.

If we turn our attention to an entire continent that is considered less developed, Africa, we find that the demographic indicators take on some extreme values relative to the rest of the world. The African death rate (15) is higher than that for the less developed countries as a group (8)—partly because AIDS has struck Africa far harder than any other continent—and the African crude birth rate is also much higher (38 compared to 24). Thus the rate of natural increase for Africa is 2.3 percent. If African living standards are to improve, the growth of GDP will have to be consistently higher than 2.3 percent—a major challenge. The infant mortality rate in Africa is 88 per thousand live births, compared to 59 for the less developed countries as a group and 6 for the more developed. The African TFR of 5.1 is far above that for the less developed regions as a whole, and life expectancy is only 52. In some AIDS-ravaged countries of southern Africa, life expectancies have fallen into the 30s, an alarming development in the twenty-first century. The last demographic measure to report should come as no surprise, given several of the others: while 68 percent of women in the rich regions use some form of contraception and 58 percent in the poor regions do the same, only 28 percent of women in Africa currently use any form of birth control (PRB 2005).

World Population—Future

How large will the world's population grow in the future? It's an easy question to ask, yet no one, expert or prophet, can answer it with any certainty. In the near term, of course, we know that population will continue to grow. At present, the worldwide birth rate of 21 per thousand stands well above the death rate of 9 per thousand, yielding a 1.2 percent (or 12 per thousand) rate of natural increase. The rate of natural increase has been trending downward since the mid-1960s when it peaked at about 2.2 percent annually. By 1980, it had fallen to 1.7 percent, and by 1990, to around 1.5 percent. As long as the growth rate remains above *zero*, population will keep on growing. And as long as the total fertility rate stays as high as its current level of 2.7, the world will be on course not merely to replace its existing population but to *expand* it (PRB 2005).

When demographers make projections of future population levels, they are careful to specify that such projections are only as good as the assumptions on which they are based. At the United Nations, the Population Division issues long-term projections every two years. These are perhaps the most "official" estimates of future population available and also the most frequently cited by governments and the media. The most critical assumptions are those made about fertility rates, which tend to be more variable than mortality rates. UN demographers assume that fertility will continue to decline over the next several decades; mortality decreases will also occur but will be smaller. As Table 1.3 shows, the United Nations offers three variants of its global population projections, based on high, medium, and low future paths of fertility rates. It should be noted that all three paths, even the high-fertility variant, track fertility *downward* from current levels. Note also that the lowest fertility assumption made by the United Nations is a level well below replacement. This possibility should be taken seriously, given the fact that demographers have been consistently caught off guard by the rapid decline of fertility rates in recent decades. Most attention, however, usually centers on the medium-fertility assumption, which in the 2004 revision results in a world population of 9.1 billion by the middle of this century.

TABLE 1.3
UN World Population Projections for 2050

	Total fertility rate	World population (billions)
High-fertility variant	2.53	10.6
Medium-fertility variant	2.05	9.1
Low-fertility variant	1.56	7.6

Source: Population Division 2005, vi, 6.

UN demographers now expect five countries to contribute the most to population growth in the coming half-century: India, Pakistan, Nigeria, the Democratic Republic of Congo, and Bangladesh. India's contribution alone will be equal to the combined total of the next *four* nations. Note that none of the top five is presently considered a "more developed" nation—nor is No. 6, Uganda. Only when you reach No. 7 on the list, the United States, do you have a more developed country contributing in a major way to world population growth. China, with its current 1.4 billion people, is only eighth on the list and will not add as many people to the world's population as Ethiopia between now and 2050.

Virtually all of the net population gains of the coming half-century will come from the less developed nations. As a result, their share of the world's population will rise from 81 percent today to 86 percent in the year 2050. The richer nations, with their much smaller family sizes, will recede in demographic importance. For example, Europe and North America, which together represented 28.5 percent of world population in 1950, are projected to represent a mere 12 percent by 2050. Of course, we do not know how many nations or which nations presently categorized as less developed will cross into more-developed status in coming decades, or whether some nations may be recategorized downward from more to less developed. But UN experts studying global demographic trends are making a remarkable prediction: by the middle of the century, the more developed regions will be losing 1 million people annually, while the less developed regions will be gaining *35 million* (Population Division 2005, vi, 1).

Do we have any idea what the world's population might be in the distant future, say, 300 years from now, and is there really any point in trying to determine it? The answers coming from the United Nations Population Division are yes to both questions. These UN analysts believe that policymakers and environmental scientists, among others, may find some value in truly long-range projections of global population. Accordingly, they produced such projections for the first time in 2004 (see World Population in 2300 in Chapter 7). As is true of all such exercises, the results depend entirely on the assumptions made. In this case, the key assumptions are (1) that life expectancies will continue to rise without limit and (2) that fertility rates around the world will continue to fall for many decades, eventually recovering to replacement levels everywhere. No catastrophic events— collisions with asteroids, global military conflicts, uncontrollable epidemics, or devastating climatic changes—are incorporated into this demographic exercise. The medium-fertility projection for world population in 2300 turns out to be very close to what the United Nations anticipates for 2050, that is, 9.0 billion as compared to 9.1 billion. But if fertility were lower by 0.2 children, total population would end up a mere 2.3 billion. If it were higher by 0.3 children, total population would reach the almost unthinkable *36.4 billion* (Population Division 2004a, 2005).

In a future measured by decades rather than centuries, one of the most troubling factors affecting population is AIDS. This twentieth-century plague now carried into the twenty-first century has already claimed millions of lives and will certainly claim many more. How substantial will the AIDS effect be on world population? Experts say the largest impact will continue to be felt in sub-Saharan Africa, which has far and away the highest HIV prevalence rate of any region in the world. Of the roughly 39 million persons living with HIV/AIDS worldwide in 2004, over 25 million were in sub-Saharan Africa. The most seriously affected countries, with adult prevalence rates of 20 percent or more, were Swaziland, Botswana, Lesotho, Zimbabwe, South Africa, and Namibia, all in southern Africa. All of these countries and a number of others in the region will experience slower population growth for the next several decades as a result of AIDS (UNAIDS 2004, 191).

One of the grim demographic results of AIDS has been lower life expectancies in some countries. Until the mid-1990s, most African nations, like the rest of the world, were experiencing a rising trend in life expectancy, but AIDS cut short and in some cases reversed that trend. Between 1990 and 2002, according to UN data, thirteen sub-Saharan African countries suffered severe declines in life expectancies. In seven of those countries, life expectancy fell below 40 years. The worst case of all was Zimbabwe, which saw its life expectancy drop from 56.6 to 33.9 years, making lives briefer in that country, statistically speaking, than they were 250 years ago in England and Sweden (Livi Bacci 2000, 135). Given the high fertility rates in most of these countries, it remains unclear whether there will be any absolute population *declines* because of the disease. Experts foresee declines in Botswana, Lesotho, Namibia, and Swaziland between now and 2050 but acknowledge that there is considerable uncertainty about population developments in Africa. Much depends on what governments there do with AIDS awareness programs and what donor countries offer in the way of technical and financial assistance (United Nations Development Program 2004; PRB 2005; Dugger 2004).

Migration

So far, we have sidestepped the topic of migration. Migratory flows have no direct impact on *total* world population because one country's loss is another's gain. If migration involves movement within a country, that country's total population is likewise unaffected. Migration does redistribute some people across national borders, however, thereby affecting population growth

rates in the sending and receiving countries just as surely as fertility and mortality do. Demographers use a "balancing equation" to make all of this clear: for any individual country, births
minus deaths, plus immigrants minus emigrants, or (B - D) + (I -
E), equals the yearly change in population. Using the United
States as an example, we find that the respective numbers from
July 1, 2001, to July 1, 2002, in millions, were: (4.0 - 2.4) + (1.7 -
0.2) = 3.1. Thus population change for the year was a positive 3.1
million. Note that the natural increase of births minus deaths accounted for a little over half the overall population gain. Net immigration, legal and illegal, provided the rest (McFalls 2003, 20).

There are roughly 190 million migrants in the world today
(mid-2005), representing about 2.9 percent of the global population. For almost half a century, the level of international migration has been on the increase. It has grown decade by decade
since 1960. Because people normally migrate for economic reasons, the direction of migration has tended to be from less developed to more developed regions, where higher incomes may be
earned—at least in theory. A secondary but sadly frequent motivation for migrating is to seek asylum or refuge, and this also
tends to take people from less developed to more developed regions. The rate of migration into richer areas for the last fifteen to
twenty years has been so heavy, and birth rates have fallen so
low in these areas, that the more developed regions have experienced a remarkably swift turnaround in the sources of population growth. In 1960, these regions got most of their population
growth from natural increase, not immigration; today the reverse
is true. Indeed, Europe, where more international migrants have
settled than anywhere else, would have experienced a net population *loss* in 1995–2000 had it not been for immigration (IOM
2005, 13; DESA 2004, viii–x).

Although the greatest number of global migrants has settled
in Europe, at least for now, migrants have had their largest *proportional* impact in Oceania, where in Australia and New Zealand
they represented over 20 percent of the population in the year
2000. Comparable figures for Canada and the United States in
2000 were 19 percent and just over 12 percent, respectively. Migrants are becoming more diversified in terms of destination: the
number of countries where immigrants are over 10 percent of the
population has risen from 43 in 1960 to 70 at the start of this
decade. Distances traveled by migrants are getting shorter on average than they were 100 years ago. At that time, the heaviest

flow of migration was from Europe across oceans to either North America or Oceania. More recently, the largest numbers of migrants have been moving from Latin America to North America; from North Africa and Eastern Europe to Western Europe; and from former republics of the USSR back to the central Russian state (DESA 2004, vii–viii).

The United States remains, year in and year out, the world's highest-volume destination for migrants. When considering the total number of immigrants received over the past one, three, or five decades—or even the past 200 years—no country comes close to the United States. The immigrant flow of the 1990s, legal and illegal, was in the range of 1 million per year, and the number is undoubtedly higher now. High rates of immigration are expected to continue. Most immigrants today are admitted on the basis of family ties to U.S. residents—a preference system that dates back to 1965. This system has changed the regional origin of immigrants from mainly European to mainly Latin American and Asian. Because of the changing immigrant pattern, by 2050 Hispanics are projected to represent 24 percent of U.S. population, and Asians 8 percent, compared with 11 and 4 percent, respectively, in 2000 (Martin and Midgley 1999, 23). Without immigration, the United States would much more closely resemble the other more developed nations in its TFR and population growth rate, with total population likely to stabilize much earlier.

Urbanization

As the world grows more populous, it also grows more urbanized. One underlying reason is that as agriculture becomes more intensive and productive, demand for labor in rural areas declines. Worsening job prospects loosen people's ties to the countryside. At the same time, the economic opportunities that cities are perceived to offer exert a "pull" on rural populations. Different countries define "urban" in different ways, but according to one common criterion, populations living in towns of at least 2,000 are considered to be urban. (In the United States, the cutoff line is 2,500.) The extent of urbanization varies considerably from nation to nation. At one extreme is the 100 percent urbanization of certain small nations such as Guadeloupe, Monaco, and Singapore. Australia and Uruguay, with above 90 percent urbanization, and Argentina, United Kingdom, Libya, Saudi Arabia, Germany, and Lebanon, in the 85–90 percent range, would also have to be considered highly urbanized. At the other extreme is a handful of nations with less than 15 percent urbanization: Burundi, Malawi, Nepal, and Uganda. The two population giants, China and India, appear to be urbanizing at different rates: China, with surging internal migration toward coastal cities, has already reached 37 percent urbanization, whereas India is holding steady at 28 percent. Not surprisingly, Africa and Asia are the least urbanized continents, while North America, South America, and Europe are the most urbanized (PRB 2005).

Although cities have existed for many centuries, the *urban transition* that is redistributing so much of the world's population from rural to urban areas is relatively recent. In 1950, the world's three largest cities, New York, London, and Tokyo, had a combined population of about 28 million. By 2005, the three largest cities—now Tokyo, São Paulo, and Mexico City—numbered about 65 million. In the late 1990s, about 45 percent of the world's people lived in urban places. This figure continues its steady climb; by one estimate, the world should be more than half urban by 2007 and over 60 percent urban by 2030 (Population Division 2004c). According to UN demographers, the major part of global population growth during the next few decades will occur in urban areas of less developed countries. The more developed regions will see urbanization rise from 74 to 82 percent between 2003 and 2030, while urbanization of less developed regions will increase from 42 to 57 percent (Weeks 2005, 471; Population Division 2004c).

The effects of the continuing global trend toward urbanization have been both good and bad. On the positive side, urban residents achieve higher levels of health and education; they also have smaller families. (The so-called urban transition seems to be an integral part of the demographic transition discussed earlier.) The economic well-being of urban dwellers often exceeds that of the rural population. On the other hand, living conditions in many Third World cities are appalling, in part because the rapidity of urban growth has made it impossible for governments to provide an adequate infrastructure of streets, schools, housing, hospitals, and sanitation. A broader concern, and one that relates to both developed and developing nations, is that urban growth (or "sprawl") is encroaching ever more deeply on lands needed for agriculture or valued for natural habitat.

Carrying Capacity

Is there an upper limit to the population of humans that the Earth can sustain? Joel Cohen presents an exhaustive analysis of this question in his 1995 book *How Many People Can the Earth Support?* One might wonder why Cohen needs over 500 pages to answer such a simple question, but in fact the question is not simple at all. There are many possible constraints on population: ecological, biological, social, and technological. There are also many ways to define *carrying capacity* because there are many different views of what constitutes an acceptable standard of living for human beings. If everyone must live at the U.S. standard of consumption, global carrying capacity will be lower than if everyone is living at, say, the Bolivian standard, or the Ethiopian standard.

Estimates of global carrying capacity have ranged from less than 1 billion to more than 1 trillion (or 1,000 billion)! The earliest estimate cited by Cohen, that of the Dutch scientist Anton van Leeuwenhoek in 1679, is 13.4 billion people. The four most recent estimates, all from 1994, vary between 3 and 44 billion people. Before we despair of such wild diversity of opinion on carrying capacity, it is worth pointing out that the majority of the over sixty separate estimates gathered by Cohen cluster in a much narrower range, between 7.7 and 12 billion. This raises some concern for Cohen, who notes that the planet's current population has "entered the zone" that the majority of scholars believe represents the sustainable upper limit. As he puts it, "the possibility must be considered seriously that the number of people on earth has reached, or will reach within half a century, the maximum number the Earth can support" at an acceptable living standard (Cohen 1995, 367). When one considers the ongoing trend toward urbanization and the view of one expert that "cities tend to grow on the best agricultural land" (Evans 1998, 201), the level of concern about carrying capacity is raised even higher. Still, there is at present nothing approaching consensus among scholars as to the true upper limit of the Earth's population.

Population Policies: Pronatalist

Throughout history, governments have attempted to modify the direction of population change, both upward and downward.

Pronatalist polices, aiming for more births and faster population growth, have been pursued in times and places where national well-being has been equated with population size. People have sometimes believed that military power would be enhanced with a larger population base—more recruits for the army and navy. Likewise, economic prosperity has sometimes been thought to depend on a good-sized population—lots of workers, lots of consumers, and so on. And of course a bigger population constitutes a bigger potential tax base, yielding more tax revenues to be spent on whatever the government, or sovereign, considers worthwhile. At times pronatalist efforts have been driven by the fear of *de*population, with consequent loss of national power and influence. France is an example of a nation given to worrying about the size of its population (Spengler 1938). On the other hand, *anti*natalist policies—those policies that aim for fewer births and *slower* population growth—have been favored in some places out of concern about the economic and social costs of rapid population growth. Typically, this policy perspective has been applied to less developed countries, though some environmentalists have claimed that richer nations, with their high per capita consumption rates, are in some ways as overpopulated as the poorer, high-fertility countries of Africa, south Asia, and Latin America.

Through surveys conducted by UN agencies we now have data on how governments around the world regard their current levels of fertility. Among the more developed countries, mainly in Europe, North America, and East Asia, three-fifths consider their current fertility rates too *low*. This view should come as no surprise, since most of the forty-four countries belonging to this group have fertility rates well below the replacement level of two children per woman. Low TFRs are bound to raise concerns about labor shortages, tax revenues, long-term capacity to support a growing elderly population, and so on. Forty percent of these governments have adopted policies aimed at raising the birth rate. In Europe and Japan, especially, where attitudes toward immigration have historically been more hostile than in the United States, higher birth rates offer an appealing means of halting an eventual decline in population. Sweden's array of pronatalist policies has garnered a lot of attention since the 1970s. Family benefits were made quite generous, in the form of cash payments, tax incentives, and extended maternity leaves. The effort seemed to pay off during the 1980s, as the Swedish fertility rate (TFR) rose from 1.7 to 2.1, but during the 1990s fertility slumped to its lowest rate ever (1.5), perhaps due to adverse economic conditions (Population Division 2004b; Kent 1999, 4–5). At this point, no one really knows how to effectively promote higher birth rates—a point we pursue further in the next chapter.

Although in recent years the United States has seen its fertility rate drop to approximately replacement level, and even briefly below that level, there is little chance of U.S. depopulation in this century. Hence one hears few calls for a pronatalist policy in the United States. The Census Bureau actually projects a more than doubling of the U.S. population, to 571 million, by the end of the century (see Chapter 7). What differentiates the United States from most other developed nations is a heavy and continuous rate of net immigration. Without immigration, as noted before, the United States' demographic future would much more closely resemble that of the other industrialized countries. With it, the nation will see population expand significantly, owing to the number of immigrants themselves, their relative youthfulness, and their high rates of fertility. If immigration policy can be thought of as a form of population policy, then the United States has accepted (if only implicitly) a policy strongly favoring a larger national population.

Population Policies: Antinatalist

For over half a century, policies aimed at slowing population growth in the developing countries have been discussed, debated, and, with wide variations, implemented. An influential rationale for antinatalist policies was provided in a 1958 study by Ansley Coale and Edgar Hoover, who argued that high rates of population growth jeopardized long-term economic development by diverting resources from growth-enhancing investments to the mere maintenance of population. Reduced fertility, on the other hand, could speed economic development by freeing more resources for investment in productivity-enhancing activities (Coale and Hoover, 1958). On the basis of this kind of thinking, the industrialized nations began funding population programs for the less developed countries (LDCs) in the 1960s and 1970s, with the United States playing a leading role.

In 2003, three-fifths of the world's less developed, poorer countries were on record as considering their fertility rates too high. For Africa that figure rises to three-quarters. Some obvious responses to the perception of too-high fertility are: postponement of marriage, abstinence, and birth control. At this point, the first two options have not yet become the bases for national population policy (although the Bush administration has heavily promoted abstinence at home and abroad, as we discuss further in Chapter 3). Birth control, on the other hand, is widely accepted, though the term itself has gone out of favor—even the expression "family planning" is now avoided in some quarters.

About 90 percent of governments around the world support the provision of contraceptive services to their citizens. Somewhat different approaches to the distribution of such services are taken in the more developed as compared to the less developed regions. In richer countries, contraceptives are obtained primarily through private health networks and the private market. In poorer countries, people depend more on subsidized provision of contraceptives by the government or nongovernmental organizations (NGOs) (Population Division 2004b). The developing countries have received considerable financial and technical support for family planning from the United Nations Population Fund (UNFPA), the United States Agency for International Development (USAID), NGOs such as International Planned Parenthood, and private foundations, such as the Ford and Rockefeller Foundations. On one principle all sides agree: no single family-planning model fits every country. Each country's efforts must be tailored to its own traditions, culture, and perceptions of what needs to be done. In addition to providing information about contraceptive choices and actually delivering contraceptive services to clients, some family-planning programs offer more general health services to women and children, and some engage in efforts to change attitudes about family size. (Radio and television soap operas delivering messages about the benefits of smaller families seem to have been quite effective in changing attitudes and behavior in some countries.) In recent years, the trend has been away from placing a narrow emphasis on birth control per se. Policymakers have come to understand that fertility is inextricably linked to women's status in society, and that higher levels of education and opportunity for women usually result in later childbearing and smaller completed families. A study by the Alan Guttmacher Institute found that in countries as diverse as Peru, Egypt, and Indonesia teenage child-bearing was *far* more prevalent among women who had less than seven years of schooling than among those who had more than seven years. Maternal education has also been shown to be correlated with lower mortality rates for children in most societies—another benefit of expanding educational opportunity for girls (Gelbard, Haub, and Kent 1999, 21–24).

Population Policy: China and India

What population policies have the world's two population giants, China and India, followed? China, with approximately 1.3 billion people in 2005 and a TFR now below replacement level at 1.7, has pursued a forceful national program of slower population growth for more than two and a half decades. India, with around 1.1 billion people and a TFR of 2.8, has followed a more decentralized system of family planning in the years since India became the first developing nation to offer family-planning services in 1951. A comparison of the two cases will be instructive.

China's fertility rate began falling first in its cities during the 1960s. There was no explicit national policy aiming for smaller families until 1971, when the *wan xi shao* campaign began. The translation of this expression is: *later* (marriage), *longer* (intervals between births), *fewer* (children). This program evolved into the "one-child policy" of 1979 that has become the focus of much international attention. Under the one-child policy, couples are given incentives and disincentives to limit themselves to a single child. Urban couples with one child who pledge not to have any more children receive monthly child-support allowances until the child reaches the age of fourteen. They are also promised more spacious housing and higher pensions when they retire. The child receives preferential treatment in applying to schools and for jobs. In rural areas, a modified policy offers couples who pledge to stop at one child added monthly payments in cash and kind. One-child families also get the same grain ration and the same size plots for private cultivation as larger families, thus reaping an indirect advantage. The Chinese provinces may implement additional policies on an individual basis, and some of these policies have included higher taxes on families who have more than two children, and even imposition on the parents of full maternity costs and medical and educational costs for such children (Weeks 2005, 258–259; Attane 2002).

Whether the one-child policy has been a success is debatable. China once set a goal of capping national population at 1.2 billion by the year 2000. The goal was not met, and while China's TFR has fallen below replacement level, its current population is so youthful, with so many young adults entering their childbearing years, that the total population is bound to increase for a few more decades at least. Some observers also question how much of the fall in fertility has been due to the one-child policy. Much of the extraordinary drop from a TFR of 7.5 in 1963 to 2.5 in 1983 occurred *before* the new policy was announced in 1979. And much of China's fertility decline might have occurred even in the absence of a strict antinatalist policy. But criticism of the one-child policy has been directed less at its efficacy than at its "coercive" features. When incentives and disincentives become strong enough, the policy looks like compulsory birth control. One of the policy's worst side effects, in a culture that values male children above female, can be seen in the neglect of infant girls and sex-selective abortion of female fetuses (Weeks 2005, 62, 258–260; Sen 1999, 220–221).

The world's most populous democracy, India, has been seeking slower population growth ever since its first five-year plan (for 1951–1956) called for the creation of family-planning centers throughout the country. At that time, the Indian TFR stood at 6.0. Early efforts were focused on information, education, and research into contraceptive methods. Results, however, were disappointing, with fertility declines seen mainly in a few states, in the upper classes, and in cities. Determined to do better, Indira Gandhi's government in 1976 revamped the program, increased the monetary incentives to participants, and suggested that state legislatures consider passing laws that ordered compulsory sterilization after the birth of a couple's third child. (Only one state actually did so.) Controversy and violence ensued, and Gandhi's party was defeated in elections a year later. Her return to office in 1980 brought a renewed commitment to the national family-planning effort, as did her son's rise to power in 1984. Rajiv Gandhi promised a broader, higher-quality national program, with more generous rewards to women who limited their family sizes. But demographic results at the national level were, and have continued to be, less than impressive. Ac-

cording to some observers, the program has been overly bureau-
cratic, inconsistent, and inflexible. Too much reliance has been
placed on sterilization (first male, later female) rather than on offering couples an array of contraceptive choices (Livi-Bacci 2001,
154–157; Weeks 2005, 565–567; Jain 1998, ch. 3).

Fertility *has* declined in India but not nearly as quickly as
policymakers once anticipated. Although at one time they hoped
to achieve replacement-level fertility by the end of the twentieth
century, the revised official goal is to reach that mark by 2010.
This looks increasingly unlikely to happen. Even if India's TFR
moved downward to replacement level by 2010, as called for in
the National Population Policy of 2000, it would not prevent continued population growth for decades to come. Demographers
expect an increase of over 500 million between 2005 and 2050
owing to the "demographic momentum" of large numbers of In-
dians about to enter or already in their reproductive years.

As with China, it is unclear how much of India's fertility decline so far should be attributed to its population policy and how
much to general modernization trends. Rates of fertility reduction vary widely across the states of India. It has been observed
that where fertility is highest, for example, in the northern states
of Uttar Pradesh, Bihar, and Rajasthan, educational levels, especially for females, are low. By contrast, in the southern states of
Kerala and Tamil Nadu, fertility is low (TFRs of 1.7 and 2.2, respectively) while education levels and literacy rates are high.
Women are accorded more economic rights and opportunities
here than in other Indian states, and family-planning programs
are less heavy-handed than they are in states with much higher
fertility rates (Sen 1999, 221–224; Jain 1998, 73).

Global Population Policy

The world has no super-government with the authority to im-
pose population policies on sovereign states around the globe,
nor is anyone seriously suggesting the desirability of such a
thing. But the views of the international community on population matters can have an impact on the deliberations of national
policymakers and on the academic, media, and political elites
who shape the policies. Over the years, the most important forum for debating population policy has been a series of decen-

nial, UN-sponsored world population conferences. The first was held in Bucharest (1974), the second in Mexico City (1984), and what may turn out to be the last, the International Conference on Population and Development, in Cairo (1994). Most nations sent official delegations to these conferences.

Each conference generated a distinct political atmosphere. At Bucharest, ideology dominated the proceedings. Some delegates attacked the rich countries' financial support of family-planning programs in the poorer ones as self-serving, if not imperialistic. A number of national delegations made clear their opposition to policies aimed at lowering population growth rates. "Economic development is the best contraceptive," in the words of one slogan voiced at the conference. Acrimony aside, the Bucharest meetings did put the nations assembled there on record as approving, for the first time, an international population "plan of action." The plan included a numerical target for reduced birth rates in the developing countries, a statement of the basic human right of all couples to make their own decisions about family size, and support for full gender equality in education, politics, and economic life (Weeks 2005, 550–551; Livi-Bacci 2001, 149).

In Mexico City ten years later, delegates were startled by the announcement of a new U.S. position that population was a "neutral phenomenon" that was neither helpful nor harmful to economic advancement. Many developing nations had come to the conclusion since 1974 that rapid population growth could indeed pose a threat to their chances for social and economic progress. The new, less activist U.S. position could be traced to anti-abortion politics in the United States and to the intellectual influence of Julian Simon (see Chapters 2 and 5) in the Reagan administration. Population experts saw the main significance of the conference in the unanimous acceptance of the idea that population growth was a matter of concern apart from economic development.

The most recent conference (Cairo, 1994) drew delegates from 183 nations. The program of action that emerged from this meeting was lengthier than previous plans of action; it was also more ambitious and wide-ranging. Topics addressed include the empowerment of women, internal and international migration, the environment, technology, NGOs, education, and more. No numerical goals were set for fertility or population growth rates, although goals *were* set for life expectancies and (reduced) child mortality rates. One expert concluded that Cairo produced three major accomplishments: it firmly removed the taboo against public discussion of family planning and birth control; it elevated the concerns and rights of women in the control of fertility; and it saw the return of the United States to a position of shared leadership on issues of world population (Cohen 1995, 71–72). The last accomplishment was short-lived: almost no one sees the United States, as led by the Bush administration, as a leader on world population issues. As of now, there are no plans for more UN-sponsored population conferences.

References

Attane, Isabell. 2002. "China's Family-Planning Policy: An Overview of Its Past and Future." *Studies in Family Planning* 33:1, 103–113.

Coale, Ansley J., and Edgar M. Hoover. 1958. *Population Growth and Economic Development in Low-Income Countries: A Case Study of India's Prospects*. Princeton, NJ: Princeton University Press.

Cohen, Joel E. 1995. *How Many People Can the Earth Support?* New York: W. W. Norton.

Department of Economic and Social Affairs (DESA), United Nations Secretariat. 2004. *World Economic and Social Survey 2004: International Migration*. New York: United Nations.

Dugger, Celia W. 2004, July 16. "Devastated by AIDS, Africa Sees Life Expectancy Plunge." *New York Times*, A3.

Evans, L. T. 1998. *Feeding the Ten Billion: Plants and Population Growth*. Cambridge: Cambridge University Press.

Gelbard, Alene, Carl Haub, and Mary M. Kent. 1999. "World Population beyond Six Billion." *Population Bulletin* 54:1, 1–44.

Haupt, Arthur, and Thomas T. Kane. 1998. *The Population Handbook*, 3rd ed. Washington, DC: Population Reference Bureau.

International Organization for Migration (IOM). 2005. *World Migration 2005: Costs and Benefits of International Migration*. Geneva: IOM.

International Programs Center of the U.S. Census Bureau. 2005. *International Data Base*. Accessed 7/05 at http://www.census.gov/ipc/www/idbnew.html.

Jain, Anrudh (ed.). 1998. *Do Population Policies Matter? Fertility and Politics in Egypt, India, Kenya, and Mexico*. New York: Population Council.

Kent, Mary Mederios. 1999. "Shrinking Societies Favor Procreation." *Population Today* 27:12, 4–5.

Livi-Bacci, Massimo. 2000. *The Population of Europe.* Malden, MA.: Basil Blackwell.

Livi-Bacci, Massimo. 2001. *A Concise History of World Population,* 3rd ed. Malden, MA: Basil Blackwell.

Martin, Philip, and Elizabeth Midgley. 1999. "Immigration to the United States." *Population Bulletin* 54:2, 1–44.

McFalls, Joseph A., Jr. 2003. *Population: A Lively Introduction,* 4th ed. Washington, DC: Population Reference Bureau.

Population Division of the Department of Economic and Social Affairs, United Nations Secretariat. 2004a. *World Population in 2300: Proceedings of the United Nations Expert Meeting on World Population in 2300.* New York: United Nations.

Population Division of the Department of Economic and Social Affairs, United Nations Secretariat. 2004b. *World Population Policies 2003.* New York: United Nations.

Population Division of the Department of Economic and Social Affairs, United Nations Secretariat. 2004c. *World Urbanization Prospects: The 2003 Revision. Highlights.* New York: United Nations.

Population Division of the Department of Economic and Social Affairs, United Nations Secretariat. 2005. *World Population Prospects: The 2004 Revision. Highlights.* New York: United Nations.

Population Reference Bureau (PRB). 2005. *2005 World Population Data Sheet.* Washington, DC.

Sen, Amartya. 1999. *Development as Freedom.* New York: Alfred A. Knopf.

Spengler, Joseph J. 1938. *France Faces Depopulation.* Durham, NC: Duke University Press.

UNAIDS. 2004. *2004 Report on the Global AIDS Epidemic: 4th Global Report.* Geneva: Joint United Nations/World Health Organization Program on HIV/AIDS.

United Nations Development Program. 2004. "HIV/AIDS Crisis Drives Down Life Expectancy, Human Development Rankings in Sub-Saharan Africa." July 14 press release.

Weeks, John R. 2005. *Population: An Introduction to Concepts and Issues,* 9th ed. Belmont, CA: Wadsworth.

2

Problems and Controversies

Controversies about population began long before we had even the roughest idea of the true size of the human race. A famous British debate of the mid-eighteenth century, for example, involved the question of how many people there had been in "ancient times," with one side believing there had been many *fewer* people than at present and the other believing there had been many *more*. In the absence of demographic data, each side had free rein to speculate at will, and there was no reluctance to do so! Most modern population controversies still begin at the numerical level: Is the present population the right size for a society (or the world)? Too large? Too small? Growing too fast? Too slowly? Once the facts or assumptions about population are settled, it quickly becomes apparent that the really interesting issues are those relating to the political, economic, and environmental consequences of population. Disagreements tend to hinge on people's personal values, politics, and attitudes about the future.

Malthus and Overpopulation Fears

One of the most widespread opinions people hold about world population is that it is *just too large*. Those who express anxiety about population size find justification in the writings of the English clergyman and economist Thomas Malthus (1766–1834), in particular, his 1798 *Essay on the Principle of Population*. Malthus did offer some gloomy, even scary, thoughts about population—

31

see the excerpt from the *Essay* in Chapter 7—but what he said has often been misunderstood or misrepresented. His basic position was that population tends to increase at a "geometric" rate, such as 1, 2, 4, 8, 16, whereas food production, at best, can only increase at an "arithmetic" rate, such as 1, 2, 3, 4, 5. This suggests an ever-present threat of a gap opening up between the actual food supply and the food requirements of a growing population. Hasty readers might conclude from this that Malthus foresaw such a gap actually materializing in his own country or perhaps for the world as a whole. Indeed, the most common misconception about Malthus is that he predicted mass famine. He did not. Malthus identified a variety of "checks" on population, such as disease, hunger, war, infanticide, and even the simple act of postponing marriage. He made clear that he approved of only one of the checks—the last. The point he stressed repeatedly was that population *must* be restrained by checks of some kind, and if the milder ones are insufficiently effective, then the harsher ones, like starvation and war, will be called into operation.

In two ways Malthusian analysis now appears out of date. First, Malthus adamantly rejected the most obvious means of restraining population—artificial birth control—on moral grounds. The only acceptable way to achieve smaller families and thus slower population growth, he said, was through the postponement of marriage. Malthus's position on this issue was not unusual either for his time or for a clergyman of the Church of England, which he was. But clearly he was on the wrong side of history in this regard. While some religious fundamentalists still do not fully accept contraception in principle, in practice most people do. Italy, for example, is one of the world's most Catholic countries, yet Italians are clearly defying (or ignoring) Roman Catholic dogma against contraception, since the country has one of the world's lowest birth rates.

The second way in which Malthus seems premodern to us today concerns his view of the environment. We can discuss this in a very few words—he had no view at all! Environmental concerns were completely absent from the original Malthusian framework. For Malthus the consequences of a population growing too rapidly took the form of depressed wages, urban crowding, infectious diseases, stunted growth among children, and other conventional miseries—never pollution, ecological degradation, or the loss of open space. Had he lived a century later,

Malthus *still* would not have been an environmentalist because modern environmentalism only dates from the 1960s.

Modern Malthusians

In the 100 years following Malthus's death, it seemed that the Malthusian specter of overpopulation had been banished. Agricultural production grew at a remarkable rate and appeared fully capable of keeping pace with rising population. Famines were increasingly infrequent and confined to parts of Asia and Africa. But in the 1950s and 1960s, as public health improvements in the less developed nations sent mortality rates dramatically downward with no corresponding decrease in fertility rates, concerns about unsustainable population growth were voiced once again. The loudest Malthusian "echo," though hardly the first of the postwar era, was Paul Ehrlich's *The Population Bomb*, published in 1968. "The battle to feed all of humanity is over," warned the Stanford biologist. "In the 1970s the world will undergo famines—hundreds of millions of people are going to starve to death" (Ehrlich 1968, xi). Just as grim a message had been delivered the previous year in William and Paul Paddock's starkly titled *Famine 1975!* At the same time, Malthusian fears about the possible destabilizing effects of rapid population growth in Third World countries were having an impact on American foreign policy—hence the support for family-planning efforts in the U.S. foreign aid program (Ross 1998, ch. 4; see also National Security Study Memorandum 200 in Chapter 7 of this volume).

For Ehrlich, unlike Malthus, the concern about population has been environmental, global, and immediate. His *Population Bomb* gave a powerful added boost to the environmental movement launched by Rachel Carson's *Silent Spring* (1962). The first Earth Day, in 1970, was inspired largely by the messages in these two books. Since then, Ehrlich has continued to voice concerns about the depletion of renewable and nonrenewable resources, the degradation of the environment, and the international tensions that can be attributed, often directly, to population growth. He warns that current population trends will lead not just to poverty and misery, as depicted by Malthus, but to ecological disaster. Given the Earth's finite carrying capacity, human population can grow only so large. At the limit there can be only two possible solutions (short of migration to other planets): lower birth rates or higher death rates. Although Ehrlich sees the second solution as more likely, he takes every opportunity to advocate those personal and public actions that could lower birth rates. He was an enthusiastic co-founder of the advocacy group Zero Population Growth, or ZPG, in 1968.

Hard on the heels of *The Population Bomb* came the sensational *Limits to Growth* (1972), a report by a team of M.I.T. scientists who used computer modeling to simulate the future direction of the global economy, environment, and population. The scholars began, reasonably enough, by assuming that population growth, agricultural production, resource depletion, industrial production, and pollution were interdependent processes, each affecting the others through "feedback loops." The computer model, with its capacity for sorting out the complex connections among a large number of variables and projecting current trends far into the future, signaled a series of crises ahead. Global population was already so large and fast-growing, nonrenewable resources were being exploited so rapidly, and pollution rates were likely to increase so substantially in coming decades that by the year 2100 economic growth would have halted. Worse yet, population would have gone into worldwide decline owing to "food crises" and rising death rates. The future depicted in *Limits to Growth* was alarming indeed.

Population Optimists

Gloomy views about population growth have undoubtedly been influential in recent times, and those espousing them are sometimes called *gloomsters, doomsters,* or simply *Malthusians.* But their views have not gone unchallenged. On the opposing side are the *boomsters* or *cornucopians.* Two of the strongest *anti-*Malthusian voices have been those of Ester Boserup (1910–1999), a Danish development economist, and Julian Simon (1932–1998), an American demographic thinker. Boserup, in her classic study, *The Conditions of Agricultural Growth* (1965), noted that Malthus and his followers saw population change as dependent on agricultural conditions. Population would grow if land was abundant or crop yields were generous, but not otherwise. Her own research, however, convinced Boserup that the direction of causation frequently ran the other way: population change could lead to changes in agricultural practices. In particular, by putting pressure on resources, rapid population growth could *induce* changes in agricultural techniques, such as shifts from slash-and-burn methods to settled cultivation, or innovations in plant varieties, more systematic crop rotations, or improvements in farm tools (Boserup 1965). In short, population pressure could be a force for dynamic, positive change.

Julian Simon offers a broader and an even more optimistic view of world population trends than Boserup. A growing population, he argues, tends to raise, not lower, the standard of living. Why? Because the most critical resource for improving human welfare is, quite simply, human ingenuity and imagination. And the way to have more of this resource is to expand population. (That is the "message" behind the title of Simon's controversial 1981 book, *The Ultimate Resource*.) Simon disputes many of the pessimistic claims made by the neo-Malthusians regarding the impact of population. He asserts, for example, that contrary to the warnings of environmentalists like Ehrlich, natural resources and energy are *not* becoming scarcer, or more expensive in constant-dollar terms, as population continues to grow. Advances in technology have brought down the extraction costs, in labor hours per unit, for most resources and thereby have actually increased the known and available reserves of those resources. Similarly, pollution in the United States has abated in recent decades, despite a growing population. Meanwhile, the world's per capita food production has been on the rise for many years, and famines have become less frequent. Hence population growth ought to be seen, according to Simon, more as a means for solving problems than as a problem in itself.

Problems of Population Density

Growth of population almost always leads to rising population density, that is, more people per unit of physical space. Only if growing numbers were matched by increased land availability, through reclamation or conquest, would this not be true. Depending on your perspective, rising population density can be either a bad or a good thing. It will be bad if it causes overcrowded housing, traffic congestion, inadequate sanitation facilities, antisocial behavior, and so on. It will be good if it creates larger markets, higher levels of business interaction, more intellectual exchange, division of labor, and other economies of scale. Population pessimists tend to emphasize the negative aspects of density; population optimists, like Julian Simon, emphasize the positive. There are no simple patterns when it comes to evaluating population densities. *High* densities may be found in countries as affluent as the Netherlands (1,033 people per square mile) and as poor as Bangladesh (2,542). *Low* densities may be seen in countries as rich as Canada (8 people per square mile) and as poor as Angola (28) in southern Africa. The Netherlands is more than 100 times as densely settled as Canada but neither richer nor poorer than Canada; likewise, Bangladesh is almost 100 times as densely populated as Angola but not much different in per capita income (PRB 2005).

Concerns about rising global population densities relate mainly to cities in the developing world. Here an ongoing rural-to-urban migration of workers and families is putting enormous strains on urban centers that are ill-equipped to accommodate the influx. Squatter settlements ring nearly every big city in the Third World. Living conditions in these *favelas, colonias,* and shantytowns can be grim, with no running water, sewage treatment, or electricity. Public transportation is often scattered and minimal, making for exhausting daily treks to places of employment. Historically, health and mortality indicators in such places have been very poor—contagious diseases, after all, spread most quickly where people are living at close quarters. Where all of the conditions just listed are found, it is easy to conclude, as population pessimists generally do, that we are faced with an "overpopulation" problem. And whatever the scale of the problem today, it seems all too likely that it will grow in the coming half-century, when nearly all the net gain in the world's population is slated to occur in the urban parts of the developing world.

Before we allow the gloom to settle too firmly on our thinking about the rising population densities of the Third World, however, we need to remind ourselves of a simple fact: when people move from rural to urban places, it is generally by choice. Cities offer the rural migrant hope of a better life. Urban living conditions may be abysmal and still an improvement on the village left behind. A UN study in 1997 found that 96 percent of urban dwellers in the developing countries had access to health care, while only 76 percent of rural residents did. Other comparisons were equally in the cities' favor: urban dwellers had better access to water by an 87 to 60 percent margin and a huge advantage in access to sanitation services—72 percent compared to 20 percent (Weeks 2005, 487). This is not to say that the poorest, most recently arrived migrants into cities invariably improve their living standards. Many do not. In any case, it may take time for real improvement to be seen, perhaps decades or generations. But there is undoubtedly some truth to what demographer John Weeks has to say about such migrants into cities: "[T]hey bring their poverty with them to a place where it is exposed to public view and, as a consequence, is more likely to be acted upon by governments and NGOs (non-governmental organizations)" (487).

Population and the Environment

These days it is beyond dispute that human population has an effect on the natural environment. Everything that we do—indeed every breath we take—has an impact, big or small, on the planet's biosphere. Some regard the human impact as large and harmful. They tend to be in the "gloomster" camp described above, and because they see human activity as tending to damage the environment, they favor slower population growth. Some would like to see an outright *reduction* in world population from current levels. The well-known nature writer Bill McKibben and his wife chose to have only one child out of concern for the impact human beings, including the McKibbens, are having on the natural world (1998). At the other end of the spectrum, "boomsters" are more sanguine, believing that nature is resilient, always in flux, and not affected by human activity in an especially pernicious way. They see no need to restrain population. The disagreement between the worried environmentalist side and the unperturbed, frequently pro-business, if not pro-corporate, side of this debate plays out on a number of issues, from global warming to endangered species to urban and suburban sprawl.

Hundreds of pages would be required to detail the various ways that human population growth has been implicated in the degradation of our environment, and hundreds more to summarize the vast literature on issues relating to population, development, and sustainability. It would probably be more useful at this point to outline a way of thinking about the population–environment linkage. The most influential simple framework for analyzing this issue is the IPAT equation presented originally (in slightly different notation) by John Holdren and Paul Ehrlich in 1971. The equation $I = PAT$ captures the idea that the impact on the environment, I, is equal to the human population, P, times the average consumption level or affluence, A, times a technical factor, T, that expresses the average pollution effects from consumption activities. Things will go badly for the environment if population increases, if people consume more on average, or if a certain type of technological change occurs. The technology factor is a bit tricky, since it can work either for or against the environment. If a technological breakthrough allows for more efficient (or "cleaner") production, using fewer resources, T goes down—a good thing. But if technology changes in a wasteful, more heavily resource-consuming direction, T goes up—a bad thing.

Several interesting scenarios can be sketched from the IPAT equation. For example, if a society feels it needs to reduce its impact on the environment over time, it faces a hard choice: reduce population, reduce consumption, improve technology, or find an acceptable combination of the three factors. A coordinated policy might permit one or more of the factors to *increase*, as long as another factor fell by a sufficient amount. Alternatively, a society that believed it had reached a tolerable ("sustainable") degree of impact on the environment and did not foresee any net change in the technology term, T, might debate the future courses open to it with respect to the remaining variables, P and A. One course might be to enjoy more individual affluence (higher A) but with smaller families (lower P). Another might be to pursue a more frugal lifestyle (lower A), with the compensating pleasures of larger families (higher P). A third mental exercise: if we feel that we cannot permit I to go any higher and that P will continue increasing for some time into the future, then it becomes clear that either there must be retrenching on consumption (lower A) or a favorable development of technology (lower T). By manipulating the IPAT equation in this manner, one gains a deeper understanding of the environmental, demographic, and economic constraints Ehrlich and Holdren were trying to model.

The IPAT equation has always lent itself more to general theorizing and policy "brainstorming" than to specific applications.

At the general level, it can provide some insights into the global impacts that the more developed regions (MDRs) and the less developed regions (LDRs) are having on the environment, and it can give some hints of what the future may bring. As we saw in Chapter 1, the less developed countries today represent about 81 percent of the world's population, and the more developed, around 19 percent. If all else were equal, this would mean that the world's poor had about four times the global environmental impact that the world's rich have. Yet we know they do not. The per capita consumption levels of the LDRs are far lower than those of the MDRs. In 2003, the World Bank listed sixty-six countries with per capita incomes of $745 or less, while the fifty-two wealthiest nations enjoyed per capita incomes *at least* twelve times higher and generally twenty-five to forty times higher (Gilbert 2004, 132–134). So while the world's poor greatly outnumber the world's rich, their environmental impact may well be less than that of the rich.

In coming decades the picture will change. Between now and 2050, the LDR population will grow much more rapidly than the MDR population. That demographic fact in itself would lead us, by the logic of IPAT, to believe the world's environment may take a "heavier hit" from the LDRs than from the MDRs. What about consumption, or A? At present the richer countries far outdistance the poorer when it comes to ownership and use of automobiles, computers, cell phones, air travel, housing, and the like. We can see the gap clearly, but we do not yet know whether or how much it will be closed in the next half-century. One clue: China and India have both experienced far more rapid economic advancement over the past decade and a half than the developed nations, and by every indication they will continue their economic surge. On the other hand, Africa's economic progress has lagged; its consumption levels may rise very little in the years ahead. But its population will climb rapidly, to almost 2 billion by 2050.

What conclusion are we led to? Although we have no firm knowledge of what will happen to any of the four variables in the IPAT equation at the global level, we are reasonably certain that population will increase, especially—and overwhelmingly—in the less developed countries. Consumption levels (A) in those countries have the potential to rise substantially also, at least among the over 2.4 billion residents of economically dynamic India and China, and perhaps in many other countries.

Thus P times A seems sure to increase among the less developed nations. For the more developed nations as a group, environmental impact may be smaller. Population is expected to grow hardly at all. But it would be surprising if per capita consumption did not continue to rise, at least slowly, as it has for well over a century. Hence P times A should also rise among the rich nations. All of this puts a clear burden on technology: unless we see big technological improvements (lowering T), the rising values of P and A around the world will give environmental pessimists—and everybody else—much to worry about.

Optimum Population

The idea of an optimum population—the best population size for a given society or for the planet—has been a subject of speculation by thinkers as ancient as Plato and as current as Paul Ehrlich. Until recent times it was mainly philosophers and economists who debated the issue of optimum population. Political philosophers have wondered what size of society would best support a democratic model of governance; economists have wondered how large a population would maximize per capita output or income. With the advent of ecological thinking and the modern environmentalist movement there has been some renewed interest in the question of the optimum size of population, especially at the global level.

Note the difference between *optimum* and *maximum* population. We have already seen in Chapter 1 that the question of how many people the Earth could possibly support has been analyzed at length by Joel Cohen. He notes that the maximum population estimates of the most prominent scientists in the past seem to converge on a range of 7.7 to 12 billion (Cohen 1995, 368–369). By current UN projections, the world will enter this central estimated range of maximum population between 2020 and 2025. But that leaves unanswered the question of whether a population of 7.7 billion plus is the *best* one for the Earth.

In the mid-1990s, Paul and Anne Ehrlich and Gretchen Daily offered some preliminary thoughts on optimum human population (Daily, Ehrlich, and Ehrlich 1994). They argued that the optimum would have to lie somewhere between the "minimum viable size" and the "biophysical carrying capacity of the planet"—and then asserted that the current world population "clearly exceeded the capacity of Earth to sustain it" (469). (World population has increased another billion since they made that assertion!) They proceeded to lay out a number of criteria that would have to be met in order for the global population to be considered optimal. For example, it would not exceed the level needed to guarantee a decent standard of living to every person, nor be too large to make it possible for everyone to enjoy freedom from sexism, racism, religious intolerance, and so on. It would be large enough to allow a good distribution of population centers, with a "critical mass" of people in each—one might call this the "cultural diversity" criterion. Importantly, an optimum human population would have to be small enough to assure the continuation of biodiversity. (The scholars did not specify any acceptable rate of species loss, but then exercises of this kind rarely descend into messy details.) In the end they stated a range of populations they believed would represent the current optimum: 1.5 to 2 billion. Two billion would, of course, be less than one-third of the world's current population and less than one-quarter of the number projected for mid-century.

One might expect the Ehrlichs to be troubled by the growing gap between the actual world population and their sense of the optimal level. Indeed, the tone of pessimistic alarm first displayed in Paul Ehrlich's 1968 best-seller, *The Population Bomb*, is still much in evidence in the population chapter of the Ehrlichs' latest book, *One with Ninevah: Politics, Consumption, and the Human Future* (2004). Yet they are able to find some glimmers of hope in present demographic trends. How so? Because the impending shrinkage of population in Europe and Japan, generally regarded as bad news in those areas, is considered "an incredibly positive trend" by the Ehrlichs, who see the world's most affluent nations as overconsumers of resources (Ehrlich and Ehrlich 2004, 99). Hence, the fewer Germans, Italians, Belgians, and Japanese, the better for global equity and for environmental sustainability.

The Great Population Slowdown

Almost as extraordinary as the explosion of human numbers during the past two centuries is the current *slowdown* in world population growth. We saw in the last chapter that the world's population reached its fastest rate of growth ever, about 2.2 percent annually, in the mid-1960s. From there the rate has declined almost continuously to the present rate of 1.15 percent, and most projections have it continuing to slide, dropping below 0.5 percent by mid-century. Considering the three basic demographic variables—fertility, mortality, and migration—only the first one could possibly account for a steady deceleration of population growth. Favorable trends in mortality—that is, longer life expectancies—would tend to *raise* the population growth rate, and migration, on a global level, has no direct effect on the growth rate. So the focus is on changes in fertility, the childbearing preferences and practices of the world's reproductive couples.

As we see in Table 2.1, total fertility rates have fallen substantially during the past half-century. For the world as a whole, the TFR has dropped by nearly one-half since 1950, from 5.02 to 2.65. If girls born today went through their reproductive years bearing children at the same age-specific rates that the world's women of all ages are now bearing children, they would have, on average, 2.65 children each. This would keep the global population growing, of course, since 2.65 is well above the 2.1 TFR that is needed to maintain a stable population. Although fertility has declined in every region of the world, it has fallen farthest in Asia and Latin America (including the Caribbean)—by over half in both areas. This is a quite significant drop, but since the TFR was so high to start with, it doesn't yet reach the replacement level in either area. Europe and North America have experienced smaller relative declines in their TFRs, but given their lower starting point, both areas have ended up below replacement level. Europe is *well* below that level. Africa, with the highest initial TFR of any region, has seen the smallest fertility reduction during the past fifty years and continues to have remarkably high fertility, about five children per woman.

Going forward, we can expect some interesting developments in fertility trends around the world, if the United Nations' demographic experts are right. For the world as a whole, fertility should reach replacement level around 2040 (see Table 2.2). Every continent except Africa will have fallen *below* replacement level, though not very far below. African fertility will be divergent from, but moving gradually into line with, the rest of the world. Note the bold assumption that Europe in 2005 has already reached its lowest level of fertility and will be registering in-

TABLE 2.1
Total Fertility Rates, Global and Regional, 1950–2005

	World	Latin America/ Africa	Asia	Europe	Carib.	North America
1950–1955	5.02	6.72	5.89	2.66	5.89	3.47
1955–1960	4.96	6.79	5.64	2.66	5.94	3.72
1960–1965	4.97	6.86	5.64	2.58	5.97	3.34
1965–1970	4.91	6.81	5.69	2.36	5.55	2.54
1970–1975	4.49	6.72	5.08	2.16	5.05	2.01
1975–1980	3.92	6.60	4.18	1.97	4.50	1.78
1980–1985	3.58	6.45	3.67	1.88	3.93	1.81
1985–1990	3.38	6.11	3.40	1.83	3.43	1.90
1990–1995	3.04	5.67	2.96	1.57	3.03	1.99
1995–2000	2.79	5.26	2.67	1.40	2.75	1.95
2000–2005	2.65	4.97	2.47	1.40	2.55	1.99

Source: United Nations Population Division, *World Population Prospects: The 2004 Revision,* accessed online at http://esa.un.org/unpp/p2k0data.asp.

creases in its TFR from now on. It would be well to regard that assumption with some skepticism, since there is little evidence that any country or region of the world has ever staged such a sustained demographic "comeback" in the past, except from catastrophes like wars, plagues, and famines.

Since it is ordinarily *nations* that formulate policies to address problems relating to population, we look next at the fertility experiences, past and future, of seven individual countries (Table 2.3). The seven are chosen somewhat arbitrarily, but note that the list includes the world's three most populous countries, as well as Latin America's biggest country, Africa's biggest, and a two-nation sample of Europe. The data presented in Table 2.3 will be useful in subsequent sections of the chapter. Reductions in fertility have been recorded by all seven countries over the forty years from 1965 to 2005, but with big variations. China and Brazil stand out, with reductions of around 70 and 60 percent, respectively. Nigeria's modest drop of 23 percent is typical of sub-Saharan Africa during this period. Russia and Italy have fallen to such low fertility rates that they face depopulation. The similarity of TFRs across the bottom of the table simply reflects a decision by the UN demographic team to make a simplifying assumption that global fertility rates will converge on 1.85 by the middle of the century. No one should place any bets that such a global identity of childbearing behavior will actually occur.

TABLE 2.2
Total Fertility Rates, Global and Regional, 2000–2050

	World	Latin America/ Africa	Asia	Europe	Carib.	North America
2000–2005	2.65	4.97	2.47	1.40	2.55	1.99
2005–2010	2.55	4.68	2.35	1.43	2.38	1.98
2010–2015	2.46	4.35	2.26	1.47	2.26	1.93
2015–2020	2.38	4.00	2.17	1.53	2.15	1.87
2020–2025	2.31	3.68	2.09	1.59	2.06	1.83
2025–2030	2.23	3.39	2.02	1.65	1.99	1.83
2030–2035	2.17	3.13	1.97	1.71	1.93	1.84
2035–2040	2.12	2.90	1.95	1.76	1.89	1.85
2040–2045	2.09	2.69	1.93	1.81	1.87	1.85
2045–2050	2.05	2.52	1.91	1.83	1.86	1.85

Source: United Nations Population Division, *World Population Prospects: The 2004 Revision,* accessed online at http://esa.un.org/unpp/p2k0data.asp.

TABLE 2.3
Total Fertility Rates for Seven Selected Countries, 1965–2050

	China	India	Nigeria	Russian Federation	Italy	Brazil	United States
1965–1970	6.06	5.69	6.90	2.02	2.49	5.38	2.55
1985–1990	2.46	4.15	6.83	2.13	1.35	3.10	1.92
2005–2010	1.74	2.76	5.32	1.40	1.38	2.25	2.04
2025–2030	1.85	1.95	3.24	1.65	1.59	1.92	1.85
2045–2050	1.85	1.85	2.40	1.85	1.85	1.85	1.85

Source: United Nations Population Division, *World Population Prospects: The 2004 Revision,* accessed online at http://esa.un.org/unpp/p2k0data.asp.

Depopulation Worries

In this era of population slowdown, the most immediate worry for countries with below-replacement fertility is the actual *loss of population*. No country wants to go out of business. National pride rests in part on national numbers. Fewer people means fewer customers, fewer investors, fewer taxpayers, a smaller workforce, and a smaller pool of military recruits. It has to be deeply disquieting to a nation like Russia to be losing around 750,000 people per year. President Vladimir Putin calls it a national crisis, and that does not seem an exaggeration. U.S. Census Bureau demographers now project Russia's 2050 population to be one-quarter below its 2005 level. This would be a loss of 33 million people. Japan faces a slightly smaller decline of 27 million between 2005 and 2050, but again that represents a shrinkage of more than 20 percent. Ukraine's projected loss comes closer to 30 percent, and a similar drop is expected in the Baltic states (Estonia, Latvia, Lithuania) by mid-century. Were the United States to experience the same proportional loss of population as Russia, it would be 67 million people. It is difficult to imagine the economic and social consequences of such a contraction.

Here is an apparent paradox: most countries with below-replacement fertility are not yet losing population as Russia is. The explanation is not terribly complicated. Population in any country keeps growing as long as births exceed deaths (ignoring migration). Even if the TFR is below 2.1, births can be numerous if there is a large enough cohort of young people coming into their reproductive years. When this happens, demographers call it *momentum*. There is a lot of positive momentum in the world at present. In many if not most countries, birth rates a generation ago were higher than today (see Tables 2.1 and 2.3), and those newborns have grown up to be today's young adults forming unions and having children. This kind of positive momentum offers a buffer against outright depopulation, but eventually it erodes and disappears if fertility rates remain low.

Just as there can be momentum in the upward direction, there can be momentum *downward* as well. With many nations spending years and even decades at subreplacement levels of fertility, their future cohorts of potential parents are getting smaller. As time passes and national populations begin to decline, it will become progressively more difficult to turn things around. Even if attitudes about childbearing changed in the future and the TFR rose above 2.1—and bear in mind that it is now *below* that level in scores of countries—population might continue to decline for many years for lack of enough reproductive-age parents. This is not merely an abstract possibility: a leading demographer, Wolfgang Lutz, and two colleagues have published a paper indicating that Europe's positive population momentum turned *negative* around the year 2000 (Lutz, O'Neill, and Scherbov 2003). Europe, it appears, is on a demographic slippery slope.

Population and economic prospects are, of course, intertwined. In a variety of ways, things go well for business when the population is expanding—and badly when the population is contracting. Ben Wattenberg has discussed this phenomenon in a recent book where he contrasts the easy successes of American CEOs "riding high on a mighty demographic wave," their expanding sales anchored in a steadily growing customer base, with the gloomy experience awaiting European businesspersons in coming decades. The latter will face declining sales, revenues, and profits as Europe's population declines—by 100 million, according to Wattenberg. Real estate will be hard hit. Fewer people means lower demand for housing and lower prices. As property values decline, the loans that so often are collateralized by real estate will have to shrink as well, and that may force a drop in investment. (Consider what happened in Japan during the 1990s.) A falling population will also bring slumping sales and profits for Europe's furniture- and carpet-makers and auto mechanics (Wattenberg 2004, 136–138). There have to be *some* economic benefits from population declines, but they are much harder to identify than the costs—and surely much smaller.

Older and Older

There's no getting around it: the world's population is growing older. When this development is expressed in terms of rising life expectancies, we see it as a thoroughly positive thing, a sign of economic and medical progress. When it is seen as enlarging the group of dependents in society who, like those too young to work, must be supported by the adult working population, it's a different story—we tend to grumble and worry. However we view it, the rising median age of our species is an established fact, not just in the rich nations but nearly everywhere. We will have to adjust to it, however painful that adjustment may prove to be.

The aging of humanity is linked to fertility trends. When fertility rates fall as low as they have for as long as they have in most of the developed nations, it strongly affects the age structure of the population. The proportion of children and adolescents in the population recedes, while the proportion of elderly expands. With age-adjusted mortality rates also declining, life expectancy has to rise. You get an older, "grayer" population on average. These trends, while affecting most of the world's poorer nations to some degree, are most clearly seen at present in the richer ones. In many of the developed nations, 15 percent of the population is over the age of 64, while in the less developed nations a more common figure is 5 percent or less in the senior category. Table 2.4 provides examples of age structures in some more developed and less developed countries. The countries were not randomly chosen: the first section displays a nearly complete listing of the more developed countries in which the over–64 population in 2004 outnumbered the youth under age 15. (As time goes on, more and more countries will be added to the list.) The second section lists half a dozen less developed countries chosen from all points of the compass. Note the extreme youthfulness of these populations by comparison with the first section.

TABLE 2.4
Age Structures of Twelve Selected Countries, 2004

COUNTRIES	Percent < 15	Percent > 64
More developed		
Germany	15	18
Greece	15	18
Italy	14	19
Japan	14	20
Portugal	16	17
Spain	15	17
Less developed		
Colombia	32	5
Ethiopia	44	3
Ghana	40	3
Indonesia	30	5
Pakistan	42	4
Yemen	46	4

Source: PRB (2005).

The *very* long-run prospect for world aging has been touched upon in Chapter 1. UN demographic experts now estimate that by 2100 life expectancies around the world will rise to a range of 66 to 97 years, depending on the country. Given that the world's longest-living people today, the Japanese, have a life expectancy of only 82, it is remarkable to think that an entire country could have a life expectancy approaching 100 in less than ten decades. But even *more* amazing is the prospect held out by the United Nations that in the year 2300 life expectancies will range from 87 to 106! Less dramatic, but significant nevertheless, are the projections on median age of the world's population: from 26 in the year 2000 to 44 by the year 2100 and 48 by 2300 (Population Division 2004).

Problems of a Graying Population

An obvious concern with aging populations is how to support the growing number of citizens who are no longer active in the labor force. Many national pension systems, including Social Security in the United States, were established long ago, when life expectancies were much shorter than they are today. Pay-as-you-go systems, under which the taxes paid by current workers are used to fund current benefits to retirees, function well when there are many workers per retired person but less well when the worker/retiree ratio falls. If that ratio falls far enough—it is now below two to one in Austria and Belgium, and headed toward one to one by 2030—the system may collapse.

Of course, pension systems of any kind are almost never found in the *developing* world, and that poses a different kind of problem: how can the elderly be assured of support in a future of lower fertility, fewer adult children to lean on, and no government pension system? This is a huge concern because the largest increases in elderly populations over the coming half-century will be found among the developing countries. By mid-century, three-quarters of the world's elderly will live in such countries. Yet these are precisely the societies least able to bear the financial burden of a growing senior citizenry. The issue is often expressed as follows: the world's developed countries got rich before they grew old, while the developing countries are in danger of growing old before they get rich.

Besides the demographic problem of a shrinking number of children per aging parent in the developing world, there is the added problem of weakening kinship ties and growing physical distances between generations. It is young adults who generally migrate from rural to urban areas seeking employment. Aging parents are left behind. The traditional patterns of intergenerational support are disrupted or at least attenuated. Call it part of modernization, but unless new support structures are found to replace the traditional practice of elders being looked after by their children, the outlook for the aged in the developing nations will be worrisome at best.

Finally, aging populations raise difficult issues of fairness in the allocation of a society's resources. As the elderly population continues to expand, requiring increased amounts of social services, there will inevitably be strains on private and public sources of funding to provide those services. Some believe that a shift of social resources away from the young and toward the older generations has been under way for years. If this continues, intergenerational conflicts of interest may prove hard to avoid. The political process will be put to the test. It has been clear for some time in the Western democracies that senior citizens, by virtue of their high participation rates in the electoral process, wield enormous influence over legislation that affects their well-being. Such political clout can only increase in the coming decades as the so-called gray lobby increases in size. With the "senior" voice growing louder, who will speak for the young?

Pronatal Policies: Can They Work?

In Chapter 1 we considered a few of the ways that governments may try to influence population in an upward or a downward direction through the encouragement of births (pronatal policies) or the discouragement of births (antinatal policies). In today's demographic environment, some countries, particularly those with fertility rates well below replacement level, are shifting from pronatalist theory to practice in an effort to boost their birth rates. The options available to them are several. Governments may ban abortion and contraception, as Romania did forty years ago under the dictator Nicolae Ceausescu—a policy that increased births almost immediately. They may outlaw divorce. They may coerce young women to conceive by, for example, imposing a tax on those who don't. And they may forbid or discontinue sex education in the schools (Levitt and Dubner 2005, ch. 4). Although such policies might prove marginally effective in raising the birth rate, they are not what we would expect any democratic government to propose, and it is highly doubtful they would be accepted in the societies that are currently trying to lift fertility rates back to replacement levels.

When it comes to encouraging more births, governments in recent decades have favored the carrot over the stick. The most obvious carrot is a monetary payment to women for having a baby. To some this may sound crude, even insulting, but it has been tried. In 1988, the Canadian province of Quebec, which had long worried about the size of the Francophone population relative to English-speakers in Canada, offered cash payments for births: $500 for the first birth, $1,000 for the second, and $8,000 for a third and every subsequent birth (Canadian dollars). Additional benefits were offered under the program, such as cash allowances and housing subsidies, all of which contributed to a very high price tag. Did it work? Initial results were favorable: the TFR rose from 1.49 in 1988 to 1.72 in 1990—still below the replacement level of 2.1 but an encouraging turnaround. After 1990, however, fertility fell back again to lower levels. It appears that Quebecois women altered the timing of their births rather than the ultimate number of births. In 1997 the program was discontinued, replaced by a cheaper and less pronatally focused program (Krull 2001).

Australia recently offered a cash bonus for births—$3,000 for a birth during 2004 or 2005, rising to $4,000 in mid-2006 (Australian dollars). Again, as in Quebec, there was a positive short-term response. The TFR in 2004 increased significantly for the first time since 1961. It is much too early to call the program a success, since women "down under" may simply be speeding up the conception and birth of children they were going to have anyway, without bonuses, at a later time. The clock is still running on this pronatalist experiment (Lalasz 2005).

Sweden and France are two European nations that have had policies in place for several decades to ease the burdens on mothers. These pronatalist policies, in fact if not in name, include paid maternal leave, day care allowances, and family cash allowances. As it happens, Sweden and France today have among the highest total fertility rates in Europe—1.7 and 1.9, respectively. While they still fall short of replacement fertility, they are doing much better than countries such as Spain and Italy that lack such policies. One expert, Phillip Longman, argues that the failure of even a highly pronatalist country like France to stabilize its population on a long-term basis demonstrates that the incentives held out for motherhood are not yet sufficiently attractive (2004, 177–178). The cost to a woman of having a child goes far beyond diapers and formula. If she leaves the labor force, the "opportunity cost" of lost wages will be steep. Indeed, that cost has been rising for many years as women have advanced educationally and professionally. If a European woman wants to combine motherhood and work in the paid labor force, there is the further problem of rigid labor market practices. The lack of flexible hours and part-time jobs, according to Longman, may well be preventing some would-be mothers from having children (2004, 178).

It is gradually becoming clear, as the evidence outlined above suggests, that pronatal policies have only a limited effectiveness. When their introduction is followed by a rise in the TFR, typically the change is relatively small and short-lived. No country has yet found a policy that can bring its fertility rate back up to replacement level on a long-term basis. That does not mean such a policy cannot be found or that it is not worth trying to find one. As nations continue to experience low fertility and, one by one, begin to actually depopulate (initially at a slow pace, then faster)—and this now appears almost inevitable—policymakers will surely return to the question of how to make parenthood more attractive. In the meantime, it is worth noting that many of the policies that have been tried so far are defensible on their own terms, regardless of whether they have raised the fertility rate.

References

Boserup, Ester. 1993 (1965). *The Conditions of Agricultural Growth: The Economics of Agrarian Change under Population Pressure.* London: Earthscan Publications.

Cohen, Joel E. 1995. *How Many People Can the Earth Support?* New York: W. W. Norton.

Daily, Gretchen C., Anne H. Ehrlich, and Paul R. Ehrlich. 1994. "Optimum Human Population Size." *Population and Environment: A Journal of Interdisciplinary Studies* 15:6, 469–475.

Ehrlich, Paul. 1968. *The Population Bomb.* New York: Ballantine.

Ehrlich, Paul, and Anne Ehrlich. 2004. *One with Ninevah: Politics, Consumption, and the Human Future.* Washington, DC: Island Press.

Gilbert, Geoffrey. 2004. *World Poverty: A Reference Handbook.* Santa Barbara, CA: ABC-CLIO.

Holdren, John P., and Paul R. Ehrlich. 1971. "Impact of Population Growth." *Science* 171:1212–1217.

Krull, Catherine. 2001, November/December. "Quebec's Alternative to Pronatalism." *Population Today* 29:8, 3–4. Available at PRB's website, www.prb.org.

Lalasz, Robert. 2005. "Baby Bonus Credited with Boosting Australia's Fertility Rate." Web news, July 2005, from PRB at www.prb.org.

Levitt, Steven D., and Stephen J. Dubner. 2005. *Freakonomics: A Rogue Economist Explores the Hidden Side of Everything.* New York: William Morrow.

Longman, Phillip. 2004. *The Empty Cradle: How Falling Birthrates Threaten World Prosperity and What to Do about It.* New York: Basic Books.

Lutz, Wolfgang, Brian C. O'Neill, and Sergei Scherbov. 2003, March 28. "Europe's Population at a Turning Point." *Science* 299:5615.

Malthus, Thomas Robert. 1993 (1798). *An Essay on the Principle of Population.* Edited by Geoffrey Gilbert. New York: Oxford University Press.

McKibben, Bill. 1998. *Maybe One: A Personal and Environmental Argument for Single Child Families.* New York: Simon & Schuster.

Meadows, Donella H., et al. 1974 (1972). *The Limits to Growth.* New York: Universe Books.

Meyer, Michael. 2004, September 27. "Birth Dearth." *Newsweek International,* 56.

Paddock, William, and Paul Paddock. 1967. *Famine 1975!* London: Weidenfeld & Nicholson.

Population Division of the Department of Economic and Social Affairs, United Nations Secretariat. 2004. *World Population in 2300: Proceedings of the United Nations Expert Meeting on World Population in 2300.* New York: United Nations.

Population Reference Bureau (PRB). 2005. *2005 World Population Data Sheet.* Washington, DC: PRB.

Ross, Eric B. 1998. *The Malthus Factor: Poverty, Politics and Population in Capitalist Development.* New York: Zed Books.

Simon, Julian. 1981. *The Ultimate Resource.* Princeton, NJ: Princeton University Press.

Simon, Julian. 1996. *The Ultimate Resource 2.* Princeton, NJ: Princeton University Press.

Specter, Michael. 1998, July 10. "The Baby Bust: A Special Report; Population Implosion Worries a Graying Europe." *New York Times,* A1.

Wattenberg, Ben. 2004. *Fewer: How the New Demography of Depopulation Will Shape Our Future.* Chicago: Ivan R. Dee.

Weeks, John R. 2005. *Population: An Introduction to Concepts and Issues,* 9th ed. Belmont, CA: Wadsworth.

Yaukey, David, and Douglas L. Anderton. 2001. *Demography: The Study of Human Population,* 2nd ed. Prospect Heights, IL: Waveland Press.

3

Special U.S. Issues

Each country faces its own population issues, which vary according to its size, location, history, and position vis-à-vis the rest of the world. Some of the population questions that interest people in the United States flow from the fact that the United States is currently the world's sole superpower. Thus the question can arise: will U.S. population levels in the future sustain America's global influence, or will they undermine it? (A well-known commentator on politics and demography, Ben Wattenberg, among others, has raised serious concerns on this point.) Partly because of its wealth and superpower status, the United States has long been a leader in the funding of international family-planning efforts. How long can this be expected to continue, given the current state of American politics? The answer could well depend on the outcome of the next election—or the one after that. Another set of population questions for Americans is actually not so different from what various other industrial democracies must confront, for example: Is the birth rate high enough? Will the labor force grow at a rate sufficient to keep the economy strong? Will low fertility and the aging of the population jeopardize the public and private pension systems now in place? Will the nation be able to provide health care to its elderly as their numbers continue to increase? These are several of the questions addressed in the present chapter.

Is the United States an Exceptional Nation, Demographically Speaking?

We saw in Chapter 2 that nearly every modern industrialized nation has a total fertility rate that is below replacement level. Examples are Germany (1.39), Italy (1.28), United Kingdom (1.66), France (1.85), Spain (1.28), Taiwan (1.57), and South Korea (1.26). A quick reminder: the total fertility rate, or TFR, is the number of children a girl born today would bear during her lifetime if she ended up having children at the same rate that women in each age category are having them right now. Thus girls born in Taiwan today would average, over the course of their reproductive years, slightly more than one and a half children each if their childbearing experiences in future decades mirrored those of Taiwanese women in the present period. Clearly, however, a TFR of 1.57 would not replenish the island's population through natural means. In fact, the next generation could end up roughly one-quarter smaller than the current one. Shrinkage of each new generation will be the long-run fate of every country whose TFR remains below 2.1 unless it receives enough *immigrants* to make up the population loss caused by low birth rates.

What about the United States? With respect to its birth rate, the United States is a notable exception to the rule of below-replacement fertility for the world's most advanced economies. For more than a decade now, the U.S. total fertility rate has fluctuated between 2.0 and 2.1; in other words, it has stayed consistently at, or just shy of, replacement level. At the height of the famed "baby boom," in the late 1950s, America's TFR rose above 3.7—higher than the average for all *developing* nations of the world today. But after the end of the boom in 1964, the fertility rate dropped to as low as 1.8 in the mid-1970s and remained at that level until the late 1980s, after which it moved gradually to its current level. Two features of the American TFR that emerge clearly are: (1) it has become less volatile with the passage of time, and (2) it is now higher than the rates seen in all other major high-income nations and appears likely to remain that way (Downs 2003).

Details of the U.S. fertility picture can be gleaned from data published by the Census Bureau. The age category in which American women bear the most children is 25–29, followed in descending order by ages 20–24, 30–34, 15–19, 35–39, and 40–44. In spite of much publicity about high-profile older women achieving pregnancies, the fertility rate per thousand women in the 40–44 age category is really quite low—only about one-eighth the rate for women in the 25–29 age range. Teen pregnancies, once a source of much comment and concern in the United States, have declined by 28 percent since 1990. Experts credit the drop to better contraception and possibly a reduction in the riskiest types of sexual activity (Bernstein 2004).

Fertility variations by race and ethnicity in the United States are smaller than variations by age, with non-Hispanic Whites and Asians/Pacific Islanders having the lowest fertility rates. Blacks have about 15 percent higher fertility, and Hispanics, about 46 percent higher than Whites. Only Hispanic women in the United States currently bear children at an above-replacement rate. National origin also makes a difference. Foreign-born women have more births per thousand than native-born women, and among both foreign-born and native-born women it is Hispanic women who currently bear the most children, by a wide margin (Downs 2003).

European fertility patterns are in some ways similar to U.S. patterns and in other ways quite dissimilar. Foreign-born women have higher birth rates than native-born women in European countries, as in the United States. Fertility is higher for women in their 20s than in their 30s and 40s in Europe, as in the United States. Three-quarters of married women aged 15–49 in Western Europe use some form of contraception, the same proportion as in the United States. (In Northern Europe contraceptive use is somewhat higher than in the United States, and in Eastern and Southern Europe it is somewhat lower.) But overall fertility rates are much lower in Europe than in the United States. Only three small European countries, Iceland, Ireland, and Albania, have TFRs as high as 2.0, and their combined populations were less than eight million people in 2005. For all of Europe, the TFR as of 2005 was a mere 1.4. Little wonder that the population of that continent is expected to *drop* by at least 50 million people between now and 2050 (PRB 2005).

Although the United States is most often compared, economically and demographically, to Europe, it would be almost as relevant to compare it to East Asia given the rapidly rising position of China in the global economy and the already solid "wealthy nation" status of Japan. Here, too, the contrast reveals the United States as quite exceptional among the economically most successful nations. Whereas American women are just about at replacement-level TFR, those of East Asia (China, Japan, the Koreas, Mongolia, and Taiwan) have a composite TFR of only 1.6. The East Asian rate of contraceptive use actually *exceeds* that of the United States. As might be expected, East Asia's population is projected to shrink by almost 70 million between 2025 and

2050—an amount that is nearly identical to the *gain* in population expected for the United States during the same time period (PRB 2005).

What Makes American Fertility Different?

We have established that the United States is indeed different from other modern, economically advanced nations in having a fertility rate that very nearly replaces the population. This, in combination with a robust rate of net immigration, ensures that American population is growing now and will continue to grow for a long time to come, as best we can foresee. High U.S. fertility is a somewhat puzzling phenomenon. Most observers see Americans and Canadians, for example, as relatively alike on a personal level and can find no easy explanation for the fact that Canadian women tend to have, on average, 0.5 fewer children than American women. Similarly, the broad comparability of living conditions, democratic politics, and capitalist economic systems in the United States and much of Europe makes the TFR gap of at least 0.6 between the two areas hard to understand. What special circumstances might explain the high U.S. fertility?

Two preliminary comments are in order. First, Americans have always been noted for their high fertility. Benjamin Franklin wrote about high colonial fertility in 1751. The British demographer Thomas Malthus, who wrote the famous *Essay on Population* (1798) mentioned in Chapter 2, believed that the growth rate of population in the British North American colonies had been "probably without parallel in history"—a judgment with which modern demographers concur (Malthus 1993, 47). In the late colonial period and even as late as 1800, American women were having about eight children each. Perhaps only one nation in the world today, the sub-Saharan African country of Niger, matches that lofty rate. The long-term fertility trend in the United States, however, was downward from the early nineteenth century onward and particularly after the Civil War ended in 1865. Second, in any period of human history before about 1980, it would have been considered quite odd to ask what accounted for a fertility rate as *high* as 2.0 or 2.1. Only in the context of recent decades and by comparison with Europe and parts of East Asia does it make any sense to ask how the American TFR can be as "high" as the replacement level.

There is no easy answer to the question. One line of thought—perhaps speculation is a better word here—centers on the optimism that has long been considered a defining characteristic of the American people. Other things being equal, if Americans tend for whatever reasons to be more optimistic than Europeans, one way in which they might demonstrate that optimism is through decisions to marry, to have children, to have *more* children, and the like. Virginia Abernethy (1994) has developed this line of thinking in a cogent way, but it has not been systematically applied to the issue of relatively high U.S. fertility in recent years. Another hypothesis, perhaps related to the one just proposed, would make religion a key factor in explaining fertility differences between the United States and Europe. If more religious people tend to have bigger families, and if Americans are more religious in the early twenty-first century than Europeans, both of which assumptions appear to be true, then we may have at least a partial explanation for the fertility gap. Phillip Longman, in his recent book *The Empty Cradle* (2004), offers some support to this line of thought. He notes that regular churchgoers, when polled, are 20 percent more likely than non-churchgoers to say that three or more children would be an ideal family size, and he cites the state of Utah, where 69 percent of residents are Mormon, as having the highest fertility rate of any state in the country (34).

One of the central forces at work in buoying up the U.S. fertility rate is *ethnicity.* As mentioned in the previous section, Hispanics in the United States have a much higher fertility rate than other groups. Those of Mexican origin have the highest rate of fertility. They also dominate current immigrant flows into the United States. Over half of the births in both Texas and California now are to women of Mexican origin. Researchers have asked whether high Mexican-origin fertility might be due to cost considerations. Contraception has a financial cost, and therefore groups with below-average incomes, such as recent immigrants from Mexico, might be expected to make less use of it and thus experience higher birth rates. Recent research, however, suggests that even more important than financial considerations are the cultural factors at work among Mexican immigrants. Women's use of English, for example, along with their youthfulness when they entered the United States have been found to be key predictors of contraceptive use. When Mexican-origin women are engaged in English-speaking networks, it gives an indication of weakened ties to traditional Mexican culture, which values fertility more highly than contemporary U.S. culture does. Similarly, when women enter the United States from Mexico at a young age (under 18), it appears they may assimilate more quickly into the dominant American culture, causing, again, a lowering of fertility toward the U.S. norm (Weeks 2005, 266; Faulkner 2004, 26–32).

The Graying of America

We noted in Chapter 1 that the world is getting older, or, as journalists often like to say, "grayer." According to UN projections, the global median age will rise to about 38 by the middle of this century, which is *14 years* above the median age at the middle of the last century. When the United Nations extends its projections all the way to the year 2300—an intriguing if perilous flight of speculation—it arrives at a global median age of *almost 50*. Life expectancy at birth for the world as a whole is also increasing. From the current level of 66, five years should be added by 2025 and another five years by 2050. Humans will be older on average, and living longer, in 2050 than ever before.

Is the United States in step with these global aging trends? It is. The United Nations estimates the median age of Americans in 1950, 2005, and 2050 (projected) at 30, 36, and 41, respectively. The fastest-growing age bracket will be those over 85, whose numbers in the United States will more than quadruple by mid-century to over 20 million. The number of people in the age range of 65 to 84 will more than double, while in all younger age ranges the numbers will grow much more slowly (U.S. Census Bureau 2004). By the middle of the century, more than one-fifth of all Americans will be over the age of 65, a fact that leads one author to characterize the nation in 2050 as being like "fifty Floridas," since America as a whole will be much older than the population of Florida is today (Longman 2004, 18).

UN projections of life expectancy at birth in the United States are consistent with the rising median age and other demographic data cited above. U.S. life expectancy should rise by roughly two years between now and 2025, and another three years by 2050.

One reason demographers believe there is a good chance of longevity increasing in the United States is that people in at least twenty other developed countries, including the United Kingdom, France, and Japan, already live longer than Americans by up to four years. Rising life expectancy in the United States could be derailed, however, or even thrown into reverse, by a public health condition that is receiving increased attention: rising rates of obesity. That is the subject of important research done by Dr. S. J. Olshansky and others (2005), which links the rise in childhood and young-adult obesity to health problems later in life that could pare years off the average lifespan.

Threat to Social Security Pensions

The increasing number and proportion of elderly in the American population would make Social Security a prominent political issue in the United States even if President George W. Bush had not chosen to make the "reform" of the system a key item in his second-term domestic agenda. Millions of words have been written about the Bush proposal, both for and against. We will put that entire controversy aside, however, since the question of private retirement accounts is fundamentally separate from the demographic problems confronting the system. (Even the president has admitted as much.) The basic issue is simple. Social Security was designed to be a pay-as-you-go system, with taxes paid by current workers going to finance monthly pension checks to the nation's retirees. In such a system, if there are plenty of worker-taxpayers and not many retirees, everything works well. Benefits can be ample; tax rates can be low. On the other hand, if there are declining numbers of workers paying taxes and growing numbers of retirees drawing benefits, we may run into a problem. That is precisely what is projected for the coming decades, largely due to the impending retirement of the so-called baby boom generation, the huge cohort of Americans born between 1946 and 1964. The youngest of the "boomers" will reach age 65 and begin drawing full benefits in the year 2011.

Specific numbers will be helpful in understanding the issue. In 1950 there were about 16 workers for every retiree in the United States. The ratio declined over time as more and more Americans reached retirement age. Today the worker-to-retiree ratio is about 3.3 to 1 and projected to fall to about 2 to 1 by 2040. Simply put, each taxpaying American now supports more elderly than ever before through the Social Security system. The burden is certain to increase in coming years. It is ironic that the demographic "good news" of more people surviving to retirement age, and then living a longer time in retirement (collecting Social Security), translates to "bad news" for the younger generation that must pay the taxes to support their retired parents and grandparents.

Strains on the Social Security system will begin to appear in 2018. Before then, tax payments flowing into the system will be more than adequate to cover payouts to recipients, with surplus tax revenues being accumulated in something called the Social Security Trust Fund. Money in the trust fund is actually invested in U.S. Treasury securities, which means in effect that the current Social Security surpluses are being used to finance other kinds of government spending. (Critics of the system consider this a fiscal shell game, and they have a point.) In 2018 current tax revenues will, for the first time, be insufficient to pay the benefits due to retirees, so it will become necessary to start liquidating the Treasury securities held in the trust fund. This will place immediate pressure on federal finances. The government will have little choice but to cut spending on other programs, raise taxes, or borrow more funds to cover the emerging Social Security deficits. In 2042, by current projections, the trust fund will be exhausted. This does not mean that Social Security recipients will suddenly stop getting their monthly checks, only that if Congress does nothing, those checks will have to be *reduced*, probably by around 25 percent.

Social Security Fixes

To recap: The United States faces a serious challenge in funding its public pension system. Retirees are living longer and collecting benefits longer than ever before, and lower rates of fertility are restraining the growth of the working-age population who pay Social Security taxes. But there is much debate about when the crunch will occur (if ever), how severe it will be, and even what words are most appropriate to use in describing the problem. One side depicts an impending "crisis" for Social Security and argues that the system will go "flat broke" in 2042. These tend to be the people who would like to see big changes in the traditional Social Security program, notably the introduction of private or personal accounts. Others are less worried about Social Security's prospects—or do not approve of the big changes advocated by the first group—and see only stresses on the system that can be managed in various ways.

If current projections prove correct and Social Security begins going into deficit in 2018, policymakers will have several options to consider. Benefits could be cut. Such a step would be fiercely resisted by the "gray lobby"—AARP and others—and appears highly unlikely to happen, given the voting power of the elderly. It should also be kept in mind that Social Security has been one of the government's most effective antipoverty programs, and that large cuts in pension payments would almost certainly raise the poverty rate among older Americans. Perhaps more feasible would be a modification of the current methods used to establish initial Social Security benefit levels. At present, the level of payments to each new group of retirees depends on wage trends in the U.S. economy. Some complex plans have been put forward that would alter the formula used in determining these payments in a way that would save the government money but over the course of time deliver lower benefits to retirees. Cash benefits would not actually be *cut*; they simply would grow more slowly in the future than would otherwise be the case.

An alternative approach to shoring up Social Security's finances would be to leave benefits alone but raise taxes on workers. There is precedent for this approach; indeed, it has been taken repeatedly in the past. The current tax rate for the old-age-pension part of Social Security is 10.6 percent on annual wages up to, and not beyond, $90,000 (in 2005). This is the combined contributory rate of employee and employer. On top of that, there is a 2.9 percent tax for Medicare and a 1.8 percent tax for the disability portion of Social Security, bringing the total FICA tax rate to 15.3 percent. One economist has argued that a tax approach to maintaining the solvency of the Social Security pension system would require that the payroll tax rate be raised by a hefty 7.1 percent (Feldstein 2005, 36). But higher taxes on labor have an adverse effect on the labor market as well as introducing other distortions into the economy. Hence there is little enthusiasm for the idea of big tax increases to keep Social Security afloat.

We have not quite exhausted the possible ways of keeping the system solvent. Aside from cutting benefits or raising taxes, there is the option of increasing the eligibility age for receiving Social Security. By keeping workers contributing for a longer time and shortening the period during which they receive benefits, such a policy change would doubly strengthen Social Security's balance sheet. It also appears to be an entirely reasonable change given the greatly increased life expectancy in recent years as compared with 1935 when the system was established. But much of the increased U.S. life expectancy has been the result of lowered infant mortality, *not* people living a lot longer after they reach retirement age. As Table 3.1 shows, men reaching age 65 in 1990 had a remaining life expectancy of about fifteen years, a gain of less than three years compared to 1940. Women had a gain of about five years.

TABLE 3.1
Demographic Statistics on Social Security, 1940–1990

Year Cohort Turned 65	Percentage of Population Surviving from Age 21 to Age 65		Average Remaining Life Expectancy for Those Surviving to Age 65	
	Male	*Female*	*Male*	*Female*
1940	53.9	60.6	12.7	14.7
1950	56.2	65.5	13.1	16.2
1960	60.1	71.3	13.2	17.4
1970	63.7	76.9	13.8	18.6
1980	67.8	80.9	14.6	19.1
1990	72.3	83.6	15.3	19.6

Source: Social Security online, at http://www.ssa.gov/history/lifeexpect.html, accessed 9/05.

Perhaps in the end a grand compromise, forged by a non-partisan, blue-ribbon commission, will have to be struck to keep the system solvent. The compromise might allow for an adjustment to the formula for initial pension payments in the future, producing some reduction in benefit growth; the FICA tax rate might be raised a bit; and the retirement age might be bumped up. A small adjustment to the retirement age could be politically acceptable if U.S. life expectancies continue to rise, something that is widely anticipated, though at a much slower rate than in the twentieth century. Keep in mind, however, that the age for regular Social Security eligibility has *already* been increased from 65 to 67, a change that will be fully in effect by the year 2025.

Medicare and Medicaid

As the population of the United States grows older, not only do its Social Security pension costs escalate, but so do its medical bills for elder care. Since 1965, Americans over the age of 65 have had a federal program, Medicare, to help them meet their medical expenses. As mentioned in the previous section, the program is financed through a payroll tax of 2.9 percent split evenly between employees and employers. (There is no upper limit to the income subject to the Medicare tax, unlike the old-age portion of FICA.) In early 2005, about 42 million people were covered by Medicare, and program finances were solidly in the black. In the long run, however, the black ink turns to red—in fact, the program will begin running deficits years before Social Security will!

Medicare's problems stem from two sources: the rising number of enrollees and the rapidly climbing costs of medical treatment. The expansion of the elder population would not in itself be a problem if the number of workers paying into the program were growing at an equally rapid pace. Unfortunately, the labor force will be growing much more slowly than the retiree population for decades after 2010. It all comes back to the baby boom phenomenon. The enormous cohort of babies born between 1946 and 1964 grew up to become the biggest labor force the United States had ever seen, and in the not too distant future they will be transformed into the biggest retired generation in history. But because the boomers were less prolific than their parents, the working population available to pay their Medicare expenses will be heavily burdened. The other half of Medicare's funding problem is the cost of medical care itself, which for many years has consistently risen faster than the general cost of living. One expert has estimated that Medicare's bite out of the national GDP will rise from 2.5 percent in 2002 to 9.2 percent in 2075. Roughly one-third of the increase will be due to the aging of the population; the other two-thirds will be due to rising health care costs (Holtz-Eakin 2003).

In some sense, the looming Social Security deficits present a simpler problem to grapple with than the Medicare deficits we will soon be facing. With pension payments, getting fiscal control is a matter of ratcheting certain formulas upward or downward in order to get the dollar flows in the system into balance. With Medicare, on the other hand, *real* goods and services must be provided under law to a vast benefit-entitled population, and the pricing of those services is both difficult to predict and difficult to control. Who could have predicted, for example, that in 2003 the president would propose, and Congress would approve, a generous new prescription drug benefit for the elderly? The White House, which originally estimated the new program's cost at $400 billion for the first ten years, now puts the cost at about $720 billion! It should come as no surprise, then, that Medicare's annual costs are on track to surpass those of Social Security itself by 2024. Very few people are aware that Medicare's cumulative deficit between now and 2075 is twice as large as the cumulative Social Security deficit (Lazarus 2005).

If Medicare's fiscal woes do not provide a stiff enough challenge to the wisdom and ingenuity of U.S. policymakers as they try to cope with the aging population, there is another program to which they can turn their attention: Medicaid. Passed by Congress in 1965 and benefiting some 53 million persons in 2005, this is a state-federal government partnership to ensure that medical care is available to the nation's low-income individuals and families. One might at first wonder what the connection is between a low-income program and the over–65 population, since, broadly speaking, U.S. elders have *improved* their economic standing relative to younger age groups over the past three decades. (This is most clearly the case when comparing the welfare of seniors to that of children.) The explanation lies in a key feature of Medicaid—its coverage of the costs of long-term care for low-income seniors. About two-thirds of the folks in nursing homes have their bills paid by Medicaid.

Nursing-home care is extremely expensive, with annual costs in 2004 averaging about $70,000 per year and rising steadily. In their 70s, 80s, and 90s, most Americans lack the private resources to cover a lengthy stay in a managed-care facility. If they end up in such a place, they must pay the tab out of their own pockets until they have essentially burned through all their financial assets, at which point Medicaid takes over. The high and rising costs of nursing-home care are one of the main reasons why the elderly, constituting only about one-quarter of the Medicaid beneficiary population, absorb more than 70 percent of the program's budget. Unlike Medicare and Social Security, Medicaid gets no support from a payroll tax. It is funded by general state and federal revenues. That means that when Medicaid costs rise year after year at rates well above the growth rate of tax revenues, states—and in some cases *counties*—are put under increasingly severe fiscal stress. Some states are beginning to look for ways to ration health care among their Medicaid recipients. *Every* state is thinking about ways to implement cost controls in this program.

Medicaid's financial problems are not solely attributable to the aging of the U.S. population. Rising health care costs and growing numbers of uninsured people are two other factors worsening the situation. When all these factors are combined, you have a policy challenge almost without precedent. And when you stand back and consider that all three foundational programs of the U.S. welfare state, namely, Social Security, Medicare, and Medicaid, face severe financial pressures in coming years as the population ages, you can only wonder whether the American political system will be able to contain those pressures. To date there has not been much vision, leadership, or discussion of hard choices on these questions from elected politicians. They have had the luxury of waiting until a real crisis arrives. At some point they will no longer have that luxury.

International Family Planning: Early U.S. Support

The politics of U.S. government support for international family planning has become so controversial in recent years that it is hard to believe how *non*controversial this issue once was. Back in the 1960s and 1970s, Democrats and Republicans alike supported what were then called "population control" efforts in the developing countries. President John F. Kennedy expressed concern about population growth occurring most rapidly in those parts of the world where hunger was already most prevalent. In 1965, under Kennedy's successor, Lyndon Johnson, the United States Agency for International Development (USAID) began supporting international family planning on a regular basis. Three years later, USAID funds were used for the first time to purchase contraceptive supplies for distribution in developing nations. Congressional support for the effort was bipartisan (USAID timeline).

In 1968, the year Paul Erhlich's *Population Bomb* put an exclamation point on rising public worries about global population growth, Richard Nixon was elected president. Like his predecessors, Nixon viewed the population issue as one that affected U.S. national security in real and potentially critical ways. In his first year in office, he sent to Congress a "special message" on world population in which he declared that population growth was "one of the most serious challenges to human destiny in the last third of this century" (Nixon 1969, 530). Nixon's interest in population continued into his second term. In 1974, he ordered a group of top administration officials to carry out a study of the impact of world population growth on American interests abroad, with a time frame extending to at least the year 2000. The classified report they produced in December 1974, "National Security Study Memorandum 200"—or, more briefly, "NSSM 200"—was delivered to Nixon's post-Watergate successor, Gerald Ford, though it was not released to the public for another fifteen years. One of the alarming conclusions of the report—excerpted in our Documents chapter—was that population pressures might destabilize countries that supplied strategic minerals and fuels to the United States (USAID timeline).

President Ford considered the population issue important enough to justify personally attending the 1974 world population conference held in Bucharest. There he declared population growth trends to be "vital to the future of mankind." At this conference, population policies and programs came under heavy attack by some delegates, journalists, and activists as a veiled assault on the Third World, undertaken to advance the interests and hegemony of the capitalist, neocolonialist First World. Needless to say, such rhetoric was rarely heard in the chambers of the U.S. Congress, but the opening salvo of a long-running campaign against international family planning had already been fired on Capitol Hill in 1973, and it came not from the left but from the right. This was the Helms amendment to the foreign aid program, sponsored by North Carolina Senator Jesse Helms. The amendment prohibited U.S. funds from being used by foreign NGOs to perform abortions or even to counsel clients on abortion as a means of family planning. It is not clear what impact the Helms amendment had on NGOs such as International Planned Parenthood. In some cases, they were probably able to engage in "creative accounting" to avoid any explicit violation of the new rule while continuing to offer the same services as before.

"Mexico City" and Abortion Politics

The Reagan administration announced a much tougher U.S. anti-abortion stance at the world population conference held in Mexico City in 1984. Henceforth no U.S. aid funds would go to any international agency that performed abortions, offered counseling on abortion, or advocated for legalized access to abortion in any country in the world—even if these activities were carried out with non-U.S. funds. The new policy ran counter to expert opinion within government agencies. It was opposed by most NGOs and by the reproductive health community, and it was universally regarded as a political concession to religious conservatives within the Republican Party. (The new policy had been foreshadowed by provisions the religious right had insisted be included in the party's 1980 platform.) With "Mexico City," as the policy came to be known, bipartisanship on international family planning came to an end. George H. W. Bush continued the policy during his single term as president, but when a Democrat, Bill Clinton, was elected to the White House in 1992, one of his first acts in office was to rescind the policy. Eight years later, George Bush reinstated the policy on his first day in office.

Critics of "Mexico City" are particularly disturbed by the prohibition of any *counseling* on the abortion option, even in places where abortion is legal. Nowhere in the United States itself are health professionals barred by the government from discussing any medical option with their patients, including abortion. This provision of the policy seems (to many) out of keeping with the value Americans place on free speech. Given the policy's added ban on any political advocacy in favor of legalizing, or improving access to, abortion in foreign countries, the term *global gag rule* comes as no surprise. Several major international family-planning agencies, including the International Planned Parenthood Federation (IFFP) and Marie Stopes International, have refused to accept the terms of "Mexico City" and thus have lost U.S. government funding. In the case of the IPPF, this brought an end to seventeen years of continuous financial support from the United States.

Of a piece with the Mexico City policy implemented by the Reagan administration was another action taken by that administration: the denial of U.S. funding to the United Nations Population Fund (UNFPA) in 1986. The UNFPA, currently supported by 166 nations, is the world's largest provider of population assistance, with an annual budget of around $500 million. Prior to 1986, the United States had been a regular financial supporter of the UNFPA—indeed it had been instrumental in the *creation* of that agency in 1967. But in 1985 Congress passed the Kemp-Kasten amendment disallowing U.S. funding to any organization that participated in coercive abortions or involuntary sterilizations. The one-child policy adopted by China in 1979 has been administered coercively at times, almost all observers agree, and the UNFPA has worked on projects in China. Through a kind of guilt-by-association logic, the Reagan administration decided that Kemp-Kasten required a cutoff of U.S. funding to the UNFPA itself. The ban on UNFPA funding continued through the remaining Reagan–Bush years, 1986–1992. Funding was partially restored under President Clinton, but the ban was put back in place under the younger President Bush in 2002.

The role of politics in the UNFPA de-funding decision is almost beyond dispute. During its first year and a half, the Bush administration supported the UN agency without objection. Then an obscure organization called the Population Research Institute leveled charges that the UNFPA was complicit in Chinese coercive practices. A delegation of British MPs made a visit to China in early 2002 to investigate the charges and concluded that the UNFPA did *not* condone, fund, or participate in coercive activities. The Bush administration's own State Department sent a three-person team of experts to China on a similar mission in May 2002, and it came to similar conclusions. But in the end the White House yielded to domestic pro-life political pressures. U.S. funding for the UNFPA was halted in July 2002. The irony here is that outside observers have actually credited the UNFPA with pushing China *away* from coercion and toward more voluntary, client-centered family-planning and reproductive health services. For more on the politics and arguments on both sides of this issue, see the biographical sketches of Representatives Chris Smith (R-NJ) and Carolyn Maloney (D-NY) in Chapter 5.

Principle and Practice

The United States still supports international family planning both in principle and in practice. Polls have consistently shown that Americans favor aid to population programs in developing nations. USAID remains the world's biggest governmental funding source for family-planning programs (as well as programs to combat AIDS). And Congress, although mainly controlled by Republicans since 1994, has not stopped appropriating funds for the UNFPA. As recently as November 2004, Congress approved $34 million for that UN agency. But the money will not go where Congress wants it to go. President Bush will almost certainly continue withholding such funds until he leaves office. Whether U.S. support for the UNFPA is restored in 2009 or not will probably depend on whether the next president is a Democrat or a Republican.

Those who define and support the current administration's positions on population policy take their stand on one overriding moral principle: preserving the lives of the unborn. They oppose abortion within the United States—seeking, for example, to overturn the Supreme Court's 1973 *Roe v. Wade* decision—and with equal vehemence they oppose abortion overseas. Both domestically and on the international scene, they get powerful support from the hierarchy (if not always the laity) of the Roman Catholic Church. Vatican diplomats have worked energetically, and with considerable success, at world population conferences to weaken, or even eliminate, the language affirming women's reproductive rights in the official documents emerging from such meetings. For pro-lifers, there can be no compromise on the issue of the unborn. They believe life begins at conception, so abortion is—not to mince words—murder. Holding such beliefs, pro-lifers naturally find it absolutely unacceptable for U.S. funds to support in any way agencies or organizations that condone, offer counseling on, or perform abortions.

On the other side of the argument are those who disagree in principle with the pro-life position. Although everyone can stipulate that biological "life" begins at conception, it is much less clear at what point the fetus becomes "viable," or at what point it acquires the status of a human being—a soul. (Even Thomas Aquinas puzzled over this question.) Those on the pro-choice side consider the fetus's right to life to be potentially in conflict with the right of a woman to control her own body. Which right takes precedence? That is a legal, philosophical, and theological debate that is unlikely to be settled anytime soon, with an impact sure to be felt in U.S. politics for years to come.

One of the moral conundrums that pro-lifers must face is that when you deprive family-planning NGOs of funding on the grounds that they are involved with abortion, the actual result may be an increased number of abortions! Organizations such as the IPPF and Marie Stopes International offer a full array of family-planning options, so if their funding is cut, they are less able to provide, among other things, the ordinary kinds of contraceptives that would make unintended pregnancies less likely. If they experience funding cutbacks, their clients' risk of becoming pregnant rises. With more unplanned pregnancies comes, inevitably, a greater number of abortions. In 2002, the UNFPA projected that the loss of U.S. funding to its various programs could cause an additional 2 million pregnancies and 800,000 abortions around the world, with accompanying increases in maternal and child mortality (Crossette 2004/2005, 59). In its own defense, the Bush administration can claim that the funds it withholds from the UNFPA are redirected into USAID programs to, among other things, reduce infant mortality. But that "compromise" is unlikely to satisfy either side. Why? Because on the one hand it probably does not reduce (and for reasons just given, may *increase*) the number of abortions, and on the other, it deprives many women of the full range of family-planning choices they might otherwise have had.

Fewer People, Declining Influence?

A final population question of special interest to Americans is whether current population trends threaten the global power and influence of their country. The more interesting version of this question is not whether the United States will remain the world's sole superpower, capable of getting its way on every issue, but whether the core values of Western civilization, proclaimed and promoted by the United States, will have less cogency, less influence, in a world with shrunken Western populations. The political-demographic commentator Ben Wattenberg has voiced this concern repeatedly. In his 1987 book *The Birth Dearth: What Happens When People in Free Countries Don't Have Enough Babies,* and again in his recent *Fewer: How the New Demography of Depopulation Will Shape Our Future* (2004), Wattenberg has worried about the geopolitical implications of low Western birth rates. He is by no means the only person to have raised an alarm on this point, but because his comments have been bracingly direct and free of "political correctness," we focus mainly on him in the following discussion.

In the late 1980s the United States was still engaged in a deadly serious Cold War with a formidable adversary, the Soviet Union. The U.S. fertility rate had languished below replacement level for a number of years—it was about 1.8 in 1987—while in the Soviet Union the TFR was 2.5. As Wattenberg noted in *Birth Dearth*, the U.S. and Soviet populations were roughly on a par at that time, with the Soviets ahead by only 15 percent. But current demographic trends, if projected into the future, would raise Soviet numbers to 365 million *and rising* by 2065, while the U.S. population in that year would be only 278 million *and falling* (Wattenberg 1987, 90). Changes in the two superpowers' age structures would widen the gap even further: the Soviet labor force was headed for a 50 percent advantage over the Americans by 2065. From a global perspective, with Western numbers viewed as a proportion of world population, things looked just as bad. The industrial democracies, which had accounted for 22 percent of world population in 1950, were down to 15 percent in 1985 and shrinking toward a 5 percent share in 2100 (Wattenberg 1987, 47). Western values would be under challenge if "our numbers go down, and down, and down [and] if our economic and military power go down, and down, and down" (Wattenberg 1987, 98).

Much has changed in the world since 1987, as Wattenberg would be the first to admit. The Soviet Union has disintegrated, Russia's population is in absolute decline, and the United States now stands apart from the other industrial democracies, with a fertility rate that remains at replacement level (just barely). But the challenge to the West continues. "In the next half century or so," Wattenberg warns, "Western civilization will become an ever-smaller fraction of total world population" (Wattenberg 2004, 160). Modern democratic nations, as he calls them, will post little if any net growth in numbers between now and 2050, with a U.S. gain of 100 million neutralized by a roughly equal loss among the rest of the group (Wattenberg 2004, 175). Meanwhile, the nondemocratic, non-Western countries will increase their global numbers and their proportion of the world population. Equating Western civilization with the countries designated by the United Nations as "more developed," Wattenberg foresees a diminution of the West's global share from 32 percent in 1950 to a mere 14 percent in 2050 (Wattenberg 2004, 161).

A variation on Wattenberg's theme—still very much in the minor key!—is the scenario sketched by Peter G. Peterson in his 1999 book *Gray Dawn: How the Coming Age Wave Will Transform America—and the World.* As every demographer knows, a slower-growing population tends quickly to become an older population. With a rising number of seniors in the developed world, and with mounting health and pension costs for those seniors, the resulting calls on the public purse may force cutbacks in spending on defense and other international priorities, as Peterson sees it. In places like Japan and Europe, labor forces may actually decline, leading to proportional declines in GDP. Under these circumstances it will be very difficult for governments to maintain their combat forces and other instruments of global influence. The older, richer countries will have a hard time retaining their "leadership roles" on the world stage (Peterson 1999, 17, 20–21).

Human Numbers — Not the Whole Story

It is hard to quarrel with the numbers cited by Peterson and Wattenberg (2004). They are in line with the most recent UN projections. The more developed, "Western" countries are indeed growing older, and their share of the world's population is all but certain to continue shrinking for decades to come. Whether this will mean diminished power for the United States and its allies, or diminished influence for Western ideas, is less clear. Military power *is* built to some degree on a demographic base. An army of one makes a nice slogan for the U.S. Army, but it takes more than one soldier to win a firefight on the battlefield. Numbers matter when it comes to projecting military power. With that acknowledged, it is also true that human numbers can be leveraged with technology. One of the key strategic principles adopted by the North Atlantic Treaty Organization (NATO) during the Cold War was to develop and deploy enough high-tech weaponry to offset the superior numbers of Red Army troops. The nation of Israel has adopted much the same strategy in the decades since it was founded, so far successfully.

It does not appear that the United States, in the next few decades, will be crippled militarily by insufficient numbers of personnel in its armed forces. (If it becomes involved in more conflicts like Iraq and Afghanistan, however, all bets are off.) The United States will remain the world's third most populous country in 2050, after India and China, with a mid-century population of 420 million. Although it will be an older population than at present, there should not be any undue difficulty in recruiting adequate numbers to meet the country's national defense needs as well as its international commitments.

What about Peter Peterson's concern that fiscal constraints on the military will loom larger in a graying America? If Medicare, Medicaid, and Social Security for an aging U.S. population eat up too much of the federal budget in coming years, there may not be much left for the Pentagon. So goes the argument. Those for whom this is a genuine worry should be reassured by this reality: through cycles of war and peace, economic upturns and downturns, and rotations of national administration between the two major political parties, the Pentagon always seems to receive a healthy share of the federal budget. By some respectable estimates, the United States spends about as much on its military as all other countries in the world *combined*. Thus, if a conflict emerges between the needs of the elderly and the needs of the Pentagon, it's probably the elderly who should worry.

On the broader question of Western values and their survival in a world with diminished numbers of Westerners, one need not be a neoconservative like Ben Wattenberg to feel invested in this issue. Western democracies proclaim high ideals: freedom of speech, freedom of the press, freedom of assembly, freedom of religion, freedom of workers to organize, and so on. Sometimes the Western nations (including the United States) live up to these ideals, sometimes not. Wattenberg believes it is important for the global spread of liberty that there be an "exemplar nation," a democratic nation that is successful both economically and demographically. He sees the United States as the exemplar nation of our time and doubts it would fulfill that role if it were losing population. Doubters might ask how a gradual stabilization or even a modest decline in population would render the United States less "exemplary." Foreigners probably rate the exemplariness of the United States on *several* criteria weightier than its current demographic status.

One of those criteria undoubtedly is the extent to which the United States is perceived to conform its own policies and conduct to its stated democratic ideals. American history offers a mixed record in this regard. The American rhetoric of liberty has been lofty and inspiring from the start; the performance has often lagged behind. When people in the "Less Developed Countries" (as Wattenberg calls them) believe the United States is lecturing them on principles of democracy that it is failing to meet within its own borders—or in its international dealings—then the "exemplar nation" ends up looking hypocritical. In any case, the ideals of Western civilization have long since become universal ideals, overwhelmingly accepted by national leaders from every part of the world, at least in their public declarations. The United Nations has been the scene and sponsor of a whole range of declarations on human rights, not all of which have been endorsed by the United States. The real task ahead, for the United States as for all nations, is to close the gap between the principles of freedom we proclaim and those we truly attain.

References

Abernethy, Virginia. 1994. "Optimism and Overpopulation." *The Atlantic Monthly* 274:6, 84–91.

Bernstein, Nina. 2004, February 20. "Teenage Rate of Pregnancy Drops in U.S." *New York Times*, A22.

Crossette, Barbara. 2004/2005. "Hurting the World's Poor in Morality's Name." *World Policy Journal* 21:4 (Winter), 57–62.

Downs, Barbara. 2003. "Fertility of American Women: June 2002." *Current Population Reports, P20–548*. Washington, DC: U.S. Census Bureau.

Faulkner, Caroline L. 2004. "Understanding Minority Fertility: Contraceptive Use among First Generation Mexican Immigrant Couples in Houston, Texas, and San Diego, California." Paper presented at Population Association of America meetings.

Feldstein, Martin. 2005. "Structural Reform of Social Security." *The Journal of Economic Perspectives* 19:2, 33–55.

Holtz-Eakin, Douglas. 2003, April 10. "Medicare's Long-Term Financial Condition." Testimony by the CBO director before the Joint Economic Committee.

Lazarus, David. 2005, February 18. "Medicare Facing Fiscal Ills." *San Francisco Chronicle*, C1.

Longman, Phillip. 2004. *The Empty Cradle: How Falling Birthrates Threaten World Prosperity [and What to Do about It]*. New York: New America Books.

Malthus, Thomas Robert. 1993 [1798]. *An Essay on the Principle of Population*. Edited by Geoffrey Gilbert for Oxford World's Classics. New York: Oxford University Press.

Nixon, Richard. 1969, July 18. "Special Message to the Congress on Problems of Population Growth," in *Public Papers of the Presidents of the United States: Richard Nixon*. Washington, DC: Office of the Federal Register, National Archives,. pp. 521–530.

Olshansky, S.J., et al. 2005. "A Potential Decline in Life Expectancy in the United States in the 21st Century." *New England Journal of Medicine* 352:11, 1138–1145.

Peterson, Peter G. 1999. *Gray Dawn: How the Coming Age Wave Will Transform America—and the World*. New York: Times Books.

Population Reference Bureau. (PRB). 2005. *2005 World Population Data Sheet*. Washington, DC: PRB.

United States Agency for International Development (USAID). n.d. "USAID's Family Planning Program Timeline: Before 1965 to the Present." Accessed at http://www.usaid.gov/our_work/global_health/pop/timeline.html

United States Census Bureau. 2004, March. "U.S. Interim Projections by Age, Sex, Race, and Hispanic Origin." Accessed at http://www.census.gov/ipc/www/usinterimproj/natprojtab02a.pdf

Wattenberg, Ben J. 1987. *The Birth Dearth: What Happens When People in Free Countries Don't Have Enough Babies*. New York: Pharos Books.

Wattenberg, Ben J. 2004. *Fewer: How the New Demography of Depopulation Will Shape Our Future*. Chicago: Ivan R. Dee.

Weeks, John R. 2005. *Population: An Introduction to Concepts and Issues*, 9th ed. Belmont, CA: Wadsworth.

4

Chronology

One of the best ways to get one's footing on a topic like world population is to scan a listing of key events that have contributed to our understanding of it. An "event" might be an international conference, the publication of an influential book, the passage of a law, the conduct of a national census, or the occurrence of a lethal epidemic. This chapter presents just such a timeline of events that have either affected world population or shaped the way we look at it. Sources for the chronology are given at the end of the chapter. Obviously, there is no single place to find a complete history of world population. Three books, however, by Cohen (1995), Livi-Bacci (2001), and Weeks (2004), are especially informative not only on the history of population but on many other aspects of the subject.

8000 B.C.   The agricultural revolution begins, with about 4 million humans on Earth; hunter-gatherers shift to more settled patterns of living, which include livestock-herding and the cultivation of grains; population begins growing more rapidly.

1000 B.C.   Egyptians are using a primitive form of contraception (condoms).

5 B.C.   Caesar Augustus orders a census of the entire Roman Empire.

A.D. 1   World population stands at about 210 million.

A.D. 2   Under the Han Dynasty, China counts the number of households, that is, conducts a primitive census.

A.D. 100 The city of Rome's population of 650,000 is unrivaled by any other city in the world.

1086   William the Conqueror orders a survey of English lands and landholdings, from which modern historians have derived a population estimate for England of around 1.5 million.

1347   The bubonic plague, or "Black Death," returns to Europe after an absence of six or seven centuries, appearing first in Sicily and spreading rapidly in the following years. Its cause is the bacillus *Yersinia pestis,* spread by rodent-borne fleas. By 1400 the plague has wiped out nearly one-third of Europe's population.

1492   Christopher Columbus's arrival in the West Indies marks the opening stage of a long-term population catastrophe for the indigenous American peoples as a result of their vulnerability to the pathogens carried by Europeans. The population of Aztecs in central Mexico, for example, falls from about 6.3 million in 1548 to 1.9 million in 1580.

1500   The population of Europe, battered by periodic returns of the plague, still has not recovered to the level it reached in 1300.

1666   The first census in Canada, known to contemporaries as "New France," is conducted by Jean Talon, intendant of Quebec City; the count is 3,918 persons.

1679   Dutch scientist A. van Leeuwenhoek offers an early quantitative estimate of Earth's maximum population, or carrying capacity: 13.4 billion

1721   Japan conducts a nationwide count of population; scholars believe population surveys were undertaken in Japan as early as the ninth century A.D.

The practice of inoculating people against smallpox is introduced in rural England: a small extract from a smallpox pustule is transferred from an infected individual to one who has not previously been infected. A mild case of the disease results, but thereafter the inoculee enjoys a natural immunity to smallpox.

1749   Sweden is among the first nations in Europe to establish a population register and census, conducted locally by clergymen.

1771   An outbreak of bubonic plague in Moscow takes 57,000 lives in one season.

1774   With the death of Louis XV from smallpox, popular opposition to smallpox inoculation in France crumbles.

1776   George Washington orders smallpox inoculation for all troops in the Continental Army.

1787   The kingdom of Spain, in its first census, counts 10.4 million people.

1790   The first U.S. census, mandated by the just-ratified Constitution, finds a total national population of about 3.9 million.

1797   Edward Jenner, an English country doctor, notices that milkmaids rarely contract smallpox. He assumes that by getting cowpox, milkmaids acquire immunity to the more deadly smallpox. Jenner develops a vaccine for humans based on cowpox that proves to be fully protective against smallpox. Thus, vaccination replaces inoculation in the prevention of smallpox.

1798   The publication of Thomas Robert Malthus's *Essay on the Principle of Population* marks a milestone in the study of human population and the social, economic, and moral implications of population size. Malthus warns that pop-

1798, ulation tends to increase more rapidly than the means of
cont. subsistence and that in the absence of other checks, famine and disease will act as the ultimate checks.

1800 Only one city in the world has 1 million people—London; two centuries later there will be 325 additional cities of that size or larger.

1801 The United Kingdom conducts its first census and counts a total of 16.3 million persons living in England, Scotland, Wales, and Ireland. The count for England alone is 8.9 million, or less than double the U.S. total for 1800 (5.3 million). The British census is repeated every ten years with the exception of the war year, 1941.

1804 There are 1 billion people on Earth.

1817 An outbreak of cholera in Calcutta spreads beyond its usual bounds; British colonial troops pass the disease to Nepalese and Afghan foes. Within a few years, ships' crews carry it even further, to Ceylon, Indonesia, China, and Japan, as well as into the Middle East and down the east African coast.

1831 An outbreak of cholera at Mecca during the annual Muslim pilgrimage leads to a widespread epidemic throughout the Islamic world. In many subsequent years, cholera outbreaks accompany the annual pilgrimage—for a final time in 1912.

1843 Vulcanization of rubber opens the way to mass production of inexpensive condoms.

1846 Failure of the potato crop initiates a great famine in Ireland; within a few years, over a million Irish die, and over a million emigrate from the island.

1854 English physician John Snow discovers, during a cholera outbreak in London, that the disease is caused *not* by "miasma," or "bad air," but rather by the presence of fecal waste in drinking water. Snow publishes his finding in 1855; not until 1883 is the actual bacterium, *Vibrio cholerae*, observed under the microscope by Robert Koch.

The Dutch establish plantations of quinchona trees in Java; an extract from the trees' bark, quinine, is effective in treating malaria.

1873   Congress passes the Comstock Act banning the distribution of contraceptive devices or birth-control information across state lines.

1882   Robert Koch announces his discovery of the bacillus responsible for tuberculosis.

1883   Francis Galton, English statistician and amateur scientist and cousin of Charles Darwin, proposes a new word, "eugenics," to denote the conscious improvement of human populations through selective breeding. The idea spreads quickly in England, Europe, and the United States—its enthusiasts include Teddy Roosevelt, Margaret Sanger, and economist John Maynard Keynes—but falls into disrepute after the 1930s.

1891   E. G. Ravenstein, a well-known British scholar, publishes a carefully calculated estimate of the world's current population as well as its future supportable population; his first estimate is later judged to have been remarkably accurate, but not his figure for the Earth's maximum population, 5.99 billion (surpassed in 1999).

1909   The International Office of Public Hygiene is established in Paris to monitor worldwide outbreaks of such diseases as cholera, typhus, yellow fever, and smallpox.

1915   The newly established Rockefeller Foundation undertakes to study and bring under control the deadly mosquito-borne "yellow fever," sending teams of scientists to Latin America and Africa. By 1935, an effective vaccine for prevention of the disease has been developed in the Rockefeller Foundation laboratories; in 1950 Max Theiler is awarded the Nobel Prize in medicine for this work.

1916   Margaret Sanger opens the first U.S. birth-control clinic in Brooklyn.

1918–   Global influenza pandemic takes an estimated 25–40
1919   million lives. U.S. servicemen heading to war in Europe take the virus with them on troop ships. Returning home, they bring the flu back to its country of origin. Total deaths from the so-called Spanish flu in the United States are estimated at 550,000.

1921   The first family-planning clinic in the United Kingdom is opened by Marie Stopes, English feminist, birth-control activist, and author of the pioneering sex manual *Married Love* (1919).

        The first vaccine effective against tuberculosis is produced.

1927   World population reaches 2 billion.

1928   Alexander Fleming's discovery of penicillin opens the way to control of pneumonia, toxic shock syndrome, and other bacterial illnesses.

1929   Population Reference Bureau (PRB) is founded in Washington, D.C., eventually becoming the most respected independent source of unbiased, accurate information on population in the United States.

1930   At a conference in Lambeth (London), the worldwide Anglican communion resolves that contraception, under appropriate circumstances, is morally acceptable.

        In reaction to the Anglican decision earlier in the year, Pope Pius XI issues the encyclical *Casti Connubii*, reasserting the traditional Roman Catholic position that contraception is contrary to the purpose of the conjugal act and therefore immoral.

1931   Population Association of America is founded by Alfred Lotka and others; it becomes the leading professional society of demographers in the United States.

1943   The Great Bengal (India) Famine claims roughly 3 million lives, mostly due to lowered resistance to disease.

1944   Norman Borlaug arrives at the Mexican research center later known as Centro Internacional de Mejoramiento de Mais y Trigo (CIMMYT), or International Maize and Wheat Improvement Center. Borlaug leads efforts to develop high-yield wheat and maize, with major funding from the Rockefeller Foundation.

1945   Demographer Frank Notestein formulates the theory of "demographic transition"; it soon becomes an influential framework for analyzing national trends in mortality, fertility, and population growth.

1946   The U.S. baby boom (also experienced in several other countries heavily involved in World War II) begins; the peak year of the boom in the United States is 1957.

United Nations Population Division is established, with Frank Notestein, an architect of the modern science of demography, as its first director.

1948   The publication of *Our Plundered Planet*, by Fairfield Osborn, raises the issue of a correlation between rapid population increase and environmental degradation; William Vogt's *Road to Survival* warns of the impact of a population explosion among the "backward billion" of the world.

The passage of the Eugenics Protection Act in postwar Japan legalizes abortion; an already declining Japanese birthrate falls even faster.

The World Health Organization is established.

1951   The draft outline of India's first Five-Year Plan calls for a national population policy that includes family planning, and specifically the provision of facilities for sterilization. The final draft of the plan, released in 1952, states that a reduction in the country's birthrate would benefit the economy as well as the health of mothers and children.

1952   Population Council is founded in New York at the instigation and under the sponsorship of John D. Rockefeller III.

India launches its Family Planning Program, the first such national effort in the world. The program is part of the country's First Five-Year Plan. It envisions family planning as part of a broader health program to be funded by the central government.

International Planned Parenthood Federation (IPPF) is established, with headquarters in London and birth-control pioneer Margaret Sanger as its first president. Its original members are from India, the United States, the United Kingdom, the Netherlands, Sweden, West Germany, Singapore, and Hong Kong. By 2005, the IPPF has 149 member organizations working in 166 countries. It is active in sixteen additional countries where it does not currently have a member association.

1955   A vaccine against polio, developed by Dr. Jonas Salk of the University of Pittsburgh Medical School, is proved effective in human trials.

1958   Coale and Hoover's book *Population Growth and Economic Development in Low-Income Countries* argues that population growth hinders poor countries' prospects for economic growth; the view becomes highly influential in government and academic circles.

1958–   Mao Zedong's crash industrialization program in China,
1961   known as the Great Leap Forward, leads to famine deaths in the range of 30 million. The estimate of 30 million is based on the difference between *expected* Chinese mortality in those years and *actual* mortality. Experts consider this the worst famine in history.

1960   There are 3 billion people on Earth.

International Rice Research Institute (IRRI) is established by the Rockefeller and Ford Foundations in the Philippines to develop high-yield varieties of rice.

U.S. Food and Drug Administration (FDA) approves oral contraceptives, or "the pill"; by 1965, it is the most common form of birth control in the United States.

1961   United States Agency for International Development (USAID) is established within the U.S. State Department; within a few years it becomes the main conduit for U.S. financial assistance to global family-planning efforts.

1962   The release of dwarf, high-yield wheat inaugurates the so-called Green Revolution, raising hopes that rapid increases in world food supplies will match the high rate of population increase, especially in the developing nations.

Serious research begins on oral rehydration therapy (ORT) to combat the devastating mortality effects of diarrhea, especially for children in the poorer countries; clinical trials are conducted by the International Centre for Diarrhoeal Diseases Research in Bangladesh from 1964 to 1968. Successful results are announced in a *Lancet* journal article in 1968. ORT now offers a safe, effective, and inexpensive treatment for cholera.

1963   The growth rate of world population reaches its all-time high of about 2.2 percent annually; by 2005 it will fall to about 1.15 percent.

1964   This year marks the close of the U.S. baby boom that began in 1946.

1965   The Supreme Court, in *Griswold v. Connecticut*, gives married couples the right to practice birth control; a later decision (1972) extends the right to unmarried couples.

President Johnson declares, in his State of the Union address: "I will seek new ways to use our knowledge to help deal with the explosion in world population and the growing scarcity in world resources" (Green 1993, 305). Senate hearings are held, and USAID prepares to get involved in family-planning efforts abroad. U.S. funding of such efforts rises during LBJ's term from $2 million to $35 million annually.

1966 IRRI releases its first high-yield rice.

1967 The United Nations Population Fund (UNFPA) is authorized.

The best-selling book *Famine, 1975!* by William and Paul Paddock advocates a harsh policy of "triage" in dealing with anticipated famines: provide aid only to those countries that have a reasonable chance of bringing their population growth under control.

1968 The publication by the Sierra Club of Paul Ehrlich's *The Population Bomb* builds public awareness of the effects of rapid population increase. The book eventually sells millions of copies.

Zero Population Growth (ZPG) is founded by Paul Ehrlich and others.

Pope Paul VI issues the encyclical *Humanae Vitae,* restating traditional Catholic opposition to all forms of birth control except the "rhythm method." Polls later indicate that Catholic couples in the United States practice birth control at the same rate as the rest of the population.

UN conference on human rights held in Iran results in the Teheran Proclamation; article 16 identifies the control of one's own fertility, and access to the means of achieving this, as a basic human right.

1969 UNFPA begins operations as the major international source of family-planning assistance.

A United Nations General Assembly resolution calls on governments to provide their citizens with the knowledge and means necessary to control their fertility.

President Nixon declares in a message to Congress: "The experience of this decade has . . . shown that lower rates of population growth can be critical for speeding up economic development and social progress" (Green 1993, 308).

1970   The Nobel Peace Prize is awarded to Norman Borlaug for his work in advancing the Green Revolution, by which food crop yields have been greatly increased in many developing countries.

Global population growth is a major concern voiced on the first Earth Day, on April 22.

1972   Publication of *The Limits to Growth*, sponsored by the Club of Rome, renews worries about an unsustainable growth of world population.

The Nixon-appointed Commission on Population Growth and the American Future, chaired by John D. Rockefeller III, recommends stabilized domestic population, an end to illegal immigration, liberalized state laws on abortion, and other measures. Nixon declines to endorse the report.

1973   *Roe v. Wade* decision by the Supreme Court legalizes abortion in the United States.

1973– 1974   Famine in Ethiopia claims more than 100,000 lives, replaying on a smaller scale the terrible Ethiopian famine of 1888–1892, in which one-third of the country's population died.

1974   Famine in Bangladesh claims 26,000 lives, according to the government, but unofficial estimates place the toll at 100,000 or more.

There are 4 billion people on Earth.

The first international conference on population to be attended by official government representatives is held in Bucharest. The conference is highly contentious and politicized, but a world population plan of action is adopted. "Economic development is the best contraceptive" becomes the most quoted phrase from the conference.

President Echeverria of Mexico reverses his previous opposition to family planning. The country's General Law

1974, of Population is altered to permit the sale and purchase
cont. of contraceptives. The Catholic Church refrains from actively opposing the change of policy.

Worldwatch Institute founded in Washington, D.C.

A National Security Council memorandum, ordered by President Nixon, details the possible adverse effects on U.S. national interests from rapidly rising world population; contents are classified (declassified in 1989).

1975 At the World Conference of the International Women's Year, a "world plan of action" points to ways that improved education, status, and employment for women would affect age at marriage, as well as the spacing and number of children.

1976 India's national government, under Prime Minister Indira Gandhi, authorizes state legislatures to enact policies of compulsory sterilization to limit birthrates; the ensuing period of "national emergency" culminates in Gandhi being voted out of office.

The government of East Germany (GDR) introduces a package of pronatal measures, consisting mainly of more generous maternity leaves. The country's TFR rises from 1.64 to 1.94 by 1980, a level more than 0.4 higher than that in West Germany. A decade after implementation of the policy, the TFR continues to be significantly above its original rate. By 2005, East and West Germany are a united nation with a TFR of only 1.4, well below replacement level.

1979 China implements the one-child policy; its previous family-planning programs of the 1960s and 1970s had already lowered fertility rates substantially. In 2005, Chinese women average more than one child each, but their total fertility rate (TFR) of 1.7 is still below replacement level.

Upon taking power in Iran, the new Islamic government discontinues the nation's family-planning program, viewing it as a Western imposition. A decade later the government reverses course and reestablishes a national program of family planning, soon judged to be one of the world's most successful.

1980   Upon concluding its global smallpox eradication and vaccination project, the World Health Organization declares smallpox *eradicated*, the first such total elimination of an infectious disease in human history. During the twentieth century, smallpox took an estimated 300 to 500 million lives.

A government interagency report solicited by President Carter in 1977 and issued in 1980 as *The Global 2000 Report to the President: Entering the Twenty-First Century* warns that "if present trends continue, the world in 2000 will be more crowded, more polluted, less stable ecologically, and more vulnerable to disruption than the world we live in now" (Barney 1980, 1). Population trends are identified as a worrisome variable. In response to *Global 2000*, President Carter requests that Congress double its funding of international population assistance; it declines to do so.

1981   The first diagnosis of AIDS is made in the United States.

The Office of Management and Budget proposes eliminating U.S. funding for population assistance from the first Reagan budget, a move quashed by Secretary of State Alexander Haig and Vice-President George H. W. Bush.

1982   The first World Assembly on Aging is held in Vienna. Delegates take note of the world population's changing age structure and, specifically, the growing proportion over age 60. They adopt—and the UN General Assembly subsequently endorses—a plan of action that includes sixty-two recommendations. Recommendation 36 states: "Governments should take appropriate action to ensure to all older persons an appropriate minimum income, and should develop their economies to benefit all the population." To satisfy this recommendation, they

1982, should "develop social security schemes based on the
cont. principle of universal coverage for older people" (World
Assembly on Aging 1983, 34–35).

1984 The second UN-sponsored world population conference is held in Mexico City; it reaffirms the plan of action adopted at Bucharest ten years earlier. The U.S.
delegation asserts the Reagan administration position
that population growth is not a significant obstacle to
economic development. It also announces that henceforth no U.S. funds will go to foreign NGOs that offer
clients abortion information or services, even if they
do so at their own expense. Observers see a clear de-
parture from previous U.S. leadership on population
policy.

The International Planned Parenthood Federation, after
seventeen years of U.S. financial support, loses that
funding after it refuses to accept new U.S. conditions on
abortion provision and counseling (the so-called Mexico
City policy).

The European Parliament passes a resolution calling on
member nations to follow pronatalist policies to head off
a crisis of low birthrates.

1986 The Reagan and Bush administrations withhold U.S.
funds from UNFPA through 1992, on grounds that some
UNFPA monies help fund coercive population practices
in China (denied by UNFPA). Some of the funds are real-
located to other family-planning programs abroad.

The National Research Council publishes *Population
Growth and Economic Development: Policy Questions*,
which argues that population growth in less developed
countries can be advantageous if it triggers certain kinds
of "market reactions," such as more clearly defined
property rights. The study finds "little support for either
the most alarmist or the most complacent views concerning the economic effects of population growth" (Working Group 1986, vii).

1987 World population reaches 5 billion; "Day of Five Billion" observed on July 11.

The Governing Council of the U.N. Development Fund recommends, and the United Nations officially declares, July 11 as a permanent *World Population Day*, with themes to be chosen annually to highlight important issues (for example, in 2000, saving women's lives; and in 2005, equality empowers).

Nafis Sadik, a Pakistani obstetrician, is appointed executive director of the UNFPA; she is the first woman to be appointed the head of a UN agency.

Singapore, concerned about the slow growth of its labor force and rapid aging of its population, becomes one of the first nations to adopt pronatalist policies. While the old, antinatalist policy was encapsulated in the slogan "Boy or Girl: Two Is Enough," the new primary slogan is: "Have Three or More Children If You Can Afford It." The pronatal campaign is not successful: in 2005, the TFR has fallen to 1.0, barely half the replacement level of fertility.

Ben Wattenberg is one of the first commentators on population to warn about falling birth rates in the industrialized world, particularly the United States, in his book *The Birth Dearth*. He argues that declining fertility in the West portends declining global influence for Western ideas and values.

1988 Mifepristone, or RU 486, developed by a French pharmaceutical company in the early 1980s, is approved for use in France (in Great Britain, 1991; in Sweden, 1992). It is the first reliable chemical agent for inducing abortion early in pregnancy.

The United Nations General Assembly endorses a decision by the World Health Organization that December 1 be declared World AIDS Day; the occasion is marked every year afterward, on December 1, in hopes of raising awareness about the disease.

1988, Quebec province, having experienced a plunge in its fer-
cont. tility rate between 1961 and 1971, adopts the Allowance
for Newborn Children, a system of financial incentives
for having children. The value of the "baby bonus" by
1992 is 500 Canadian dollars, tax-free, for a first birth,
1,000 for a second, and 8,000 for a third and any subsequent birth. In addition to the birth bonus, a regular allowance is to be paid to families with children. One
study finds that the pronatal policy can be credited with
93,000 extra births in Quebec between 1989 and 1996, at
an estimated cost of $15,000 per birth (Milligan 2002, 2).
The policy is canceled in 1997.

1989 President Bush vetoes a foreign aid bill that includes $15
million for the UNFPA but later signs a revised bill that
increases the population aid budget by $20 million (with
no money for UNFPA).

1990 The FDA approves Norplant, a contraceptive implant for
women.

1992 The FDA approves the use of an injectable contraceptive
for women, Depo-Provera (previously used in eighty
other countries).

In an unprecedented step, the Royal Society of London
and the U.S. National Academy of Sciences issue a joint
statement urging a "more rapid stabilization of world
population" as a partial remedy for environmental
degradation that threatens to become irreversible (see
Chapter 7).

Another statement by scientists, this one signed by over
1,500, including half the living Nobel laureates in science, calls for stabilization of world population. This
"Warning to Humanity" stresses the damage suffered by
the environment from overconsumption by the developed nations and rapidly expanding populations among
the developing nations (see Chapter 7).

At Rio de Janeiro, the United Nations Conference on Environment and Development, popularly known as the

Earth Summit, approves a report that includes this state-ment: "The growth of world population and production, combined with unsustainable consumption patterns, places increasingly severe stress on the life-supporting capacities of our planet" (United Nations Conference on Environment and Development 1992, sec. 5.3).

1993   President Clinton issues an executive order, two days af-ter his inauguration, rescinding the Mexico City policy of 1984 and indicating an intention to restore U.S. finan-cial support for UNFPA.

A UN-sponsored Conference on Human Rights con-venes in Vienna and issues, at its conclusion, the Vienna Declaration and Programme of Action; part II, para. 41, states: "The World Conference on Human Rights reaf-firms, on the basis of equality between women and men, a woman's right to accessible and adequate health care and the widest range of family planning services, as well as equal access to education at all levels" (World Confer-ence on Human Rights 1993, II, item 41).

At an international science summit on world population held in New Delhi, representatives from fifty-eight sci-entific academies endorse a statement that reads in part: "In our judgment, humanity's ability to deal successfully with its social, economic, and environmental problems will require the achievement of zero population growth within the lifetime of our children" ("*Science Summit*" 1994, 236).

The World Health Organization declares tuberculosis (TB) to be a global emergency; at century's end, the dis-ease is claiming 2 million lives each year, with 1 billion new TB infections expected between 2000 and 2020, re-sulting in 35 million deaths.

Genocidal tribal conflict in Burundi takes 100,000 lives.

1994   The third UN-sponsored world population conference, now titled International Conference on Population and Development (ICPD), is held in Cairo; it adopts a Pro-

1944, gram of Action to be followed by all participating na-
cont. tions.

Genocidal tribal conflict in Rwanda takes an estimated 1 million lives.

The Zapatista uprising in Chiapas, Mexico, is attributed by some observers, in part, to population pressures on the available land; land scarcity in Chiapas is exacerbated by concentrated landholding patterns.

Three environmental scientists, including Paul Ehrlich, estimate the world's optimal population to be around 2 billion; this assumes consumption patterns that are more frugal, and energy and resource use more efficient, than are seen in the United States presently.

1995 According to a report issued by the United Nations' Intergovernmental Panel on Climate Change (IPCC), "The balance of evidence suggests that there is a discernible human influence on global climate."

1995– Famine in North Korea, caused by natural disasters and
1999 economic mismanagement, takes the lives of 2 million (by U.S. estimate).

1996 At the UN World Food Summit, held in Rome, delegates from 173 nations sign a Plan of Action calling for progress toward world population stabilization, as well as wiser management of natural resources and less excessive consumption. More concretely, the conference calls for a 50 percent reduction in the number of malnourished people in the world by 2015.

1997 Media mogul Ted Turner donates $1 billion to the United Nations in support of its efforts in the areas of population, health, and environment.

A U.S. Department of State Strategic Plan asserts that "stabilizing population growth is vital to U.S. interests. . . . Not only will early stabilization of the world's population promote environmentally sustainable economic development in other countries, but it will benefit the U.S. by improving trade opportunities and mitigating future global crises" (Lasher 1998, 19).

1998   The bicentennial of Malthus's *Essay on the Principle of Population* (1798) is widely noted, with commentators debating the merits, realism, and relevance of the Malthusian theory in the contemporary world.

The United Nations issues new, lower projections of world population for the year 2050; its medium (most likely) estimate is 8.9 billion.

1999   The ICPD + 5 forum held at the Hague (February 8–12) reviews progress toward the goals set at the 1994 UN population conference in Cairo, in an atmosphere of general disappointment; many goals have not been met.

Officially on October 12, Earth has 6 billion people.

In Japan, Masahiro Yamada's book *Parasaito Shinguru no Jidai (The Era of Parasite Singles)* becomes a best-seller. Yamada calls attention to the increasing tendency of Japan's young adults to get jobs and achieve financial independence, yet continue to live in their parents' home and not marry. The average age at marriage for men in Japan is almost 31, and for women, 28.5. These data imply that as many as 25 percent of men and 19 percent of women will still be single at the age of 50.

2000   The United States conducts its twenty-second decennial census. Total population is found to be 281,421,906, a 13 percent increase from 1990. Separately, the Census Bureau issues its first-ever projection of U.S. population to the end of the twenty-first century, putting the number in the year 2100 at 571 million, or about double its current level.

The FDA grants approval for the abortion drug mifepristone, or RU-486, to be marketed under the name Mifeprex; 620,000 European women have already used the drug.

2000, The United Nations predicts, in a report issued June 27,
cont. that in those African nations with the worst AIDS infection rates, between one-half and two-thirds of all current 15-year-olds will eventually die of the disease.

Nafis Sadik, executive director of the UNFPA, retires after fourteen years, to be replaced on January 1, 2001, by Thoraya Obaid of Saudi Arabia. Obaid had been in charge of the UNFPA division for Europe and the Arab States; she holds a Ph.D. in literature from Wayne State University in Detroit and has long experience in international civil service.

India becomes the second nation, after China, to reach a population of 1 billion. The country adopts a National Population Policy that envisions achievement of replacement-level fertility by 2010. Other goals include reduction to zero in the number of girls marrying before the age of 18 and sharp reductions in the infant and maternal mortality rates.

In a much firmer statement than the one issued in 1995, the Intergovernmental Panel on Climate Change now concludes that man-made gases have "contributed substantially to the observed warming over the last 50 years" (Revkin 2000, A22) and warns that by the year 2100 temperatures may be as much as 11 degrees Fahrenheit above their 1990 levels, far higher than previously estimated. The full report is unanimously approved by 150 scientists at a meeting of the IPCC in Shanghai in January 2001.

2001 Immediately upon taking office, President George W. Bush reinstates the Mexico City policy banning U.S. funds to international family-planning agencies that counsel or provide abortions. Some observers anticipate an ironic result—an *increase* in abortions from the agencies' reduced ability to provide contraceptives to their clients.

Reacting to the Bush announcement of nonsupport for the UNFPA and the International Planned Parenthood

Association, the European Union's Development and Humanitarian Aid commissioner, Poul Nielson, pledges that the European Union will fill any "decency gap" created by the U.S. funding loss. Nielson states, "The losers from this [U.S.] decision will be some of the most vulnerable people on this planet. Reproductive health services are crucial elements in the fight against poverty, and the UNFPA and the IPPF deserve strong support to continue their activities" (EuropaWorld 2002, 1).

2002   The UN Population Division lowers from 2.1 to 1.85 its baseline assumption of the TFR toward which all nations, developing and developed, are headed. High-fertility nations will fall toward a 1.85 TFR, and low-fertility nations will rise toward it. This high-level recognition of the global trend toward lower fertility is described by some as "momentous." The lower TFR number is built into the long-term projections in the 2002 and 2004 *World Population Prospects* issued by the United Nations.

Russia conducts its first census in thirteen years during one week in October. Final results are scheduled for release in 2005, but a mid-2004 estimate by the Russian government puts the total population at about 144 million. This represents a loss of some 5 million people since the collapse of the Soviet Union in late 1991.

A report on demographic developments in Europe finds that the nation with the lowest fertility is Armenia, with a TFR of only 1.02. Other low-fertility nations include Czech Republic (1.14), Slovak Republic (1.20), Slovenia (1.21), and Latvia (1.21). Only one country, Turkey, has a TFR above replacement level, at 2.51 (Council of Europe 2002).

The second World Assembly on Aging (Madrid), with representatives from 159 nations, issues a political declaration that includes this assertion: "We commit ourselves to provide older persons with universal and equal access to healthcare and services, including physical and mental health services, and we recognize that the growing needs of an ageing population require additional poli-

2002, cies, in particular care and treatment, the promotion of
cont. healthy lifestyles and supportive environments. We shall promote independence, accessibility and the empowerment of older persons to participate fully in all aspects of society" (Second World Assembly 2002, art. 14).

In its first *International Migration Report*, the United Nations finds that nearly 10 percent of the population residing in the world's more developed regions are migrants. About 2.3 million people migrate annually from the less to the more developed regions. Over half of them (1.4 million) migrate to North America. Roughly one-quarter of the world's governments regard the current immigration rate as too high.

2003 In testimony before Congress, Alan Greenspan, chairman of the Federal Reserve, warns that the rapid aging of the populations of Europe and Japan may lead to lower savings rates in those areas. This, in the future, could cause global capital flows that have sustained U.S. investment to be diverted to Europe and Japan.

China's population reaches 1.3 billion, the highest of any nation in history.

The Census Bureau announces that Latinos now surpass African Americans as the largest minority ethnic group in the United States.

2004 Despite the Bush administration's refusal to give U.S. financial support to the UNFPA, a record total of $326 million is contributed to the Population Fund by European and other governments.

2005 The United Nations releases its biennial *World Population Prospects: The 2004 Revision,* with a medium-variant projection for global population of 9.1 billion in 2050. The high-variant projection, which assumes higher fertility (by one-half child per woman), is 10.6 billion; the low-variant projection (one-half fewer children per woman) is 7.7 billion.

2007   The majority of the world's population is now urban for the first time in history, according to a UN projection issued in 2004. The trend toward urbanization is expected to continue. By 2020, three-fifths of the world's people will be urban dwellers.

2013   World population is set to pass the 7 billion mark according to UN projections.

2028   World population is set to pass 8 billion.

2050   The world's developed regions will have about the same population, 1.2 billion, as in 2005, according to United Nations projections; the less developed regions will have 7.8 billion, far more than their 5.3 billion in 2005.

The number of people aged 60 years or older (2 billion) will be greater than the number aged 14 years or younger, according to the United Nations. Over half the elderly population will live in Asia.

2300   UN demographers offered, in 2003, their first world population projections for the distant future, three centuries hence. The estimates range from 2.3 billion, if global fertility rates settle at 1.85 children per woman, to 36.4 billion, if fertility stabilizes at 2.35 children per woman. The medium estimate, based on fertility of 2 children per woman, is about 9 billion people. For illustrative purposes, demographers also projected the consequences of global fertility rates remaining exactly as they are now. By 2150, world population would grow to 244 billion, and by 2300, it would reach the unimaginable level of 134 *trillion!*

References

Barney, Gerald O. 1980. *Global 2000 Report to the President—Entering the Twenty-First Century*. Washington, DC: U.S. Government Printing Office.

Brown, Lester, et al. 1999. *Beyond Malthus: Nineteen Dimensions of the Population Challenge*. New York: W. W. Norton.

Buttner, Thomas, and Wolfgang Lutz. 1990, September. "Estimating Fertility Responses to Policy Measures in the German Democratic Republic." *Population and Development Review* 16:3, 539–555.

Coale, A., and E. Hoover. 1958. *Population Growth and Economic Development in Low-Income Countries.* Princeton, NJ: Princeton University Press.

Cohen, Joel. 1995. *How Many People Can the Earth Support?* New York: W. W. Norton.

Council of Europe. 2002. *Recent Demographic Developments in Europe, 2002.* Strasbourg, France: Council of Europe Publishing.

Daily, G. C., A. H. Ehrlich, and P. R. Ehrlich. 1994, July. "Optimum Human Population Size." *Population and Environment* 15:6, 469–475.

Eberstadt, Nicholas. 2005, Winter. "Russia: The Sick Man of Europe." *The Public Interest* 158, 3–20.

Ehrlich, Paul. 1968. *The Population Bomb.* New York: Ballantine.

EuropaWorld. 2002, July 26. "Commission Grants EUR 32 Million Towards Reproductive Health in Developing Countries." *EuropaWorld.* Accessed at http://www.europaworld.org/week92/commissiongrants 26702.htm

Evans, L. T. 1998. *Feeding the Ten Billion: Plants and Population Growth.* Cambridge: Cambridge University Press.

Green, Marshall. 1993. "The Evolution of US International Population Policy, 1965–92: A Chronological Account." *Population and Development Review* 19:2, 303–321.

Himes, N. E. 1976. *Medical History of Contraception.* New York: Schocken Books.

Hinde, T. 1995. *The Domesday Book: England's Heritage, Then & Now.* London: Tiger Books International.

Holloway, Marguerite. 2001, April. "Aborted Thinking: Reenacting the Global Gag Rule Threatens Public Health." *Scientific American* 284:4, 19–21.

Lasher, Craig. 1998. "U.S. Population Policy Since the Cairo Conference." *ECSP Report,* Issue 4, 16–23. Washington, DC: Woodrow Wilson Center, Environmental Change and Security Project.

Livi-Bacci, Massimo. 2001. *A Concise History of World Population,* 3rd ed. Malden, MA: Basil Blackwell.

Malthus, Thomas Robert. 1798. *An Essay on the Principle of Population.* Edited by Geoffrey Gilbert. New York: Oxford University Press.

McNeill, William H. 1976. *Plagues and Peoples.* New York: Anchor Press.

Meadows, Donella H., et al. 1972. *The Limits to Growth: A Report for the Club of Rome's Project on the Predicament of Mankind.* New York: Universe Books.

Milligan, Kevin. 2002, January 24. "Quebec's Baby Bonus: Can Public Policy Raise Fertility?" *C. D. Howe Institute Backgrounder.*

Noonan, John T. 1986. *Contraception: A History of Its Treatment by the Catholic Theologians and Canonists.* Cambridge, MA: Harvard University Press.

Paddock, William, and Paul Paddock. 1967. *Famine—1975! America's Decision: Who Will Survive?* Boston: Little, Brown.

Population Division of the Department of Economic and Social Affairs of the United Nations Secretariat. 2005. *World Population Prospects: The 2004 Revision.* New York: United Nations.

Retherford, Robert, and Naohiro Ogawa. 2005. "Japan's Baby Bust: Causes, Implications, and Policy Responses." East-West Center Working Papers, Population Series No. 118.

Revkin, Andrew C. 2000, October 26. "A Shift in Stance on Global Warming Theory," *New York Times,* A22.

"Science Summit" on World Population: A Joint Statement by 58 of the World's Scientific Academies. 1994, March. Reprinted in *Population and Development Review* 20:1, 233–238.

Second World Assembly on Aging. 2002. *Political Declaration.* New York: United Nations. Accessible at http://www.un.org/esa/socdev/ageing/waa/a-conf–197–9a.htm

Sen, Amartya K. 1981. *Poverty and Famines: An Essay on Entitlement and Deprivation.* Oxford: Oxford University Press.

United States Census Bureau. 2005. International Data Base, accessible at http://www.census.gov/ipc/www/idbnew.html

United Nations. 2002. *Political Declaration [Second World Assembly on Aging].* New York: United Nations.

United Nations Conference on Environment and Development. 1992. *Agenda 21.* Rio de Janeiro: UN Secretariat.

United Nations Population Division. 2002. *International Migration Report 2002.* New York: United Nations.

Wattenberg, Ben J. 1987. *The Birth Dearth.* New York: Pharos Books.

Weeks, John R. 2004. *Population: An Introduction to Concepts and Issues,* 8th ed. Belmont, CA: Wadsworth.

Working Group on Population Growth and Economic Development. 1986. *Population Growth and Economic Development: Policy Questions.* Washington, DC: National Academy Press.

World Assembly on Aging. 1983. *Vienna International Plan of Action on Aging*. New York: United Nations. Accessible at http://www.un.org/ esa/socdev/ageing/ageipaa3.htm#A

World Conference on Human Rights. 1993. *Vienna Declaration and Programme of Action*. New York: UN General Assembly.

Yamada, Masahiro. 1999. *Parasaito Shinguru no Jidai*. Tokyo: Chikuma Shobo.

5

Biographical Sketches

opulation has been the subject of speculation and debate for
hundreds of years. Even the so-called father of population
studies, Thomas Malthus (1766–1834), had numerous intellectual forebears. In this chapter, we get to know some of the
main actors and thinkers in the field of population. Some, like
Malthus, Paul Ehrlich, and Julian Simon, have forged the basic
theoretical and policy frameworks within which population issues are addressed. Others, like John Bongaarts and Paul Demeny, have refined our understanding of key demographic
processes. More practical-minded individuals, like Margaret
Sanger and Thoraya Obaid, have helped shape new population
policies at the national and international levels. And scientists
like Norman Borlaug, Walter Plowright, and M. S. Swaminathan
have led the research efforts that are making it possible to continue balancing the world's population with its food supply.
There is no master list of the "right" people to include in a biographical gallery like this. Many more individuals could have
been featured. For example, Margaret Sanger and Maria Stopes,
birth-control pioneers in the United States and Britain, respectively, had courageous counterparts in many other countries. The
scientists, activists, theorists, and leaders singled out in this
chapter have, as the saying goes, "stood on the shoulders of giants."

John Bongaarts (1945–)

Will the world's population eventually peak? One answer to that
question is: it *has* to, sooner or later. Just how soon (or late) will

105

depend, to an important degree, on how quickly the worldwide fertility rate—currently around three children per woman—falls to the replacement level of about two. As we know, such a decline in fertility has already occurred in the developed nations but not yet in most of the developing nations. Demographer John Bongaarts has presented an influential model of fertility, according to which there are four basic determinants of a society's fertility rate: the proportion of women married, the proportion who are physically unable to bear children (infecund), the rate of abortion, and the proportion of women using contraception. These four variables account for almost all observed differences in fertility among nations. At the global level, therefore, we will have to see further change in one or more of the variables before fertility, which has been declining for years, settles at (or below) replacement level. The most likely variable to change: the proportion of women using contraception.

Dutch by birth and citizenship, Dr. Bongaarts wrote his doctoral thesis on the "demographic transition" (University of Illinois, 1972). He has long been associated with the Population Council in New York City, where he is currently vice-president in the policy research division. He has served on many panels, committees, and boards, and has briefed the U.S. vice-president and secretary of state on population matters.

Further Reading. J. Bongaarts and A. Bulatao (eds.), *Beyond Six Billion: Forecasting the World's Population* (Washington, DC: National Academy Press, 2000); "Staff Biographies," Population Council website at http://www.popcouncil.org/staff/bios/jbongaarts.html

Norman Borlaug (1914–)

His admirers see in Norman Borlaug's lifework a decisive refutation of Malthus. The famed eighteenth-century English parson had worried about the danger of human numbers outpacing any possible increase in food production, with famine the ultimate control. As the populations of the developing nations shot upward in the second half of the twentieth century, a Malthusian crisis appeared imminent in Asia and Africa. The occurrence of widespread famines was taken almost for granted in the West. But the so-called Green Revolution of the 1960s, for which Borlaug was principally responsible, helped keep food supplies growing as fast as, and in many cases *faster* than, the population. Knowledgeable observers credit the agricultural innovations of Borlaug and his colleagues with saving millions of lives, especially in the developing world.

An Iowa native, Borlaug earned his bachelor's degree in forest management and his Ph.D. in plant pathology (University of Minnesota, 1942). In 1944, he accepted the invitation of the Rockefeller Foundation to lead a research effort in Mexico aimed at improving that country's wheat production. Over many years of patient experimentation, he and his team developed the dwarf, high-yielding wheat varieties that, in combination with chemical fertilizers and irrigation, allowed Mexico to greatly increase its grain output and reduce its dependency on food imports. The Mexican research center that evolved out of the original research program—known by its acronym CIMMYT—soon achieved worldwide renown. Borlaug was invited to develop similar crop varieties in India and Pakistan; his remarkable success in doing so helped move the subcontinent from famines in the 1960s to much greater food security in subsequent decades. His plant-breeding practices were also emulated at the International Rice Research Institute (IRRI) in the Philippines, and today most Asian rice bowls are filled with hybridized rice.

In 1970, Borlaug was awarded the Nobel Peace Prize for his efforts to reduce world hunger through agricultural science. He has not rested on his laurels, however. First at Cornell University, then at Texas A & M, he has held Distinguished Professorships. He continues to mentor young scientists at the CIMMYT in Mexico. And in recent years he has turned his attention to the food situation in sub-Saharan Africa. Working with Japanese philanthropist Ryoichi Sasakawa and former president Jimmy Carter, Borlaug, under the auspices of the Sasakawa–Global 2000 Foundation, initiated field trials of new varieties of wheat, sorghum, cassava, and cow peas in several African countries. As with his earlier efforts, these projects have produced startling increases in crop yields. Borlaug is the first to admit, however, that long-term success in Africa will be a challenge, given the lack of physical infrastructure, the extraordinary levels of poverty, the lack of social cohesion, and the high rates of population increase. He continues to worry about global population, in spite of all he has done to banish the Malthusian specter.

Further Reading. G. Easterbrook, "The Forgotten Benefactor of Humanity," *The Atlantic Monthly* 279:1 (January 1997); "Visit of Dr. Norman Borlaug to MSU [Michigan State University]," March 2003, at http://www.iia.msu.edu/absp/borlaugvisit.html

Ester Boserup (1910–1999)

One of the most notable demographic thinkers of the twentieth century was the Danish economist Ester Boserup. In her classic study *The Conditions of Agricultural Growth* (1965), she turned Malthusian theory on its head and in the process gave valuable ammunition to the "cornucopian" side of the population debate. Under simple Malthusian theory, population levels were thought to depend on available food supplies. Thus an improvement in agricultural techniques could pave the way to a rapid increase in population. But what if the relationship worked in a reverse direction, with faster population growth the *cause*, rather than the *effect*, of improved methods of agricultural production? That, in essence, was Boserup's contention in her 1965 book. Her empirical research convinced her that agricultural advances were spurred by population pressure, and not the other way around. In particular, the pressure of more people on the land (that is, rising population *density*) had led to such historic innovations as the plow, crop rotations, irrigation, and the use of fertilizers. These notions clearly ran counter to the neo-Malthusian orthodoxy of the 1950s, 1960s, and 1970s, which regarded population growth as likely to jeopardize economic development.

Boserup was educated at the University of Copenhagen, where she studied economic theory, sociology, and agriculture. She began her career as an economic planner in the Danish government during World War II. Later she spent a decade—much of it in the study of European agriculture—at the United Nations Economic Commission for Europe in Geneva, Switzerland. In 1957 she moved to India to assist Gunnar Myrdal (a future Nobel laureate in economics) in his research on Asian economic development. Her extensive travel as part of this project and a subsequent period of research in Africa in 1964–1965 gave Boserup a firsthand grasp of development issues and an impatience with purely theoretical approaches to development. Her interest in the way modernization affected the status of women led her to write *Woman's Role in Economic Development* (1970).

Population optimists like Julian Simon were delighted to welcome Boserup to their ranks. As they saw it, her work demonstrated that population growth need not have any negative impact on human well-being; indeed, it could be highly beneficial. Although the environmentalist camp remained skeptical, they respected the empirical and multidisciplinary qualities of Boserup's scholarship.

Further Reading. E. Boserup, "The Impact of Scarcity and Plenty on Development," in R. I. Rotberg and T. K. Rabb (eds.), *Hunger and History* (Cambridge: Cambridge University Press, 1985).

Lester R. Brown (1934–)

Few public-interest organizations have been as closely identified with their founder as the Worldwatch Institute has been with Lester Brown. For over a quarter of a century, beginning in 1974, Brown led the Institute. In a sense Worldwatch supported, and was supported by, the environmental movement. Its annual *State of the World* report, always co-authored by Brown, assumed the status of a semiofficial document; it is now translated into all of the world's major languages and used in hundreds of college and university courses in the United States and abroad. Brown has demonstrated a flair for "getting out the word" in a variety of formats: *Vital Signs* and *State of the World* annuals, monographs (the Environmental Alert series), the bimonthly magazine *World Watch*, interviews, and speeches. Consistently throughout his career, Brown has expressed concern about world population, most notably in his 1994 book *Full House: Reassessing the Earth's Population Carrying Capacity* (with H. Kane) and his 1999 book *Beyond Malthus: Nineteen Dimensions of the Population Challenge* (with G. Gardner and B. Halweil).

Educational credentials in agriculture and public administration—along with firsthand experience both in farming (tomato-growing in New Jersey) and in the federal government—may help explain Lester Brown's willingness to view environmental issues broadly. He sees the problems of the environment as complex and interrelated. Solutions will not come from specialists working only within their narrow fields of expertise. Hence the useful role of organizations like Worldwatch that can supply government officials, the media, and the public with analysis that is readable and broad-gauged rather than narrowly technical.

In 2001, the year after he gave up the presidency of World-watch, Lester Brown founded the Earth Policy Institute (EPI). The mission of EPI is to develop and disseminate a "vision of what an environmentally sustainable economy" would look like and to provide a "roadmap" of how to get there. Brown has been receiving honorary degrees, prizes, and fellowships for decades, among them, the MacArthur Fellow award (1986), the United Nations Environment Prize (1987), the Blue Planet Prize (1994), and an honorary professorship in the Chinese Academy of Sciences (2005). His board memberships include the Council on Foreign Relations and Zero Population Growth.

Further Reading. L. Brown, *Outgrowing the Earth: The Food Security Challenge in an Age of Falling Water Tables and Rising Temperatures* (New York: W. W. Norton, 2005); "World in the Balance: Voices of Concern," NOVA program broadcast on PBS, April 20, 2004, transcribed at http://www.pbs.org/wgbh/nova/worldbalance/voic-brow.html

Joel E. Cohen (1944–)

Curious people through the centuries have asked the simple question: how high can our planet's population rise? Their answers, and a fascinating review of the entire subject, may be found in Joel Cohen's 1995 book *How Many People Can the Earth Support?* With doctoral training in applied mathematics, population sciences, and tropical public health at Harvard, and as head of the Laboratory of Populations at Rockefeller University and Columbia University, Cohen is well qualified to tackle the issue. He carefully notes a host of difficulties and complications that must be overcome before one can estimate the Earth's carrying capacity. Surprisingly, the middle value (or median) of past maximum-population estimates turns out to be quite close to actual UN projections of world population by the middle of the twenty-first century. Indeed, Cohen's survey of previous estimates of maximum global population—back to 1679—strongly suggests that the world is approaching what many demographic thinkers have deemed to be the upper limits of sustainable population.

Formerly a member of Harvard's Society of Fellows, Cohen has been elected to the American Academy of Arts and Sciences, the American Philosophical Society, and the National Academy of Sciences. He has won the Tyler Prize for Environmental Achievement (1999) and a MacArthur Foundation award. His writings have ranged across demography, ecology, epidemiology, and mathematics.

Further Reading. J. Cohen, "Human Population: The Next Half Century," *Science* 302:5648 (November 2003); J. Cohen, "The Future of Population," in R. N. Cooper and R. Layard (eds.), *What the Future Holds: Insights from Social Science* (Cambridge, MA: MIT Press, 2002).

Paul Demeny (1932–)

No one will insist—with the possible exception of economists—that our most personal decisions are based on economics. Still, the demographer Paul Demeny, a Distinguished Scholar at the Population Council in New York, believes that the timing of a country's "fertility transition"—the all-important move to smaller families—is mainly determined by four economic factors. They are (1) the direct cost to parents of rearing and educating their children; (2) the indirect costs in lost earnings when a parent, usually the mother, is kept out of the job market by childrearing activities; (3) the earnings that children can bring home to their families; and (4) the contribution children can make to their parents' old-age security relative to other systems of economic support, such as state pensions. All of this suggests that government policies to speed the transition to lower fertility should be simple to devise, though perhaps not as easy to implement. For example, policies discouraging child labor and requiring children to remain in school, encouraging women to enter or reenter the labor force, or providing for old-age assistance will all tend to raise the costs and lower the benefits of childbearing.

A widely respected figure in the demographic profession, Paul Demeny immigrated to the United States from Hungary in 1956, earned his Ph.D. in economics from Princeton University in 1961, and founded the journal *Population and Development Review* *(PDR)* in 1974. He remains the journal's editor to this day, and

PDR remains a refreshingly readable source of population information and perspective. In 2003, Demeny was named Laureate of the International Union for the Scientific Study of Population.

Further Reading. P. Demeny, "Policies Seeking a Reduction of High Fertility: A Case for the Demand Side," *Population and Development Review* 18:2 (June 1992).

Nicholas Eberstadt (1955–)

At the various councils, foundations, and government agencies concerned with population matters, there has long been a dominant view about the world's population: it is growing too fast, damaging the environment, and dampening the economic prospects of poorer nations. But for years there has also been a vigorous dissent from the neo-Malthusian orthodoxy. Julian Simon, Peter Bauer, Ester Boserup, and two resident scholars at the American Enterprise Institute, Ben Wattenberg and Nicholas Eberstadt, have challenged the mainstream view. In a widely noted article in *The Public Interest* (Fall 1997), Eberstadt explored the possibility that a population "implosion" was under way nearly everywhere in the world. Fertility rates were declining on every continent, and in Europe and parts of East Asia the drop was so severe that populations might well *shrink* in the foreseeable future. The social and economic implications were immense. On its current path, Italy, for example, would become, within two generations, a place where most children had no siblings, aunts, uncles, or cousins. (China was moving in the same direction.) The concept of family would be fundamentally altered. Europe would face massive immigration pressures. Some Asian societies would have to cope with a "bride shortage" due to abortion practices that favored male offspring.

Because he does not share the view that population growth needs to be curbed, Eberstadt is not favorably impressed by the financial support that U.S. charitable foundations have given to international family planning—or "population control," as he prefers to call it. He has written about the crucial role of the Rockefeller and Ford Foundations in launching these efforts in the 1950s and 1960s, and the renewed interest shown in such activities by a more recent generation of American philanthropists, such as Ted Turner, Bill Gates, and Warren Buffett. Eberstadt believes that ordinary American taxpayers have become less supportive of aid to international population programs and that wealthy philanthropists are stepping in to make up the difference out of their own pockets.

Eberstadt presents his provocative ideas on television and radio programs, in the pages of leading public-affairs journals and newspapers, and before congressional committees. He has been a consultant to the Departments of State and Defense, the World Bank, and the Census Bureau. Holding three degrees from Harvard and one from the London School of Economics, Eberstadt has been for many years a visiting fellow at Harvard's Center for Population and Development Studies. His books include *Prosperous Paupers and Other Population Problems* (2000).

Further Reading. N. Eberstadt, "Rethinking the Population Problem," *The Public Interest* 159 (Spring 2005); N. Eberstadt, "The World Population 'Crisis': American Philanthropy's Long, Fruitless Affair with Population Control," *The Philanthropy Roundtable* (November–December 1998).

Paul R. Ehrlich (1932–)

In recent decades, the individual most responsible for sounding the alarm over the impact of human population on the natural environment has been Paul Ehrlich. His 1968 book *The Population Bomb* was an international best-seller. It has been credited, along with Rachel Carson's *Silent Spring*, with helping to launch the environmentalist movement. The urgent tone (and premature pessimism) of this work is evident in its much-quoted opening lines: "The battle to feed all of humanity is over. In the 1970s and 1980s hundreds of millions of people will starve to death in spite of any crash programs embarked upon now." Ehrlich's powerful and persuasive prose echoes the original population warning of Malthus in 1798. But while Malthus analyzed population mainly in economic terms, Ehrlich stresses the *ecological* costs of overpopulation. He points to things like pollution, depletion of the ozone layer, and species extinction as potential costs of too rapid population growth. His simple equation, $I = P \times A \times T$, makes the impact (I) on the environment depend directly on population (P), the average level of consumption or affluence (A), and the level of technology (T). Obviously, a rising population has harmful effects on the environment unless offset by lower consumption rates or more beneficent kinds of technology.

The clear role of population (P) in his formula helps account for Ehrlich's persistent emphasis, in books, articles, and television appearances, on limiting human numbers. He believes families should aim for two children at most, preferably one. Not surprisingly, he was a co-founder of the organization Zero Population Growth, later renamed Population Connection. But a broadening of Ehrlich's environmental concerns is evident in *The Stork and the Plow* (1995) and *One with Ninevah: Politics, Consumption, and the Human Future* (2004), co-authored with Anne Ehrlich, with their advocacy of less wasteful lifestyles in the developed world, a reduction of the income gap between rich and poor nations, and better education and improved status for women. Ehrlich has not hesitated to support strong government measures to achieve the limits on population and consumption that he considers imperative. This is one of several areas in which he differs sharply with the population optimists, led by Julian Simon (until the latter's death in 1998).

Ehrlich earned his Ph.D. in biology from the University of Kansas and has been for many years on the faculty at Stanford University, where he is Bing Professor of Population Studies. His special research interest has been the genetics, ecology, and population dynamics of checkerspot butterflies. His many honors include prizes from the Royal Swedish Academy of Sciences, the United Nations, the World Wildlife Fund, and the MacArthur Foundation. His writings include hundreds of articles, *The Population Explosion* (1990, with A. H. Ehrlich), *Betrayal of Science and Reason: How Anti-Environmental Rhetoric Threatens Our Future* (1996, with A. H. Ehrlich), and the books cited above.

Further Reading. B. Wattenberg, "How Should Humanity Prosper?" [interview with Ehrlich], PBS, March 17, 2005, transcribed at http://www.pbs.org/thinktank/show_1150.html; "Paul and Anne Ehrlich, 1998 Tyler Laureates," at http://www.usc.edu/dept/LAS/tylerprize/tyler98.html

Werner Fornos (1933–)

For the past quarter-century, Werner Fornos has been the Paul Revere of the population-awareness community, sounding the alarm about overpopulation to every kind of audience, attending population conferences all over the world, and serving as president of the Population Institute. As with most neo-Malthusians,

Fornos stresses the environmental degradation caused by excessive population growth. But what is distinctive in his approach to overpopulation is a clear focus on the downward trend in the *quality of life* as human numbers continue to climb. He worries about the squalor and misery experienced by millions around the world as they crowd into super-large cities. He points to the poverty, illiteracy, and disease rates found in those parts of the world where 95 to 99 percent of future population growth is expected to take place. When he looks at his adopted country—the German native was granted U.S. citizenship in 1953—Fornos sees a need for greater action on two fronts. First, the United States needs to support international family-planning programs more generously. Second, it needs to establish its own population policy. The United States has faster population growth than any other industrialized nation, with serious consequences for global warming and other environmental problems.

A graduate of the University of Maryland, Fornos served for four years as a Maryland state legislator before joining the Population Institute. In February 2000, he received the Order of Merit, the highest award granted by the German government to a noncitizen. He was co-winner of the United Nations Population Award in 2003.

Further Reading. C. N. McDaniel, *Wisdom for a Livable Planet* (San Antonio, TX: Trinity University Press, 2005).

He Kang (1923–)

To be China's minister of agriculture is to shoulder the ultimate Malthusian responsibility: keeping food supplies growing fast enough to feed the world's most populous nation. Superficially, it might not seem a difficult task, since China several years ago reached below-replacement fertility (fewer than two children per woman) as a result of its one-child policy. But the relative youthfulness of China's population gives it what demographers call momentum. With millions of Chinese entering their childbearing years, population—and the demand for food—will continue to increase for many years to come. He Kang, the Chinese minister of agriculture from 1983 to 1990 and a key agricultural planner from as early as 1979, seems never to have been daunted by the challenge. His rise to a position of high influence in the agricultural bureaucracy coincided with the similar rise to paramount political influence in China by Deng Xiaoping, a pragmatist determined to lead the country away from the deadening effects of government controls and central planning. Deng wanted peasant farmers to have more decision-making authority and a chance to make profits by their hard work.

Implementation of the new approach, under He Kang's inspired guidance, led to quick results: grain output rose from 305 million tons in 1978 to a record 407 million tons in 1984. Other types of agricultural production—meat, sugar, fish catches, cotton—also showed impressive gains. By 1986, He Kang could boast that China had achieved basic self-sufficiency in food and clothing, a welcome refutation of the gloomier predictions of some Western writers in the 1960s. He Kang was awarded the World Food Prize in 1993.

Further Reading. "He Kang: 1993 World Food Prize Laureate," accessed at http://www.worldfoodprize.org/Laureates/Past/1993.htm

Thomas Homer-Dixon (1956–)

Some neo-Malthusians have warned of famine as the logical result to be expected from the population explosion that the world has experienced since about the mid-twentieth century. But Malthus himself believed the toll taken by excessive population growth could be measured in moral degradation and political repression as often as it was in shrinking portions of food on people's plates. Thomas Homer-Dixon, director of the Trudeau Centre for Peace and Conflict Studies at the University of Toronto, has for some years now been contributing to a still more complex way of understanding what may lie ahead for poor but populous regions of the world. He argues that in many places rapid population growth is depleting and degrading the available supplies of renewable resources such as cropland, forests, and fresh water. The supplies that remain are often under the control of powerful, privileged interests who exploit them without regard for the long-term effects on the majority of the population. Growing environmental scarcities can contribute, in Homer-Dixon's view, to outbreaks of "ecoviolence." Indeed, he believes we have already seen ecoviolence occur in Chiapas (Mexico), the

Gaza Strip, South Africa, and Pakistan, and are likely to see more of it in the future.

A native and citizen of Canada, Homer-Dixon earned his Ph.D. in political science at M.I.T. (1989). He has presented his research at the World Economic Forum in Davos, Switzerland, and has twice briefed the vice-president of the United States. His most recent book is *The Ingenuity Gap* (New York: Alfred A. Knopf, 2000).

Further Reading. T. Homer-Dixon, *Environment, Scarcity and Violence* (Princeton, NJ: Princeton University Press, 1999); T. Homer-Dixon home page at http://www.homerdixon.com/

Richard Jackson (1955–)

The world's population is rapidly growing older. In 1950, the median global age was about 24 years. By 2050, the United Nations predicts, it will be around 38. For some countries, the "graying" will be more dramatic: Spain's median age may reach 51 as early as 2035. Italy and Japan could be that old even sooner. Among the experts pondering the consequences of such unprecedented global aging, one of the most prominent is Richard Jackson, director of the Global Aging Initiative at Georgetown University's Center for Strategic and International Studies. Jackson has developed an "aging vulnerability index" the purpose of which is to assess national capacities to withstand the financial burdens of rapidly aging populations. Of the twelve developed countries examined, the three most vulnerable turn out to be France, Italy, and Spain; the least vulnerable are Australia, the United Kingdom, and the United States. In separate policy studies, Dr. Jackson has explored the economic impact of aging in the United States, Germany, and China. A senior advisor to the Concord Coalition, he is particularly concerned about future entitlement program costs and the fiscal implications of those rapidly rising costs. Jackson brings an uncommon historical perspective to his current research with an undergraduate degree in classics from SUNY-Albany and a Ph.D. in economic history from Yale.

Further Reading. R. Jackson and N. Howe, "The Graying of the Middle Kingdom: The Demographics and Economics of

Retirement Policy in China" (Washington, DC: CSIS Global Aging Initiative Program, 2004); R. Jackson and N. Howe, "The 2003 Aging Vulnerability Index: An Assessment of the Capacity of Twelve Developed Countries to Meet the Aging Challenge" (Washington, DC: CSIS, 2003). Both studies are available online.

Wolfgang Lutz (1956–)

When low rates of childbirth prevail for a long enough time, population acquires something called "negative momentum." In simplest terms, this means that even if women now decide to start having more children, there are so many fewer women of childbearing age that the total population will continue to trend downward for years. Wolfgang Lutz, one of Europe's leading demographers, startled readers of the journal *Science* in 2003 by announcing that Europe had crossed over from positive to negative momentum around the year 2000. Europe's population today, therefore, has a built-in tendency to decline. If governments are concerned with the economic and other pressures likely to result from this tendency, they will need to design policies encouraging women either to have more children or to have them earlier. The only other way to bolster population in the long run would be through immigration.

Lutz is one of the most actively engaged demographers in the world. Holder of a Ph.D. in demography from the University of Pennsylvania (1983), he is currently leader of the World Population Program at the International Institute for Applied Systems Analysis in Laxenburg, Austria; director of the Vienna Institute of Demography at the Austrian Academy of Sciences; and principal investigator at the Asian MetaCentre for Population and Sustainable Development, headquartered at the National University of Singapore. Lutz's research centers on demographic forecasting and on the connections between population and the environment. He is the author of numerous books and scientific papers on population.

Further Reading. W. Lutz, B. C. O'Neill, and S. Scherbov, "Europe's Population at a Turning Point," *Science* 299:5615 (March 28, 2003); W. Lutz, *Future Population of the World: What Can We Assume Today?* 2nd ed. (London: Earthscan Publications, 1997).

Carolyn B. Maloney (1948–)

When Carolyn Maloney first got into electoral politics in 1982 with a successful run for the New York City Council, family planning was not a "hot button" issue at the local, state, or national level. That changed quickly. In 1984, the Reagan administration announced that the United States would no longer provide funding to foreign NGOs (nongovernmental organizations) that engaged in the provision of abortions or abortion counseling. In what came to be called the global gag rule, the Reagan administration also disallowed any foreign organization receiving U.S. funds from advocating for an easing of its country's legal restrictions on abortion. In addition, the U.S. contribution to the United Nations Population Fund, or UNFPA, was held back under Reagan and not restored until the election of Bill Clinton in 1992. On the day Clinton won the presidency, Maloney won a House seat representing part of New York City; she has held that seat ever since. For a number of years now, Maloney has been the most vocal Democrat on Capitol Hill in supporting the restoration of U.S. funding to the UNFPA—funding that President George W. Bush halted once again in 2002. Maloney has also spoken out strongly against the global gag rule. Global women's issues have been an ongoing concern for her. She was a member of the U.S. delegation to the Fourth World Conference on Women in Beijing (1995) and to the five- and ten-year follow-ups to the historic 1994 International Conference on Population and Development in Cairo. Maloney was born in Greensboro, North Carolina, graduated from Greensboro College (1970), and was a teacher and school administrator in New York before entering politics.

Further Reading. S. Cohen, "Global Gag Rule Threatens International Family Planning Programs," *The Guttmacher Report on Public Policy*, 3:1 (February 2000); "Biography" link at http://www.house.gov/maloney/

Thomas Robert Malthus (1766–1834)

The most commonly cited name in the history of population studies (and controversies) is Malthus. The adjective "Malthusian" has entered the English language as a term suggestive of the frightening possibilities of overpopulation. Thomas Robert Malthus came from a middle-class family in the south of England. Shortly after graduation from Cambridge University in 1788, he was ordained a clergyman in the Church of England. In 1805, he was appointed professor of history and political economy at the East India College, where he taught for the rest of his life. His *Essay on the Principle of Population* was published anonymously in 1798, with significant revisions incorporated into later editions. Malthus was an economist who shared many of the free-market views of his great classical predecessor, Adam Smith.

In his population theory, Malthus argued that human numbers tend to increase more rapidly than the food supply needed for subsistence. He pointed to the explosive rates of population growth observed under favorable conditions, for example, in the American colonies, and to the finite amount of land available for the production of food. Although it is commonly asserted that Malthus predicted famine for the human race, this is quite untrue. Malthus merely stated that population must be restrained by some combination of "checks," and that if all other checks failed to limit population, famine would do the grim job. He believed that some checks were more benign in their operation than others, and he particularly favored what he called moral restraint—the delay of marriage until a couple could afford children, with chastity in the interim.

Malthus became one of the most controversial public figures of his day, and even now the evaluations of his ideas range from highly critical to warmly appreciative. Environmentalists applaud his attention to the impact of rapid population growth and believe his concerns are even more pertinent in a world of 6.5 billion people than in a world of 1 billion. Critics, on the other hand, argue that Malthus underestimated the potential of technological progress in agriculture; that he wrongly blamed the poor for their own misery; and that, by rejecting birth control (on moral grounds), he failed to grasp the most effective and humane means of avoiding overpopulation. His *Essay* remains available in many editions and continues to invite new generations of readers to confront difficult issues.

Further Reading. T. R. Malthus, *An Essay on the Principle of Population* (1798), G. Gilbert (ed.) (Oxford: Oxford World's Classics, 1993).

Thoraya Obaid (1946–)

Half a million women in the developing world die each year from pregnancy-related complications. That the giving of new life continues to cost so many women their *own* lives is one reason the United Nations Population Fund (UNFPA) needs the best leadership it can get. On January 1, 2001, Thoraya Obaid was promoted from within UNFPA ranks to succeed Dr. Nafis Sadik as executive director. Dr. Obaid is the first Saudi Arabian national to head any UN agency. What she brings to the position is a quarter-century's experience of working with governments, mainly in western Asia, to develop programs to empower women and promote gender equality. Although a veteran practitioner of diplomatic niceties, Obaid can be blunt. When President Bush held back the funds that Congress had appropriated for the UNFPA in 2002, her response came quickly: "These $34 million could prevent two million unwanted pregnancies and 77,000 cases of infant mortality. Mr. President, women and children will die as a result of your decision."

Dr. Obaid was the first Saudi woman to receive a scholarship from her government to study at an American university. She earned her B.A. degree (1966) from Mills College in Oakland, California, with a major in English literature, and went on to earn a doctorate in the same subject at Wayne State University in 1974. The next year she began her long career at the United Nations that culminated in the announcement by Secretary-General Kofi Annan, in late 2000, that she was "the ideal candidate" to be the next head of the UNFPA.

Further Reading. S. Lohoff and R. Bernhard, "Thoraya Obaid—Working for Women," *Deutsche Welle,* July 29, 2003, transcribed at http://www.qantara.de/webcom/show_article.php/_c-307/_nr-16/_p-1/i.html; Executive Director page at UNFPA website, www.unfpa.org

Walter Plowright (1923–)

The awarding of the 1999 World Food Prize to Dr. Walter Plowright put the spotlight on a resourceful scientist and a costly disease, neither well known to the public. The disease, *rinderpest,* has plagued humankind since the era of the Roman Empire. It is a highly infectious viral disease that is nearly always fatal to cattle and other hoofed animals, and thus devastating in its impact on those who depend on livestock herds. In the eighteenth century, outbreaks of rinderpest killed 200 million cattle in Western Europe, wreaking such havoc that one result was the founding of the world's first veterinary school in Lyon, France, where veterinary science was born. An outbreak during the 1890s wiped out between 80 and 90 percent of the cattle in sub-Saharan Africa, causing untold human suffering. As recently as the 1980s, an outbreak of rinderpest in Nigeria brought losses estimated in the billions of dollars.

Walter Plowright, an English-born and -trained veterinary scientist, devoted much of his career to developing an effective vaccine against rinderpest. He did most of the research at the Mugaga Laboratory of the East African Veterinary Research Organization in Kenya, from 1956 to 1971. Ultimately, he was able to produce a vaccine known as TCRV (tissue culture rinderpest vaccine) that proved to be safe, effective, cheap to produce, and stable even in tropical climates. The resulting gains in food security and, indirectly, economic security for millions of people in Africa and Asia have been enormous. One estimate puts the value of the Plowright vaccine to the economy of India during the period 1965–1998 at close to $300 billion. So effective is the vaccine that only a few pockets of rinderpest remain in Somalia, Sudan, and Pakistan. The Food and Agriculture Organization (FAO) of the United Nations hopes to eradicate the disease from the entire world by the year 2010, a scientific accomplishment that would be on a par with the eradication of smallpox.

The World Food Prize, known unofficially as the Nobel Prize for food research, was created in 1987 to honor those who have made vital contributions to improving the quantity, quality, or availability of food in the world. The foundation that administers the prize (currently $250,000) in Des Moines, Iowa, has on its council of advisors the Nobel Peace laureate Norman Borlaug, who was instrumental in creating the prize, as well as former presidents Jimmy Carter and George H. W. Bush.

Further Reading. "Food Prize for Cattle Saviour (Extract from BBC News)," *Empres Transboundary Animal Diseases Bulletin* 11 (September 1999), available online at FAO Document Depository.

Margaret Sanger (1879–1966)

The career of Margaret Sanger, American birth-control pioneer, demands a full-length biography to be told properly. Born in Corning, New York, the sixth of eleven children, Sanger saw her mother die at the age of 50, worn out by eighteen pregnancies. (It happens that Francis Place, the great nineteenth-century advocate of birth control, also was born into a very large family.) As a young woman, Sanger trained to be a nurse. Following marriage and an early association with New York intellectuals and anarchists, as well as participation in several hard-fought labor disputes on the eve of World War I, she began working with women in some of New York's poorest neighborhoods. The plight of these women, lacking the most basic health services and sexual information, angered the young midwife. When she tried to publish an article on venereal disease in 1912, the censors suppressed it. Two years later, her advocacy of contraception in her feminist magazine, *The Woman Rebel*, earned her an indictment for breaking the postal obscenity laws. Sanger fled to Europe but returned the following year. Charges against her were dropped.

In 1916, Sanger opened the first American birth-control clinic in a Brooklyn tenement. It was modeled on a Dutch facility she had visited while in Europe. Nine days after the clinic's opening, Sanger and her colleagues were arrested for distributing contraceptive information. She served thirty days in jail but won a partial victory on appeal: the court ruled that contraception could be prescribed, for "medical reasons," by a doctor but not by a nurse as Sanger wanted. This cleared the way for Sanger to open a doctor-operated clinic in 1923. With all the publicity she had received, and a wealthy second husband willing to bankroll her cause, Sanger assumed leadership of the international birth-control movement. An overseas lecture tour took her as far away as Japan and India, where she helped found organizations that still exist today. She sponsored the first world population conference in Geneva, Switzerland, in 1927, an event that led to the establishment, the following year, of the International Union for the Scientific Study of Population.

Sanger was instrumental in the founding of Planned Parenthood in the United States and later the International Planned Parenthood Federation, of which she was the first president from 1952 to 1959. She had a lifelong interest in seeing more effective, less costly forms of birth control developed. In the early 1950s, she persuaded a wealthy friend to fund the biological research that led to the development of oral contraceptives. Today, population agencies around the world, including UNFPA, have shifted away from an emphasis on population quotas and targets, and back toward Sanger's original vision of family planning as a means of giving women, through improved health care, more control over their own lives.

Further Reading. The Margaret Sanger Papers Project website at http://www.nyu.edu/projects/sanger/index.html

Amartya K. Sen (1933–)

From Malthus's time down to the present, concerns about the size and growth rate of population have centered on the dire possibility of *famine*. The Malthusian way of thinking emphasizes the tendency toward an imbalance between total population and the means of subsistence, with people under the worst circumstances literally running out of food. Famine is seen as an issue of food availability. It arrives in the wake of drought, devastating cyclones, ravaging floods. But this is not the only way to think about famine, according to economist Amartya K. Sen. People can starve for the simple reason that they lack the financial means (or "entitlements") to purchase food, even though adequate stocks of food may be well within their reach. A shortage of purchasing power can be as lethal as an actual shortage of food. In his important 1981 study, *Poverty and Famines: An Essay on Entitlement and Deprivation,* Sen developed this line of thought not only theoretically but empirically. A careful examination of several twentieth-century famines led him to conclude that starvation had occurred in Bengal (1943), Ethiopia (1972–1974), and Bangladesh (1974) not because of a sharp drop in the supply of food available in those countries but because large numbers of people, for reasons such as inflation and unemployment, lacked sufficient monetary entitlements to purchase food. A shortage of entitlements also contributed to famine in the Sahel of Africa in the early 1970s.

This analysis points to a view of famine that makes it more the product of human institutions relating to markets and property rights than of any "natural" forces. For famine to be averted, exchange entitlements in countries prone to food insecurity must be more equally distributed than they have (often) been in the past. That is because the workings of an exchange economy cannot ensure that food will be any more equally distributed than incomes are. Absent conscious intervention, a minimal or zero income will translate to inadequate portions of food.

Born in West Bengal, India, a region hit by famine during World War II, Amartya Sen was educated at Presidency College, Calcutta, and at Trinity College, Cambridge (Ph.D., 1959). He has taught at universities in India, the United States, and Britain. In 1998, the year he won the Nobel Prize in Economics, he resigned a professorship at Harvard to return to Trinity College as its Master. Sen is a leading authority in the technical field of welfare economics, but he is better known to the public for his studies of poverty, hunger, and inequality. Beyond the 1981 book cited earlier, two notable works he co-authored with Jean Dreze are *Hunger and Public Action* (1989) and *The Political Economy of Hunger* (1990–1991, 3 vols.).

Further Reading. A. Sen, "Autobiography," at http:// nobelprize.org/economics/laureates/1998/sen-autobio.html; A. Sen, "Public Action to Remedy Hunger," Tanco Memorial Lecture, London, August 2, 1990, at http://www.thp.org/ reports/sen/sen890.htm#n1

Julian L. Simon (1932–1998)

Discussions of world population are often tinged with apprehension, gloom, and pessimism, for which the writings of T. R. Malthus are partly to blame. The strongest antidote to neo-Malthusian gloom may be found in the writings of Julian Simon, who proved to be the foremost *anti*-Malthusian of the twentieth century. In scores of articles, several books, and many television interviews and newspaper columns, Simon tried to take the curse off population growth, arguing that increased human numbers should be viewed in a *positive* light, not just as a liability but as a long-term asset. The liability came in the form of increased short-run demands on existing stocks of resources. The asset took the form of human inventiveness: more human beings meant more minds capable of innovative thinking and technological advances that could *stretch* the stocks of resources. For Simon, the evidence that population growth had in fact had a benign impact was to be seen in falling resource prices, rising life expectancies, and a host of other indicators of environmental and material well-being. For good reason he was labeled a "cornucopian."

Simon's optimism on population posed a vigorous challenge to the more sober views of environmentalists. His main opponent in the arena of demographic controversy was biologist Paul Ehrlich, author of the 1968 best-seller *The Population Bomb*. In that book and in many other forums, Ehrlich had warned of impending famines, natural resource shortages, and dangerous rates of pollution—all attributable, more or less, to excessive population growth. Simon countered with reams of data pointing to trend lines that were positive, not negative. History demonstrated that whenever a particular resource became scarce and costly, human ingenuity found ways to conserve it or substitute around it. Always Simon emphasized human creativity and adaptability, which he believed the doomsayers either ignored or underestimated. His position on immigration was fully consistent with his population optimism: he advocated an open immigration policy for the United States.

For a demographic thinker, Simon had a rather unconventional academic career. His graduate degrees were in business economics (University of Chicago), as were his early research interests. His final academic position was professor of business administration at the University of Maryland. He was also a senior fellow at the Cato Institute—which gives an indication of the free-market orientation of much of his writing. His main books were *The Economics of Population Growth* (1977), *The Ultimate Resource* (1981; revised in 1996 as *The Ultimate Resource 2*), and *The Economic Consequences of Immigration* (1989).

Further Reading. S. Moore, "Julian Simon Remembered: It's a Wonderful Life," *Cato Online Policy Report*, 20:2 (March–April 1998).

Steven W. Sinding (1943–)

The world's leading NGO in the field of family planning, the International Planned Parenthood Federation, or IPPF, got a new director-general in 2002—Dr. Steven Sinding. The IPPF, founded in 1952 with the legendary Margaret Sanger as its first president, coordinates the activities of 150 national member associations working in 180 countries. Dr. Sinding's path to the leadership of the IPPF began with undergraduate studies at Oberlin College (1965) and a Ph.D. in political science from the University of North Carolina at Chapel Hill (1970). Ironically for one who is now publicly at odds with his own government, Sinding worked for years in the United States Agency for International Development, first as its director for population and then as head of the AID mission in Kenya. He went on to serve as the population advisor to the World Bank and then to direct the population sciences program at the Rockefeller Foundation from 1991 to 1999. In 1994, he was a member of the U.S. delegation to the ICPD conference in Cairo. More recently he has been a professor at Columbia University's Mailman School of Public Health. His publications on population-related topics are extensive.

Dr. Sinding took an early opportunity following his appointment at the IPPF to attack the Bush administration for trying to undermine the program of action adopted at the Cairo conference in 1994. A key element of that program was the idea that all couples should have access to reproductive health information and services. In Dr. Sinding's view, this Cairo commitment had been simply a reaffirmation of the 1968 Teheran Proclamation on Human Rights, which included the right of married couples to determine "freely and responsibly" the number and spacing of their offspring. Sinding dismisses the current U.S. administration's push for a no-condoms, abstinence-only policy on international family planning as based on "pseudo-science" and "absurd." His organization has lost millions of dollars in U.S. financial support by refusing to accept the Reagan-era Mexico City policy (also known as the "global gag rule")—reinstated by President Bush in 2001—which cuts off U.S. funding to any foreign NGO that offers, counsels, or advocates for legal abortion.

Further Reading. N. Birdsall, A. C. Kelley, and S. Sinding, *Population Matters: Demographic Change, Economic Growth, and Poverty in the Developing World* (Oxford: Oxford University Press, 2001); S. Sinding, "Why the Cairo Programme of Action Is So Important," International Parliamentarians' Conference (Ottawa, 2002), at http://www.unfpa.org/ipci/index.htm

Christopher H. Smith (1953–)

Shortly after President Bush took office in January 2001, he sent a supportive message to the 28th annual March for Life on the Mall in Washington, D.C. It was read to over 100,000 marchers by a conservative Republican congressman from New Jersey, Christopher Smith. Appropriately so, since Rep. Smith had gained by then, as he continues to have, a reputation as perhaps the strongest opponent of abortion in the U.S. Congress. In the late 1990s, he was closely involved in political maneuvering to get the so-called Mexico City policy reinstated. Under that policy, U.S. funding was denied to any foreign NGO that engaged in abortion-related activities, even with its own money. Presidents Reagan and George H. W. Bush followed the policy from 1984 to 1992, but President Clinton reversed it immediately upon taking office in 1993. Clinton also restored the annual U.S. contribution to the United Nations Population Fund that had been withheld under Reagan and the older Bush on grounds that the UNFPA implicitly supported China's coercive one-child population policy. (The UNFPA vigorously denies the allegation.)

Although it may appear that U.S. backing for international family-planning programs has become a political football, with Democrats in favor and Republicans opposed, the truth is more complicated. Democrats in Congress and the White House typically favor generous funding of the programs, with few restrictions. Republicans in Congress and the White House will fund family planning abroad—President Bush, for example, proposed USAID spending of $425 million for population assistance in fiscal year 2005—but with "pro-life" restrictions. They prefer to steer the money, even in programs intended to combat the global AIDS epidemic, toward faith-based and abstinence programs. Many experts in the field, it should be noted, question whether abstinence programs have a proven track record of effectiveness.

Congressman Smith is a New Jersey native. His B.A. degree in business (1975) is from Trenton State College, now called the College of New Jersey. He was the executive director of the New Jersey Right to Life Committee from 1976 to 1978 and won his seat in New Jersey's Fourth District in 1980, which means he became a congressman at the youthful age of 27. For many years Smith has chaired or co-chaired the House Pro-Life Caucus; his voting record has consistently earned 100 percent ratings from the National Right to Life Committee. Smith's other legislative interests include veterans' affairs, the fight against human trafficking, and autism education.

Further Reading. C. Smith, "An Urgent Appeal to Get Involved in Politics . . ." (November 2000), accessed at http://www. priestsforlife.org/government/chrissmithspeech.htm; "About Chris" webpage at http://www.house.gov/chrissmith/

Marie Stopes (1880–1958)

Much like her contemporary Margaret Sanger on the other side of the Atlantic, Marie Stopes fought for the reproductive rights of women in Britain in the early decades of the twentieth century. In 1921, she opened the first birth-control clinic in the United Kingdom. Located in north London, the "Mothers' Clinic" employed only female nurses and doctors and had a clientele of mainly poor women. In the face of much opposition, Stopes opened other clinics around Britain, including a horse-drawn caravan. Like Sanger, Stopes took an interest in the varieties of contraceptive techniques and even designed a cervical cap that was dispensed at her clinics. She wanted family-planning clinics to be opened in every country in the world. (The international organization that today bears her name, Marie Stopes International, operates in more than thirty countries.)

Born in Edinburgh, Stopes graduated with honors from University College London and then earned her doctorate at the University of Munich. Her first marriage was a personal fiasco that prompted her to write *Married Love* (1918), a sex manual that became a best-seller. Stopes received thousands of letters from grateful readers of the book; her other book, *Wise Parenthood* (1918), dealt with the specifics of birth control. Stopes's second marriage, to Humphrey Roe, was much more successful than her first. Roe shared her commitment to the cause of birth control and helped finance the publication of her books and the operation of her clinics. The couple had one child, Harry, born in 1924.

Further Reading. M. Stopes, *Married Love*, Ross McKibbin (ed.) (Oxford: Oxford World's Classics, 2004).

M. S. Swaminathan (1925–)

In the 1950s and 1960s, India was perceived by many as a demographic train wreck waiting to happen. Its population was growing far more rapidly than its agricultural output. In some years, the only thing standing between the Indian masses and famine was the flotilla of U.S. grain ships arriving at the nation's ports. Yet the worst did not happen, and much of the credit for averting Malthusian disaster in India goes to Dr. M. S. Swaminathan. Born in the southern Indian state of Tamil Nadu and educated first in India and then at Cambridge University (Ph.D. in genetics, 1952), Swaminathan went on to the University of Wisconsin for post-graduate study. He was offered a professorship there but declined it: "I asked myself, why did I study genetics? It was to produce enough food in India. So I came back." At the Indian Agricultural Research Institute in New Delhi, of which he was the director by 1966, Swaminathan became the architect of India's Green Revolution, leading the efforts to adapt high-yield wheat varieties from Mexico to conditions in India. This involved the cross-breeding of Mexican semi-dwarf plants developed by Norman Borlaug with Japanese and local strains to create a superior wheat for Indian agriculture. But it also involved big administrative challenges, like persuading the Indian government to import sufficient quantities of wheat seeds, and getting farmers to adopt new seed varieties, chemical fertilizers, and pesticides. The success of Swaminathan's efforts is evident in a simple statistic: from a wheat output of 12 million tons in the early 1960s, India has now reached 70 million tons and is virtually self-sufficient in basic foodstuffs.

For the achievements outlined above, and for his leadership both nationally and internationally in trying to develop more eco-friendly and sustainable agricultural practices, Dr. Swaminathan has received numerous honors. These include the World Food Prize (1987), the Tyler Environment Award (1991), the Honda Award (1991), the United Nations Environment Program's Sasakawa Prize (1994), and the Volvo Environment Prize (1999). The money that came with these awards helped their recipient establish and sustain the M. S. Swaminathan Research Foundation and, under its aegis, the Centre for Research on Sustainable Agricultural Development, in Chennai, Madras. The purpose of the Centre, which has a staff of 150, is to advance the cause of environmentally sound and socially equitable agriculture. Dr. Swaminathan was named the UNESCO-Cousteau Professor in Ecotechnology for Asia in 1996.

Further Reading.   S. Kapoor, "M. S. Swaminathan: Brain Food for the Poor," *AsiaWeek.com* (June 29, 2001); M. Ganguly, "M. S. Swaminathan," *Time*, 154:7/8 (August 23–30, 1999).

Ben Wattenberg (1933–)

Everyone who ever managed to draw the public's attention to the issue of population had a knack for turning a phrase, and Ben Wattenberg is no exception. In his new book *Fewer* (2004), Wattenberg declares on the first page, *"[N]ever have birth and fertility rates fallen so far, so fast, so low, for so long, in so many places, so surprisingly"* (italics in the original). Wattenberg, a senior fellow at the American Enterprise Institute in Washington, D.C., has long been concerned about falling fertility rates in the United States and in the Western world more generally. He first sounded the alarm in 1987 with *The Birth Dearth*. A decade later, in "The Grandchild Gap," a one-hour television special for PBS, he explored the demographic and psychological issues related to low fertility in the industrialized countries. So confident is Wattenberg that the global trend toward smaller families is permanent that he dismisses the United Nations' medium-variant projection of mid-century population in favor of its *low*-variant projection. Thus he sees global population topping out at around 8 billion.

Wattenberg does not call himself a demographer but rather an admirer of demographers. His real stock-in-trade is political and intellectual dialogue, which he enters—briskly, unabashedly—from the conservative side, even though his resumé includes a stint as aide and speechwriter to President Lyndon Johnson in the 1960s and campaign advisor to two prominent Democratic senators in the 1970s. Since 1994, he has moderated "Think Tank with Ben Wattenberg" for PBS. He is the author of nine books and for many years was a syndicated columnist. His B.A. is from Hobart and William Smith Colleges (1955), from which he received an honorary degree in 1975.

Further Reading.   B. Wattenberg, *Fewer: How the New Demography of Depopulation Will Shape Our Future* (Chicago: Ivan Dee, 2004); B. Wattenberg, "It Will Be a Smaller World After All," *New York Times*, March 8, 2003; "About Ben Wattenberg" at http://www.pbs.org/thinktank/about_ben.html

6

Statistics and Graphs

Nowadays anyone with a question about some aspect of world population stands an excellent chance of being able to find an answer. Demographers are at work all the time to produce reliable data for policymakers and the public. Two organizations, the U.S. Census Bureau and the UN Population Division, issue some of the most comprehensive population estimates, allowing us to satisfy our curiosity on any number of issues. For example, how many people currently live on our planet? In what parts of the world is population expanding most rapidly, and where is it actually shrinking? How much of a slowdown in global population growth is expected to take place in the next 50 to 100 years? How many people are born and die every minute, every day, or every year, at current rates? What are the world's most populous cities and countries, and how might the rankings change over the next few decades? The tables and graphs in this chapter answer these and many other questions. We begin with Table 6.1, which shows the number of births and deaths for various time spans, from years down to seconds.

Table 6.2 presents the U.S. Census Bureau's estimates of world population, year by year, back to 1950 and forward to the middle of the current century. It also provides information on the annual percentage rates of population growth and the actual numbers of people added each year. Note that the annual growth rate peaked in 1962–1963 at 2.19 percent, while the actual numbers added to global population peaked more than two decades later, in 1989, at about 88 million. Demographers expect never again to see that large an increase in one year.

TABLE 6.1
World Vital Events per Time Unit, 2005

Time unit	Natural Births	Deaths	Increase
Year	130,013,274	56,130,242	73,883,032
Month	10,834,440	4,677,520	6,156,919
Day	356,201	153,781	202,419
Hour	14,842	6,408	8,434
Minute	247	107	141
Second	4.1	1.8	2.3

Source: U.S. Census Bureau, International Data Base; updated 4/26/05.

TABLE 6.2
Total Midyear Population for the World: 1950–2050

	Population	Average annual growth rate (%)	Average annual population change
1950	2,556,517,137	1.47	37,798,160
1951	2,594,315,297	1.61	42,072,962
1952	2,636,388,259	1.71	45,350,197
1953	2,681,738,456	1.77	47,979,452
1954	2,729,717,908	1.87	51,465,740
1955	2,781,183,648	1.89	52,974,870
1956	2,834,158,518	1.95	55,842,882
1957	2,890,001,400	1.94	56,522,767
1958	2,946,524,167	1.76	52,351,768
1959	2,998,875,935	1.39	42,090,531
1960	3,040,966,466	1.33	40,782,196
1961	3,081,748,662	1.80	55,995,030
1962	3,137,743,692	2.19	69,519,033
1963	3,207,262,725	2.19	71,119,386
1964	3,278,382,111	2.08	68,979,816
1965	3,347,361,927	2.07	70,182,601
1966	3,417,544,528	2.02	69,689,877
1967	3,487,234,405	2.04	71,794,577
1968	3,559,028,982	2.07	74,579,864
1969	3,633,608,846	2.05	75,142,514
1970	3,708,751,360	2.07	77,391,102
1971	3,786,142,462	2.00	76,476,397
1972	3,862,618,859	1.95	75,970,556
1973	3,938,589,415	1.88	74,885,210
1974	4,013,474,625	1.80	72,998,197
1975	4,086,472,822	1.73	71,516,414

TABLE 6.2, continued

	Population	Average annual growth rate (%)	Average annual population change
1976	4,157,989,236	1.72	72,098,269
1977	4,230,087,505	1.69	72,025,391
1978	4,302,112,896	1.72	74,827,692
1979	4,376,940,588	1.71	75,704,974
1980	4,452,645,562	1.69	76,038,009
1981	4,528,683,571	1.75	79,722,408
1982	4,608,405,979	1.75	81,441,019
1983	4,689,846,998	1.70	80,257,445
1984	4,770,104,443	1.70	81,750,075
1985	4,851,854,518	1.70	83,362,927
1986	4,935,217,445	1.73	86,023,275
1987	5,021,240,720	1.71	86,724,868
1988	5,107,965,588	1.68	86,758,510
1989	5,194,724,098	1.68	88,041,729
1990	5,282,765,827	1.58	84,050,074
1991	5,366,815,901	1.55	84,045,822
1992	5,450,861,723	1.49	81,716,293
1993	5,532,578,016	1.45	80,846,508
1994	5,613,424,524	1.38	79,045,988
1996	5,773,464,448	1.36	78,896,320
1997	5,852,360,768	1.31	77,375,209
1998	5,929,735,977	1.28	76,427,042
1999	6,006,163,019	1.25	75,364,877
2000	6,081,527,896	1.22	74,414,630
2001	6,155,942,526	1.19	73,686,642
2002	6,229,629,168	1.17	73,483,285
2003	6,303,112,453	1.16	73,750,665
2004	6,376,863,118	1.16	74,195,672
2005	6,451,058,790	1.15	74,427,813
2006	6,525,486,603	1.14	74,629,207
2007	6,600,115,810	1.13	74,940,532
2008	6,675,056,342	1.12	75,228,043
2009	6,750,284,385	1.11	75,466,071
2010	6,825,750,456	1.10	75,688,866
2011	6,901,439,322	1.09	75,802,963
2012	6,977,242,285	1.08	75,615,963
2013	7,052,858,248	1.06	75,167,390
2014	7,128,025,638	1.04	74,490,498
2015	7,202,516,136	1.02	73,766,792
2016	7,276,282,928	1.00	73,055,605
2017	7,349,338,533	0.98	72,230,253

(continues)

TABLE 6.2, continued

	Population	Average annual growth rate (%)	Average annual population change
2018	7,421,568,786	0.96	71,289,623
2019	7,492,858,409	0.93	70,235,773
2020	7,563,094,182	0.91	69,180,831
2021	7,632,275,013	0.89	68,144,353
2022	7,700,419,366	0.87	67,028,250
2023	7,767,447,616	0.84	65,862,519
2024	7,833,310,135	0.82	64,679,285
2025	7,897,989,420	0.80	63,596,858
2026	7,961,586,278	0.78	62,635,490
2027	8,024,221,768	0.77	61,689,308
2028	8,085,911,076	0.75	60,746,079
2029	8,146,657,155	0.73	59,800,227
2030	8,206,457,382	0.72	58,925,303
2031	8,265,382,685	0.70	58,132,001
2032	8,323,514,686	0.69	57,333,600
2033	8,380,848,286	0.67	56,512,857
2034	8,437,361,143	0.66	55,666,984
2035	8,493,028,127	0.64	54,846,652
2036	8,547,874,779	0.63	54,058,633
2037	8,601,933,412	0.62	53,249,683
2038	8,655,183,095	0.60	52,414,904
2039	8,707,597,999	0.59	51,542,658
2040	8,759,140,657	0.58	50,686,755
2041	8,809,827,412	0.56	49,847,392
2042	8,859,674,804	0.55	48,957,732
2043	8,908,632,536	0.54	48,019,825
2044	8,956,652,361	0.52	47,040,969
2045	9,003,693,330	0.51	46,074,635
2046	9,049,767,965	0.50	45,123,225
2047	9,094,891,190	0.48	44,148,176
2048	9,139,039,366	0.47	43,161,841
2049	9,182,201,207	0.46	42,174,749
2050	9,224,375,956		

Source: U.S. Census Bureau, International Data Base; updated April 2005.

In Table 6.3 the United Nations offers its first truly long-range population projections—to the year 2300! Demographers understand that more things could happen over the course of the next three centuries than any model could possibly incorporate.

TABLE 6.3
UN Long-Range World Population Projections:
Various Growth Scenarios, 2000–2300 (in millions)

Year	World Medium	High	Low	More developed regions Medium	High	Low	Less developed regions Medium	High	Low
2000	6,071	6,071	6,071	1,194	1,194	1,194	4,877	4,877	4,877
2025	7,851	8,365	7,334	1,241	1,282	1,199	6,610	7,082	6,135
2050	8,919	10,633	7,409	1,220	1,370	1,084	7,699	9,263	6,325
2075	9,221	12,494	6,601	1,153	1,467	904	8,068	11,027	5,696
2100	9,064	14,018	5,491	1.131	1,651	766	7,933	12,367	4,726
2125	8,734	15,296	4,556	1,137	1,885	679	7,597	13,411	3,877
2150	8,494	16,722	3,921	1,161	2,152	633	7,333	14,571	3,288
2175	8,434	18,696	3,481	1,185	2,454	593	7,249	16,242	2,889
2200	8,499	21,236	3,165	1,207	2,795	554	7,291	18,441	2,612
2225	8,622	24,301	2,920	1,228	3,179	517	7,395	21,122	2,403
2250	8,752	27,842	2,704	1,246	3,612	482	7,506	24,230	2,223
2275	8,868	31,868	2,501	1,263	4,100	448	7,605	27,768	2,053
2300	8,972	36,444	2,310	1,278	4,650	416	7,694	31,793	1,894

Source: United Nations Department of Economic and Social Affairs, Population Division, *World Population to 2300* (New York: United Nations, 2004), p. 28.

Hence the model they use ignores potential ecological, political, and economic discontinuities of the kind experts worried about in the 1960s and 1970s and simply rolls forward the number of people at the starting point on the basis of low-, medium-, and high-growth rate assumptions. One particular assumption the United Nations makes is that the AIDS epidemic will not run completely out of control. (How reassuring it would be to *know* this and not merely *assume* it!) Note the vast difference in the 2300 global population depending on whether a low- or high-growth rate is assumed. The world could have as few as 2.3 billion people—a fraction of the present population—or as many as 36 billion, more than five times the current level. But the most likely figure is about 9 billion, which is quite close to the population we expect to see in 2050. Under all assumptions, the share of the more developed (rich) nations in the world's total population is expected to decline, while the share of the less developed nations expands.

Table 6.4 presents the United Nations' most recent population projections, by continent, to the middle of the twenty-first century. These projections are revised and reissued every two years, in even-numbered years. The table gives only the medium-variant projections, which assume that fertility rates everywhere are trending toward the level of 1.85 children per woman. Demographers consider the medium-variant estimates more realistic than either the high- or low-variant versions. What most journalists took away from the table upon its release was the figure of 9.1 billion people on Earth by the year 2050. At mid-century nearly three out of every five humans will live in Asia—a slight proportional decrease from today. Europe will decline from about 11 percent to 7 percent of world population. The big gainer will be Africa, rising from 14 percent currently to 21 percent by 2050.

TABLE 6.4
World Population Projections to 2050 by Region (in millions)

Year	World	Africa	Asia	Europe	Latin America and Caribbean	North America	Oceania
2000	6,086	812	3,676	728	523	315	31
2005	6,465	906	3,905	728	561	331	33
2010	6,843	1,007	4,130	726	599	346	35
2015	7,219	1,115	4,351	721	634	361	37
2020	7,578	1,228	4,554	715	667	375	39
2025	7,905	1,344	4,728	707	697	388	41
2030	8,199	1,463	4,872	698	722	400	43
2035	8,463	1,584	4,992	688	744	411	44
2040	8,701	1,705	5,092	677	761	421	45
2045	8,907	1,823	5,168	666	774	430	47
2050	9,076	1,937	5,217	653	783	438	48

Source: Population Division of the Department of Economic and Social Affairs of the United Nations Secretariat, *World Population Prospects: The 2004 Revision* and *World Urbanization Prospects: The 2003 Revision,* http://esa.un.org/unpp.

In Table 6.5 we see the anticipated urban-rural breakdown of world population over the next several decades. The balance will tip—irreversibly, we think—in the urban direction by 2010, when for the first time over half (51.3 percent) of the world's population will live in cities. The urban proportion will continue to increase, reaching about 61 percent by 2030. This trend toward higher rates of city-dwelling is one of the factors leading demographers to be-

TABLE 6.5
Projected Urban-Rural Breakdown of World Population, 2000–2030

Year	Urban Population (millions)	Percent Urban	Rural Population (millions)	Percent Rural
2000	2,864	47.1	3,222	52.9
2005	3,177	49.2	3,287	50.8
2010	3,512	51.3	3,331	48.7
2015	3,868	53.6	3,352	46.4
2020	4,236	55.9	3,341	44.1
2025	4,611	58.3	3,295	41.7
2030	4,987	60.8	3,212	39.2

Source: Population Division of the Department of Economic and Social Affairs of the United Nations Secretariat, *World Population Prospects: The 2004 Revision* and *World Urbanization Prospects: The 2003 Revision*, http://esa.un.org/unpp,

lieve strongly that global fertility rates will continue to decline, since children tend to be more costly and inconvenient in an urban setting than in a rural one.

Table 6.6 provides a range of essential demographic data for all the regions and countries in the world as of 2005. For ease of use, individual countries are listed alphabetically. If we look at the big picture revealed in the regional data, what stands out most clearly is the special status of sub-Saharan Africa. That region has the highest birth rate, highest death rate, highest rate of natural increase, highest infant mortality rate, and highest total fertility rate in the world—by a wide margin in most cases.

TABLE 6.6
Key Demographic Data for the Regions and Countries of the World, 2005

Country or area	Population 2005 (millions)	Births per 1,000 population	Deaths per 1,000 population	Rate of natural increase (percent)	Infant mortality rate	Total fertility rate
WORLD	6,451	20	9	1.2	50.0	2.61
Less developed	5,242	22	8	1.4	54.9	2.84
More developed	1,210	11	10	0.1	7.5	1.59
Sub-Saharan Africa	733	39	16	2.3	89.7	5.29
Northern Africa	159	22	5	1.6	33.5	2.60
Near East	191	26	5	2.0	37.3	3.41
Asia (excluding Near East)	3,648	19	8	1.1	46.3	2.35

TABLE 6.6, continued

Country or area	Population 2005 (millions)	Births per 1,000 population	Deaths per 1,000 population	Rate of natural increase (percent)	Infant mortality rate	Total fertility rate
Latin America and the Caribbean	555	20	6	1.4	26.5	2.36
Western Europe	396	10	10	0.0	4.7	1.52
Eastern Europe	121	10	11	0.0	12.9	1.35
Commonwealth of Independent States	280	13	13	0.0	38.7	1.63
Northern America	329	14	8	0.6	6.4	2.04
Oceania	33	17	7	0.9	21.2	2.25
Afghanistan	29.9	47	21	2.6	163.1	6.75
Albania	3.6	15	5	1.0	21.5	2.04
Algeria	32.5	17	5	1.3	31.0	1.92
American Samoa	0.06	23	3	2.0	9.3	3.25
Andorra	0.07	9	6	0.3	4.0	1.29
Angola	11.8	46	25	2.1	187.5	6.42
Anguilla	0.01	14	5	0.9	21.0	1.73
Antigua and Barbuda	0.07	17	5	1.2	19.5	2.26
Argentina	39.5	17	8	0.9	15.2	2.19
Armenia	3.0	12	8	0.4	23.3	1.32
Aruba	0.07	11	7	0.5	5.9	1.79
Australia	20.1	12	7	0.5	4.7	1.76
Austria	8.2	9	10	-0.1	4.7	1.36
Azerbaijan	7.9	20	10	1.1	81.7	2.44
Bahamas, The	0.3	18	9	0.9	25.2	2.20
Bahrain	0.7	18	4	1.4	17.3	2.63
Bangladesh	144.3	30	8	2.2	62.6	3.13
Barbados	0.3	13	9	0.4	11.7	1.64
Belarus	10.3	11	14	-0.3	13.4	1.39
Belgium	10.4	10	10	0.0	4.7	1.64
Belize	0.3	29	6	2.4	25.4	3.68
Benin	7.6	40	12	2.7	81.3	5.32
Bermuda	0.07	12	8	0.4	8.5	1.89
Bhutan	2.2	34	13	2.1	100.4	4.81
Bolivia	8.9	24	8	1.6	53.1	2.94
Bosnia and Herzegovenia	4.4	9	8	0.1	10.1	1.21
Botswana	1.6	23	29	-0.6	54.6	2.85
Brazil	186.1	17	6	1.1	29.6	1.93
Brunei	0.4	19	3	1.6	12.6	2.30
Bulgaria	7.5	10	14	-0.5	20.6	1.38
Burkina Faso	13.5	46	16	3.0	92.9	6.54
Burma	47.0	18	10	0.8	63.6	2.01
Burundi	7.8	42	14	2.9	64.4	6.63

TABLE 6.6, continued

Country or area	Population 2005 (millions)	Births per 1,000 population	Deaths per 1,000 population	Rate of natural increase (percent)	Infant mortality rate	Total fertility rate
Cambodia	13.6	27	9	1.8	70.9	3.44
Cameroon	17.0	34	14	2.1	64.9	4.47
Canada	32.8	11	8	0.3	4.8	1.61
Cape Verde	0.4	25	7	1.9	47.8	3.48
Cayman Islands	0.04	13	5	0.8	8.2	1.90
Central African Republic	4.2	34	19	1.6	87.3	4.50
Chad	9.7	46	17	2.9	93.1	6.32
Chile	16.0	15	6	1.0	8.8	2.02
China	1,306.3	13	7	0.6	24.2	1.72
Colombia	43.0	21	6	1.5	21.0	2.56
Comoros	0.7	38	8	2.9	74.9	5.09
Congo (Brazzaville)	3.6	43	13	3.0	87.4	6.14
Congo (Kinshasa)	60.8	44	14	3.1	90.7	6.54
Cook Islands	0.02	22	5	1.7	NA	NA
Costa Rica	4.0	19	4	1.4	9.9	2.28
Cote d'Ivoire	17.3	36	15	2.1	90.8	4.58
Croatia	4.5	10	11	-0.2	6.8	1.39
Cuba	11.3	12	7	0.5	6.3	1.66
Cyprus	0.8	13	8	0.5	7.2	1.83
Czech Republic	10.2	9	11	-0.1	3.9	1.20
Denmark	5.4	11	10	0.1	4.6	1.74
Djibouti	0.5	40	19	2.1	104.1	5.40
Dominica	0.07	16	7	0.9	14.2	1.96
Dominican Republic	9.0	24	6	1.8	29.4	2.86
East Timor	1.0	27	6	2.1	47.4	3.61
Ecuador	13.4	23	4	1.8	23.7	2.72
Egypt	77.5	23	5	1.8	32.6	2.88
El Salvador	6.7	27	6	2.1	25.1	3.16
Equatorial Guinea	0.5	36	15	2.1	91.2	4.62
Eritrea	4.7	35	10	2.5	47.4	5.20
Estonia	1.3	10	13	-0.3	7.9	1.39
Ethiopia	73.1	39	15	2.4	95.3	5.33
Faroe Islands	0.05	14	9	0.5	6.2	2.20
Fiji	0.9	23	5	1.7	12.6	2.75
Finland	5.2	11	10	0.1	3.6	1.73
France	60.7	12	9	0.3	4.3	1.85
French Guiana	0.2	21	5	1.6	12.1	3.01
French Polynesia	0.3	17	5	1.2	8.4	2.04

(continues)

TABLE 6.6, continued

Country or area	Population 2005 (millions)	Births per 1,000 population	Deaths per 1,000 population	Rate of natural increase (percent)	Infant mortality rate	Total fertility rate
Gabon	1.4	36	12	2.4	55.4	4.77
Gambia, The	1.6	40	13	2.7	73.1	5.38
Gaza Strip	1.4	40	4	3.6	22.9	5.91
Georgia	4.7	10	9	0.1	18.6	1.41
Germany	82.4	8	11	-0.2	4.2	1.39
Ghana	21.9	31	10	2.1	56.4	4.10
Gibraltar	0.03	11	9	0.2	5.1	1.65
Greece	10.7	10	10	0.0	5.5	1.33
Greenland	0.06	16	8	0.8	15.8	2.41
Grenada	0.09	22	7	1.5	14.6	2.37
Guadeloupe	0.4	15	6	0.9	8.6	1.91
Guam	0.2	19	4	1.5	6.9	2.60
Guatemala	12.0	31	5	2.5	32.0	3.93
Guernsey	0.07	9	10	-0.1	4.7	1.38
Guinea	9.5	42	16	2.6	91.5	5.83
Guinea-Bissau	1.4	38	17	2.1	107.2	4.93
Guyana	0.8	18	8	1.0	33.3	2.05
Haiti	8.1	37	12	2.4	73.5	5.02
Honduras	7.2	29	5	2.4	26.5	3.69
Hong Kong S.A.R.	6.9	7	6	0.1	3.0	0.93
Hungary	10.0	10	13	-0.3	8.6	1.31
Iceland	0.3	14	7	0.7	3.3	1.92
India	1,080.3	22	8	1.4	56.3	2.78
Indonesia	242.0	21	6	1.4	35.6	2.44
Iran	68.0	17	6	1.1	41.6	1.82
Iraq	26.1	33	5	2.7	50.2	4.28
Ireland	4.0	14	8	0.7	5.4	1.87
Israel	6.3	18	6	1.2	7.0	2.44
Italy	58.1	9	10	-0.1	5.9	1.28
Jamaica	2.7	21	6	1.5	16.3	2.47
Japan	127.4	9	9	0.1	3.3	1.39
Jersey	0.09	10	9	0.0	5.2	1.57
Jordan	5.8	22	3	1.9	17.4	2.71
Kazakhstan	15.2	16	9	0.6	29.2	1.89
Kenya	33.8	40	15	2.5	61.5	4.96
Kiribati	0.1	31	8	2.2	48.5	4.20
Korea, North	22.9	16	7	0.9	24.0	2.15
Korea, South	48.6	10	6	0.4	6.3	1.26
Kuwait	2.3	22	2	1.9	9.9	2.97
Kyrgyzstan	5.1	22	7	1.5	35.6	2.70

TABLE 6.6, continued

Country or area	Population 2005 (millions)	Births per 1,000 population	Deaths per 1,000 population	Rate of natural increase (percent)	Infant mortality rate	Total fertility rate
Laos	6.2	36	12	2.4	85.2	4.77
Latvia	2.3	9	14	-0.5	9.6	1.26
Lebanon	3.8	19	6	1.3	24.5	1.92
Lesotho	2.0	25	29	-0.4	88.8	3.35
Liberia	2.9	46	24	2.2	162.0	6.09
Libya	5.8	27	3	2.3	24.6	3.34
Liechtenstein	0.03	10	7	0.3	4.7	1.51
Lithuania	3.6	9	11	-0.2	6.9	1.19
Luxembourg	0.5	12	8	0.4	4.8	1.79
Macau S.A.R.	0.4	8	4	0.4	4.4	1.00
Macedonia	2.0	12	9	0.3	10.1	1.57
Madagascar	18.0	42	11	3.0	76.8	5.66
Malawi	12.7	43	20	2.4	96.1	5.98
Malaysia	24.0	23	5	1.8	17.7	3.07
Maldives	0.3	35	7	2.8	56.5	5.02
Mali	11.4	50	17	3.3	109.5	7.47
Malta	0.4	10	8	0.2	3.9	1.50
Man, Isle of	0.08	11	11	0.0	5.9	1.65
Marshall Islands	0.06	34	5	2.9	29.4	3.93
Martinique	0.4	14	6	0.8	7.1	1.79
Mauritania	3.1	41	12	2.9	70.9	5.94
Mauritius	1.2	16	7	0.9	15.0	1.96
Mayotte	0.2	42	8	3.4	62.4	5.89
Mexico	106.2	21	5	1.6	20.9	2.45
Micronesia, Federated States of	0.1	25	5	2.0	30.2	3.25
Moldova	4.5	15	13	0.2	40.4	1.81
Monaco	0.03	9	13	-0.3	5.4	1.76
Mongolia	2.8	22	7	1.4	53.8	2.26
Montserrat	0.01	18	7	1.0	7.3	1.78
Morocco	32.7	22	6	1.7	41.6	2.73
Mozambique	19.4	36	21	1.5	130.8	4.70
Namibia	2.0	25	18	0.7	49.0	3.18
Nauru	0.01	25	7	1.8	9.9	3.19
Nepal	27.7	31	9	2.2	67.0	4.19
Netherlands	16.4	11	9	0.2	5.0	1.66
Netherlands Antilles	0.2	15	6	0.9	10.0	2.00
New Caledonia	0.2	18	6	1.3	7.7	2.31
New Zealand	4.0	14	8	0.6	5.8	1.79
Nicaragua	5.5	25	4	2.0	29.1	2.81
Niger	12.2	51	21	3.0	119.7	7.55

(continues)

TABLE 6.6, continued

Country or area	Population 2005 (millions)	Births per 1,000 population	Deaths per 1,000 population	Rate of natural increase (percent)	Infant mortality rate	Total fertility rate
Nigeria	128.8	41	17	2.3	98.8	5.53
Northern Mariana Islands	0.08	20	2	1.7	7.1	1.27
Norway	4.6	12	9	0.2	3.7	1.78
Oman	3.0	37	4	3.3	19.5	5.84
Pakistan	162.4	30	8	2.2	72.4	4.14
Palau	0.02	18	7	1.2	14.8	2.46
Panama	3.1	22	5	1.7	16.7	2.70
Papua New Guinea	5.5	30	7	2.3	51.5	3.96
Paraguay	6.3	29	5	2.5	25.6	3.93
Peru	27.9	21	6	1.5	31.9	2.56
Philippines	87.9	25	5	2.0	23.5	3.16
Poland	38.6	10	10	0.0	7.4	1.24
Portugal	10.6	11	10	0.0	5.0	1.47
Puerto Rico	3.9	13	8	0.5	9.3	1.75
Qatar	0.9	16	5	1.1	18.6	2.87
Reunion	0.8	19	5	1.4	7.8	2.47
Romania	22.3	11	12	-0.1	26.4	1.36
Russia	143.4	10	15	-0.5	15.4	1.27
Rwanda	8.4	41	16	2.4	91.2	5.49
Saint Helena	0.01	12	6	0.6	19.0	1.54
Saint Kitts and Nevis	0.04	18	8	1.0	14.5	2.33
Saint Lucia	0.2	20	5	1.5	13.5	2.21
Saint Pierre and Miquelon	0.01	14	7	0.7	7.5	2.03
Saint Vincent and the Grenadines	0.1	16	6	1.0	14.8	1.85
Samoa	0.2	16	7	0.9	27.7	3.01
San Marino	0.03	10	8	0.2	5.7	1.33
Sao Tome and Principe	0.2	41	7	3.4	43.1	5.71
Saudi Arabia	26.4	30	3	2.7	13.2	4.05
Senegal	11.7	33	10	2.4	54.1	4.50
Serbia and Montenegro	10.8	12	10	0.2	12.9	1.67
Seychelles	0.08	16	6	1.0	15.5	1.75
Sierra Leone	5.9	46	23	2.3	162.6	6.15
Singapore	4.4	9	4	0.5	2.3	1.05
Slovakia	5.4	11	9	0.1	7.4	1.32
Slovenia	2.0	9	10	-0.1	4.5	1.24
Solomon Islands	0.5	31	4	2.7	21.3	4.04
Somalia	8.6	46	17	2.9	116.7	6.84
South Africa	44.3	18	21	-0.3	61.8	2.24
Spain	40.3	10	10	0.0	4.4	1.28

TABLE 6.6, continued

Country or area	Population 2005 (millions)	Births per 1,000 population	Deaths per 1,000 population	Rate of natural increase (percent)	Infant mortality rate	Total fertility rate
Sri Lanka	20.1	16	6	0.9	14.3	1.85
Sudan	40.2	35	9	2.6	62.5	4.85
Suriname	0.4	18	7	1.1	23.6	2.34
Swaziland	1.1	28	29	-0.1	72.9	3.62
Sweden	9.0	10	10	0.0	2.8	1.66
Switzerland	7.5	10	8	0.1	4.4	1.43
Syria	18.4	28	5	2.3	29.5	3.50
Taiwan	22.9	13	6	0.6	6.4	1.57
Tajikistan	7.2	33	8	2.4	110.8	4.05
Tanzania	36.8	38	17	2.1	98.5	5.06
Thailand	64.2	14	7	0.7	20.2	1.63
Togo	5.4	37	10	2.7	62.2	5.01
Tonga	0.1	25	5	2.0	12.6	3.00
Trinidad and Tobago	1.1	13	10	0.2	25.8	1.75
Tunisia	10.1	16	5	1.0	24.8	1.75
Turkey	69.7	17	6	1.1	41.0	1.94
Turkmenistan	5.0	28	9	1.9	73.1	3.41
Turks and Caicos Islands	0.02	22	4	1.8	15.7	3.08
Tuvalu	0.01	22	7	1.5	20.0	3.00
Uganda	27.3	47	13	3.5	67.8	6.74
Ukraine	47.0	9	14	-0.6	10.1	1.16
United ArabEmirates	2.6	19	4	1.5	14.5	2.94
United Kingdom	60.4	11	10	0.1	5.2	1.66
United States	295.7	14	8	0.6	6.5	2.08
Uruguay	3.4	14	9	0.5	11.9	1.91
Uzbekistan	26.9	26	8	1.8	71.1	2.94
Vanuatu	0.2	23	8	1.5	55.2	2.77
Venezuela	25.4	19	5	1.4	22.2	2.26
Vietnam	83.5	17	6	1.1	25.9	1.94
Virgin Islands	0.1	14	6	0.8	8.0	2.19
Virgin Islands, British	0.02	15	4	1.0	17.3	1.72
Wallis and Futuna	0.02	22	5	1.7	NA	NA
West Bank	2.4	32	4	2.8	19.6	4.40
Western Sahara	0.3	45	16	2.9	NA	NA
Yemen	20.7	43	9	3.5	61.5	6.67
Zambia	11.3	41	20	2.1	88.3	5.47
Zimbabwe	12.2	28	22	0.6	52.3	3.18

Source: U.S. Census Bureau, International Data Base; updated April 2005.

TABLE 6.7
Projected Population of the World's Three Most Populous Countries,
2000–2050 (in millions)

	China	India	United States
2000	1,269	1,003	282
2005	1,306	1,080	296
2010	1,348	1,155	309
2015	1,393	1,227	323
2020	1,431	1,297	336
2025	1,453	1,362	350
2030	1,462	1,421	364
2035	1,461	1,474	378
2040	1,455	1,522	392
2045	1,443	1,565	406
2050	1,424	1,601	420

Source: U.S. Census Bureau, International Data Base; updated in April 2005.

Table 6.7 puts the focus on the world's three most populous nations, China, India, and the United States, and their projected population trends over the next half-century. Those trends are sharply divergent, with India expected to grow 60 percent, the United States almost 50 percent, and China a meager 12 percent, between 2000 and 2050. The rapid pace of growth in India is set to push that nation ahead of China as the world's most populous country by 2035. The United States will never be a contender for the top spot, but, unlike all the other currently industrialized nations, at least it will keep *growing*.

Table 6.8 gives the rankings of the top twenty nations by population for 1950 and 2000, and then—with the inevitable uncertainty that goes with demographic projections into the future—Table 6.9 gives the rankings for 2025 and 2050. These changing lists reveal the gradual displacement of the so-called developed nations by the developing nations. For example, in 1950 Pakistan was No. 13 and Nigeria was No. 15 in the list; by 2050 Pakistan will have climbed to No. 6 in the world and Nigeria will be No. 4! Meanwhile, Japan will have tumbled from fifth place in 1950 to seventeenth place a century later. Interestingly, the only country that retains the very same ranking throughout the entire period is the United States, at No. 3.

In Table 6.10 we have the 2005 and 2015 listings of the world's thirty largest *urban agglomerations*—a term that means, essentially, metropolitan areas. A city's ranking in such a list can

TABLE 6.8
Top Twenty Countries Ranked by Population, 1950 and 2000

1950		2000	
1 China	562,579,779	1 China	1,268,853,362
2 India	369,880,000	2 India	1,002,708,291
3 United States	152,271,000	3 United States	282,338,631
4 Russia	101,936,816	4 Indonesia	224,138,438
5 Japan	83,805,000	5 Brazil	175,552,771
6 Indonesia	82,978,392	6 Russia	146,731,774
7 Germany	68,374,572	7 Pakistan	146,342,958
8 Brazil	53,443,075	8 Bangladesh	130,406,594
9 United Kingdom	50,127,000	9 Japan	126,699,784
10 Italy	47,105,000	10 Nigeria	114,306,700
11 Bangladesh	45,645,964	11 Mexico	99,926,620
12 France	41,828,673	12 Germany	82,187,909
13 Pakistan	39,448,232	13 Philippines	79,739,825
14 Ukraine	36,774,854	14 Vietnam	79,060,410
15 Nigeria	31,796,939	15 Egypt	70,492,342
16 Mexico	28,485,180	16 Turkey	65,666,677
17 Spain	28,062,963	17 Iran	65,660,289
18 Vietnam	25,348,144	18 Ethiopia	64,690,052
19 Poland	24,824,000	19 Thailand	61,862,928
20 Egypt	21,197,691	20 United Kingdom	59,522,468

Source: U.S. Census Bureau, International Data Base; updated in April 2005.

change over time, depending not only on birth and death rates in that city but also on the rate at which people are migrating into it. The same pattern seen in Tables 6.8 and 6.9 where the more developed countries are being overtaken by the less developed countries is mirrored, to some extent, at the urban level. New York, for example, was second-ranked in the world back in 1990; by 2015, it will have fallen to sixth place. Similarly, Osaka-Kobe, eighth-ranked in 1990, is projected to fall to eighteenth place by 2015. Meanwhile, Mumbai will rise from sixth-ranked to second by 2015. Another fact of our urban future to be noted in the table is the near-universal growth in the size of individual urban agglomerations. The growth rate of some cities will be phenomenal. Lagos, Nigeria, for example, is expected to mushroom from 11.1 million in 2005 to 17.0 million in 2015. The only urban area of 2005 that will actually lose population in the next decade, if the estimates are correct, is Seoul, South Korea.

Table 6.11 documents the global extent and death toll of the HIV/AIDS epidemic, with data from the World Health Organiza-

TABLE 6.9
Top Twenty Countries Ranked by Population, 2025 and 2050

2025		2050	
1 China	1,453,123,817	1 India	1,601,004,572
2 India	1,361,625,090	2 China	1,424,161,948
3 United States	349,666,199	3 United States	420,080,587
4 Indonesia	300,277,490	4 Nigeria	356,523,597
5 Pakistan	228,822,199	5 Indonesia	336,247,428
6 Brazil	217,825,222	6 Pakistan	294,995,104
7 Nigeria	206,165,946	7 Bangladesh	279,955,405
8 Bangladesh	204,538,715	8 Brazil	228,426,737
9 Russia	130,534,651	9 Congo (Kinshasa)	183,177,415
10 Mexico	130,198,692	10 Mexico	147,907,650
11 Japan	120,001,048	11 Philippines	147,630,852
12 Philippines	118,685,776	12 Ethiopia	144,716,331
13 Congo (Kinshasa)	107,981,867	13 Uganda	132,699,173
14 Ethiopia	107,804,235	14 Egypt	126,920,512
15 Egypt	103,352,882	15 Russia	110,763,998
16 Vietnam	99,977,731	16 Vietnam	107,772,641
17 Iran	83,186,886	17 Japan	99,886,568
18 Turkey	82,204,623	18 Iran	89,691,431
19 Germany	80,637,451	19 Turkey	86,473,786
20 Thailand	70,523,958	20 Sudan	84,192,309

Source: U.S. Census Bureau, International Data Base; updated in April 2005.

tion's annual report on this disease. As noted elsewhere in this book, AIDS has taken its most devastating toll in sub-Saharan Africa, where the adult prevalence rate is twelve times greater than in North America and about twenty-five times greater than in Western and Central Europe. AIDS deaths in Africa numbered over 2 million in 2004, while an additional 3 million people became infected.

As birthrates fall and life expectancies rise, populations almost everywhere are growing grayer. The aging of the world's population can be easily grasped in Tables 6.12 and 6.13. In Table 6.12, we have the breakdown of population by age category and region for the years 2005, 2025, and 2050; in Table 6.13, the median ages are given. Conventionally, those aged 15 to 64 are judged to be "working-age"; those younger than 15 or older than 64 are considered economically dependent. Table 6.12 shows that by midcentury the old-age category will have increased from 7.3 percent to 16.4 percent of global population. The dependent fraction of population will not have changed greatly, but a much bigger part of it will consist of the elderly. The more developed na-

TABLE 6.10
World's Thirty Largest Urban Agglomerations,
2005 and 2015 (projected)

2005 population (millions)		2015 population (millions)	
1 Tokyo, Japan	35.3	1 Tokyo, Japan	36.2
2 Mexico City, Mexico	19.0	2 Mumbai (Bombay), India	22.6
3 New York–Newark, USA	18.5	3 Delhi, India	20.9
4 Mumbai (Bombay), India	18.3	4 Mexico City, Mexico	20.6
5 Sao Paulo, Brazil	18.3	5 Sao Paulo, Brazil	20.0
6 Delhi, India	15.3	6 New York–Newark, USA	19.7
7 Calcutta, India	14.3	7 Dhaka, Bangladesh	17.9
8 Buenos Aires, Argentina	13.3	8 Jakarta, Indonesia	17.5
9 Jakarta, Indonesia	13.2	9 Lagos, Nigeria	17.0
10 Shanghai, China	12.7	10 Calcutta, India	16.8
11 Dhaka, Bangladesh	12.6	11 Karachi, Pakistan	16.2
12 Los Angeles–Long Beach–		12 Buenos Aires, Argentina	14.6
Santa Ana, USA	12.1	13 Cairo, Egypt	13.1
13 Karachi, Pakistan	11.8	14 Los Angeles–Long	
14 Rio de Janeiro, Brazil	11.5	Beach–Santa Ana, USA	12.9
15 Osaka-Kobe, Japan	11.3	15 Shanghai, China	12.7
16 Cairo, Egypt	11.1	16 Metro Manila, Philippines	12.6
17 Lagos, Nigeria	11.1	17 Rio de Janeiro, Brazil	12.4
18 Beijing, China	10.8	18 Osaka-Kobe, Japan	11.4
19 Metro Manila, Philippines	10.7	19 Istanbul, Turkey	11.3
20 Moscow, Russian Federation	10.7	20 Beijing, China	11.1
21 Paris, France	9.9	21 Moscow, Russian Federation	10.9
22 Istanbul, Turkey	9.8	22 Paris, France	10.0
23 Seoul, Republic of Korea	9.6	23 Tianjin, China	9.9
24 Tianjin, China	9.3	24 Chicago, USA	9.4
25 Chicago, USA	8.7	25 Lima, Peru	9.4
26 Lima, Peru	8.2	26 Seoul, Republic of Korea	9.2
27 London, United Kingdom	7.6	27 Santa Fe de Bogota, Colombia	8.9
28 Santa Fe de Bogota, Colombia	7.6	28 Lahore, Pakistan	8.7
29 Tehran, Iran	7.4	29 Kinshasa, Dem. Republic of the Congo	8.7
30 Hong Kong, China, Hong Kong SAR	7.2	30 Tehran, Iran	8.5

Source: UN Department of Economic and Social Affairs, Population Division, *World Urbanization Prospects: The 2003 Revision* (New York: United Nations, 2004), pp. 122–123.

tions will have much older populations than the less developed in 2050, just as they do today. But because of their greater wealth, they may find it less problematic (though still a challenge) to support their elders than the less developed world will.

Table 6.13 indicates that half of the world's population is presently older than 27.6 years and half is younger. Regional

TABLE 6.11
The Worldwide HIV/AIDS Epidemic (2004)

Region	People living with HIV/AIDS, 2004	Adult prevalence (%)	People newly infected with HIV	AIDS deaths 2004
Sub-Saharan Africa	25,400,000	7.4	3,100,000	2,300,000
North Africa, Middle East	540,000	0.3	92,000	28,000
South and Southeast Asia	7,100,000	0.6	890,000	490,000
East Asia	1,100,000	0.1	290,000	51,000
Oceania	35,000	0.2	5,000	700
Latin America	1,700,000	0.6	240,000	95,000
Caribbean	440,000	2.3	53,000	36,000
Eastern Europe, Central Asia	1,400,000	0.8	210,000	60,000
Western and Central Europe	610,000	0.3	21,000	6,500
North America	1,000,000	0.6	44,000	16,000
TOTAL	39,400,000	1.1	4,900,000	3,100,000

Source: UNAIDS and World Health Organization, *AIDS Epidemic Update: December 2004* (Geneva, Switzerland: UNAIDS, 2004), pp. 76–79.

TABLE 6.12
Age Distribution of the World's Population
by Region, 2005, 2025, and 2050

	2005 population (millions)	%	2025 population (millions)	%	2050 population (millions)	%
World, total	6,451	100.0	7,898	100.0	9,224	100.0
Age 0–14	1,790	27.7	1,901	24.1	1,936	21.0
Age 15–64	4,188	64.9	5,158	65.3	5,774	62.6
Age 65+	472	7.3	838	10.6	1,514	16.4
Less developed countries, total	5,241	100.0	6,650	100.0	7,988	100.0
Age 0–14	1,585	30.2	1,705	25.6	1,742	21.8
Age 15–64	3,369	64.3	4,371	65.7	5,059	63.3
Age 65+	287	5.5	574	8.6	1,187	14.9
More developed countries, total	1,210	100.0	1,247	100.0	1,235	100.0
Age 0–14	205	16.9	196	15.7	194	15.7
Age 15–64	819	67.7	787	63.1	715	57.9
Age 65+	186	15.3	264	21.2	327	26.4

TABLE 6.12, continued

	2005 population (millions)	%	2025 population (millions)	%	2050 population (millions)	%
Sub-Saharan Africa, total	733	100.0	1,121	100.0	1,735	100.0
Age 0–14	315	43.1	434	38.7	563	32.4
Age 15–64	396	54.0	649	57.9	1,083	62.4
Age 65+	22	2.9	38	3.4	89	5.2
Northern Africa, total	159	100.0	206	100.0	245	100.0
Age 0–14	50	31.5	49	24.0	46	18.9
Age 15–64	101	63.7	141	68.2	158	64.3
Age 65+	7	4.7	16	7.9	41	16.8
Near East, total	191	100.0	267	100.0	355	100.0
Age 0–14	65	33.8	76	28.4	80	22.6
Age 15–64	118	61.5	173	64.9	228	64.4
Age 65+	9	4.6	18	6.7	46	13.0
Asia, excl. Near East, total	3,648	100.0	4,391	100.0	4,862	100.0
Age 0–14	985	27.0	980	22.3	898	18.5
Age 15–64	2,428	66.6	2,954	67.3	3,079	63.3
Age 65+	235	6.4	458	10.4	885	18.2
Latin America and Caribbean, total	555	100.0	678	100.0	760	100.0
Age 0–14	162	29.3	152	22.5	138	18.1
Age 15–64	359	64.6	456	67.3	481	63.2
Age 65+	34	6.1	69	10.2	142	18.7
Western Europe, total	396	100.0	401	100.0	378	100.0
Age 0–14	64	16.1	57	14.2	52	13.8
Age 15–64	263	66.6	253	63.1	216	57.1
Age 65+	68	17.3	91	22.7	110	29.1
Eastern Europe, total	121	100.0	117	100.0	102	100.0
Age 0–14	20	16.4	17	14.2	13	13.1
Age 15–64	84	69.5	76	65.0	58	56.4
Age 65+	17	14.1	24	20.8	31	30.5
Baltics, total	7.2	100.0	6.5	100.0	5.2	100.0
Age 0–14	1.1	15.5	0.9	14.0	0.7	12.8
Age 15–64	5.0	68.7	4.2	64.8	2.9	55.4
Age 65+	1.1	15.8	1.4	21.2	1.6	31.8

(continues)

TABLE 6.12, continued

	2005 population (millions)	%	2025 population (millions)	%	2050 population (millions)	%
Commonwealth of Independent States, total	280	100.0	282	100.0	275	100.0
Age 0–14	53	18.8	52	18.5	47	17.2
Age 15–64	193	68.8	185	65.7	166	60.5
Age 65+	35	12.5	45	15.8	61	22.4
North America, total	329	100.0	388	100.0	462	100.0
Age 0–14	67	20.3	76	19.5	89	19.2
Age 15–64	221	67.2	241	62.1	276	59.7
Age 65+	41	12.5	71	18.4	97	21.0
Oceania, total	33	100.0	40	100.0	44	100.0
Age 0–14	8	24.3	8	20.6	8	17.7
Age 15–64	21	65.2	26	64.4	28	62.2
Age 65+	3	10.4	6	15.1	9	20.1

Source: U.S. Census Bureau, International Data Base; updated April 2005.

TABLE 6.13
Global Median Ages, 2005, 2025, and 2050

	2005	2025	2050
World	27.6	32.5	36.5
Less developed countries	25.4	30.6	35.3
More developed countries	38.8	43.5	45.4
Sub-Saharan Africa	18.1	20.2	24.3
Northern Africa	24.0	31.4	38.8
Near East	23.1	27.7	33.7
Asia, excluding Near East	27.8	34.0	39.6
Latin America and the Caribbean	26.2	33.0	40.1
Western Europe	40.3	45.9	48.1
Eastern Europe	37.1	44.3	50.4
Baltics	38.4	44.6	52.8
Commonwealth of Independent States	34.2	39.1	42.4
North America	36.5	38.9	39.6
Oceania	32.0	36.1	40.6

Source: U.S. Census Bureau, International Data Base; updated April 2005.

variations are striking. In sub-Saharan Africa, the median age today is an extremely youthful 18.1, while in Western Europe the median age is over twice that figure. For each region, demographers expect higher median ages by 2025 and higher again by 2050. In all of human history, the world's median ages have never reached the levels seen and projected in this table. It is remarkable to think that by the middle of the century Eastern Europe and the Baltics will have as many people *over* the age of 50 as under the age of 50!

Like tables of data, graphs can be useful in presenting some important features of the global population picture as it stands today and as it has developed over the centuries and millennia. Figure 6.1 depicts world population over the past 7,000 years. Given the graph's vertical scale (billions), world population barely registers at all before about 2000 B.C. At that time it begins a slow ascent, so slow that in 1500—500 years ago—it remains under one-half billion. Since that time, however, there has been an astonishing acceleration. By 2000, population crosses the 6 billion line, and it is now expected to reach 9 billion by midcentury. The growth of our species has been truly explosive in recent times.

Figure 6.2 shows not only the rising curve of total world population, projected to 2050, but also the actual increments of population beginning in 1750. These increments are given on a per-decade basis. They allow us to see that the gains in population were relatively small in the eighteenth century, visibly larger in the nineteenth, and simply enormous during the twentieth century—and into the twenty-first. For those who feel some uneasiness about the magnitude of global population, the only reassuring aspect of Figure 6.2 is the decrease in decadal growth after the 1980s. Each subsequent decade adds, or will add, less to world population than the previous decade; the 2040s will give the smallest numerical boost to global population since the 1940s.

The actual and projected year-by-year growth rate of world population during the period 1950–2050 may be seen in Figure 6.3. This graph shows that the fastest population growth in history occurred in the early 1960s, at around 2.2 percent annually; growth has been slowing down ever since. The downward trend will continue steadily to the middle of this century, demographers believe. By 2050, the growth rate is expected to have fallen quite dramatically—to less than half of 1 percent annually. That will be the slowest growth rate in well over a century. (And of

FIGURE 6.1
Estimated Human Population from 5000 BC to the Present

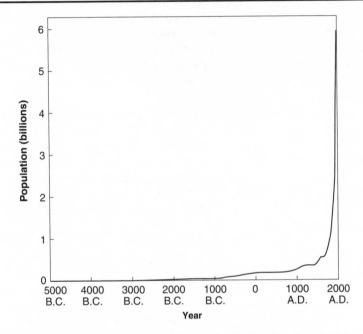

Source: Based on data given in Colin McEvedy and Richard Jones, *Atlas of World Population History* (New York: Viking Penguin, 1978).

course the *absolute* populations of several countries, mainly in Europe, will be shrinking long before 2050.)

Figures 6.4 and 6.5 illustrate the theory and reality of demographic transition, as outlined in Chapter 1. In Figure 6.4, we see high birth- and death rates before the transition begins (Stage I). Then the death rate begins to decline (Stage II). The birthrate may remain high for a period of time, but eventually it, too, starts to decline (Stage III). Finally, both rates stabilize at new lower levels (Stage IV). Actual population growth is slow or zero in Stage I, rapid in Stages II and III, and again slow or zero in Stage IV.

The demographic reality corresponding to the theory depicted in Figure 6.4 can be seen in Figure 6.5, which tracks crude birth- and death rates for a group of thirteen European countries from 1850 to 1990 and for a group of 106 less developed countries from 1950 to 1990. (Data for less developed countries were not

FIGURE 6.2
Long-Term World Population Growth, 1750–2050

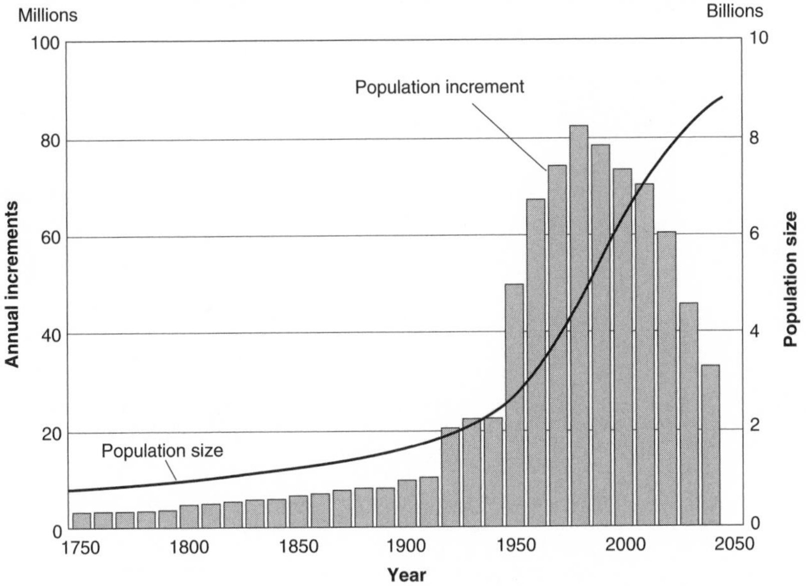

Source: U.N. Population Division, *The World at Six Billion* (1999). Reprinted by permission.

recorded as early as for the European countries.) The graph makes two things immediately evident: first, the downward trends in birth- and death rates in Europe have not been smooth, but they *have* been long-lasting and have clearly brought the continent to Stage IV of the demographic transition; and second, the less developed countries began their own mortality and fertility transitions at significantly higher death and birthrates, at mid-twentieth century, than was seen in Europe a century earlier. Although both rates have declined, birthrates remain far above death rates—more so than was ever the case in Europe—and consequently, population continues to grow rapidly in the developing world.

Finally, Figures 6.6 and 6.7 are examples of "population pyramids." Demographers use such pyramids to graphically represent age structures. A pyramid with the classic shape, broaden-

FIGURE 6.3
World Population Growth Rate, 1950–2050

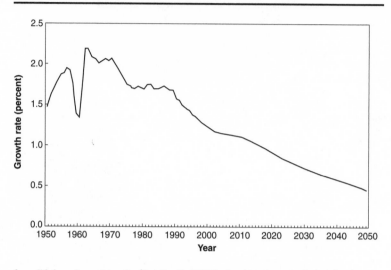

Source: U.S. Census Bureau, International Data Base (April 2005) at http://www.census.gov/ipc/www/img/worldgr.gif

FIGURE 6.4
Demographic Transition Model

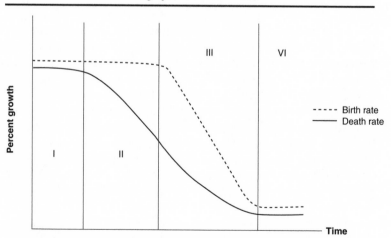

Source: Author's illustration

FIGURE 6.5
Crude Birth and Death Rates in Developed and Developing Countries

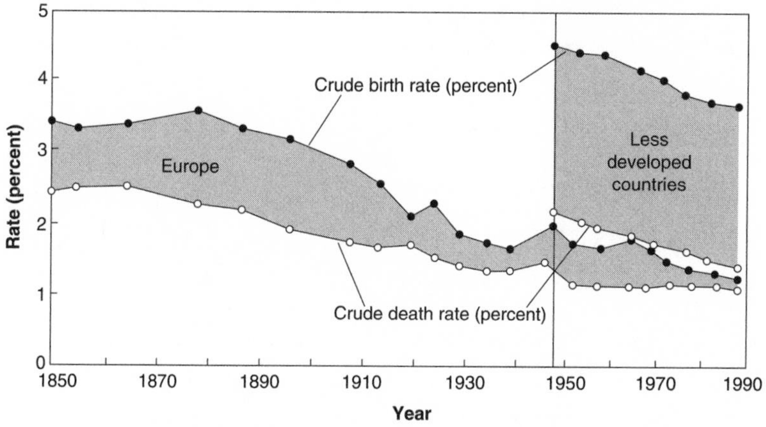

Source: Alan C. Kelley, "Economic Consequences of Population Change in the Third World," *Journal of Economic Literature,* 26:4 (1988), p. 1688. Reprinted with permission.

ing out from a narrow top to a wide bottom, indicates a population in which the fertility rate is high and the total number of people is growing, especially at the young end (base) of the pyramid. Male and female populations are shown on the left- and right-hand sides of the graph, respectively. Figure 6.6 is the population pyramid for Nigeria in 2005, and it is typical of a developing country with high fertility, one that is far from having completed its demographic transition. Many nations of Africa, Asia, and Latin America have similar population pyramids.

Figure 6.7 is the population pyramid for Sweden in 2005 and typifies many European and East Asian nations. Because fertility has been declining for some time in Sweden, the youngest cohort, those in the age range of 0 to 4, is *not* the largest—far from it. The largest cohort actually consists of Swedes born between forty and forty-four years ago. As fertility rates decline around the world in coming decades, the global age structure will gradually come to resemble Sweden's more than Nigeria's. (Even Nigeria's population pyramid will evolve away from its current shape and more toward the barrel shape of the developed nations.)

158 Statistics and Graphs

FIGURE 6.6
Population pyramid for Nigeria, 2005

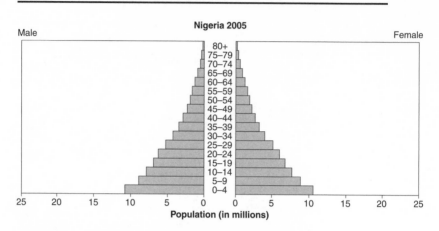

Source: U.S. Census Bureau, International Data Base at http://www.census.gov/
cgi-bin/ipc/idbpyry.pl?cty=NI&maxp=23957602&maxa=80&ymax=250&yr=2005&.submit=

FIGURE 6.7
Population pyramid for Sweden, 2005

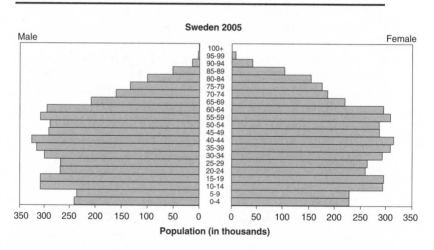

Source: U.S. Census Bureau, International Data Base at http://www.census.gov/
cgi-bin/ipc/idbpyry.pl?cty=SW&maxp=343714&maxa=100&ymax=250&yr=2005&.submit=

7

Documents

Certain books, declarations, and reports on the subject of world population have garnered a great deal of attention, either at the time of
their publication or retrospectively. Some of these important documents are presented in this chapter, mainly in excerpts. The oldest by
far is the famous 1798 Essay on the Principle of Population (often
abbreviated to Essay on Population) by the Reverend T. R. Malthus,
from which a vast array of theoretical ideas, worries, and misconcep-
tions about population were drawn in the subsequent two centuries.
The core of Malthus's demographic argument is presented in the first
two chapters of his work.

Essay on Population (1798)
Chapter I

. . . I think I may fairly make two postulata.

First, That food is necessary to the existence of man.

Secondly, That the passion between the sexes is necessary,
and will remain nearly in its present state.

These two laws, ever since we have had any knowledge of
mankind, appear to have been fixed laws of our nature, and, as
we have not hitherto seen any alteration in them, we have no
right to conclude that they will ever cease to be what they now
are, without an immediate act of power in that Being who first
arranged the system of the universe, and for the advantage of his

creatures, still executes, according to fixed laws, all its various operations. . . .

Assuming then my postulata as granted, I say, that the power of population is indefinitely greater than the power in the earth to produce subsistence for man.

Population, when unchecked, increases in a geometrical ratio. Subsistence increases only in an arithmetical ratio. A slight acquaintance with numbers will show the immensity of the first power in comparison of the second.

By that law of our nature which makes food necessary to the life of man, the effects of these two unequal powers must be kept equal.

This implies a strong and constantly operating check on population from the difficulty of subsistence. This difficulty must fall somewhere and must necessarily be severely felt by a large portion of mankind.

Through the animal and vegetable kingdoms, nature has scattered the seeds of life abroad with the most profuse and liberal hand. She has been comparatively sparing in the room and the nourishment necessary to rear them. The germs of existence contained in this spot of earth, with ample food and ample room to expand in, would fill millions of worlds in the course of a few thousand years. Necessity, that imperious all pervading law of nature, restrains them within the prescribed bounds. The race of plants and the race of animals shrink under this great restrictive law. And the race of man cannot, by any efforts of reason, escape from it. Among plants and animals its effects are waste of seed, sickness, and premature death. Among mankind, misery and vice. The former, misery, is an absolutely necessary consequence of it. Vice is a highly probable consequence, and we therefore see it abundantly prevail; but it ought not, perhaps, to be called an absolutely necessary consequence. The ordeal of virtue is to resist all temptation to evil.

This natural inequality of the two powers of population and of production in the earth, and that great law of our nature which must constantly keep their effects equal, form the great difficulty that to me appears insurmountable in the way to the perfectibility of society. All other arguments are of slight and subordinate consideration in comparison of this. I see no way by which man can escape from the weight of this law which pervades all animated nature. No fancied equality, no agrarian regulations in their utmost extent, could remove the pressure of it even for a single century. And it appears, therefore, to be decisive against the possible existence of a society, all the members of which should live in ease, happiness, and comparative leisure, and feel no anxiety about providing the means of subsistence for themselves and families.

Consequently, if the premises are just, the argument is conclusive against the perfectibility of the mass of mankind.

I have thus sketched the general outline of the argument, but I will examine it more particularly, and I think it will be found that experience, the true source and foundation of all knowledge, invariably confirms its truth.

Chapter 2

I said that population, when unchecked, increased in a geometrical ratio, and subsistence for man in an arithmetical ratio.

Let us examine whether this position be just.

I think it will be allowed, that no state has hitherto existed (at least that we have any account of) where the manners were so pure and simple, and the means of subsistence so abundant, that no check whatever has existed to early marriages; among the lower classes, from a fear of not providing well for their families; or among the higher classes, from a fear of lowering their condition in life. Consequently in no state that we have yet known has the power of population been left to exert itself with perfect freedom.

Whether the law of marriage be instituted or not, the dictate of nature and virtue seems to be an early attachment to one woman. Supposing a liberty of changing in the case of an unfortunate choice, this liberty would not affect population till it arose to a height greatly vicious; and we are now supposing the existence of a society where vice is scarcely known.

In a state therefore of great equality and virtue, where pure and simple manners prevailed, and where the means of subsistence were so abundant that no part of the society could have any fears about providing amply for a family, the power of population being left to exert itself unchecked, the increase of the human species would evidently be much greater than any increase that has been hitherto known.

In the United States of America, where the means of subsistence have been more ample, the manners of the people more pure, and consequently the checks to early marriages fewer, than in any of the modern states of Europe, the population has been found to double itself in twenty-five years.

This ratio of increase, though short of the utmost power of population, yet as the result of actual experience, we will take as our rule; and say,

That population, when unchecked, goes on doubling itself every twenty-five years, or increases in a geometrical ratio.

Let us now take any spot of earth, this Island for instance, and see in what ratio the subsistence it affords can be supposed to increase. We will begin with it under its present state of cultivation.

If I allow that by the best possible policy, by breaking up more land, and by great encouragements to agriculture, the produce of this Island may be doubled in the first twenty-five years, I think it will be allowing as much as any person can well demand.

In the next twenty-five years, it is impossible to suppose that the produce could be quadrupled. It would be contrary to all our knowledge of the qualities of land. The very utmost that we can conceive is that the increase in the second twenty-five years might equal the present produce. Let us then take this for our rule, though certainly far beyond the truth, and allow that by great exertion, the whole produce of the Island might be increased every twenty-five years, by a quantity of subsistence equal to what it at present produces. The most enthusiastic speculator cannot suppose a greater increase than this. In a few centuries it would make every acre of land in the Island like a garden.

Yet this ratio of increase is evidently arithmetical.

It may be fairly said, therefore, that the means of subsistence increase in an arithmetical ratio.

Let us now bring the effects of these two ratios together.

The population of the Island is computed to be about seven millions; and we will suppose the present produce equal to the support of such a number. In the first twenty-five years the population would be fourteen millions, and the food being also doubled, the means of subsistence would be equal to this increase. In the next twenty-five years the population would be twenty-eight millions, and the means of subsistence only equal to the support of twenty-one millions. In the next period, the population would be fifty-six millions, and the means of subsistence just sufficient for half that number. And at the conclusion of the first century the population would be one hundred and twelve millions and the means of subsistence only equal to the support of thirty-five millions, which would leave a population of seventy-seven millions totally unprovided for.

A great emigration necessarily implies unhappiness of some kind or other in the country that is deserted. For few persons will leave their families, connections, friends, and native land, to seek a settlement in untried foreign climes, without some strong subsisting causes of uneasiness where they are, or the hope of some great advantages in the place to which they are going.

But to make the argument more general, and less interrupted by the partial views of emigration, let us take the whole earth, instead of one spot, and suppose that the restraints to population were universally removed. If the subsistence for man that the earth affords was to be increased every twenty-five years by a quantity equal to what the whole world at present produces, this would allow the power of production in the earth to be absolutely unlimited, and its ratio of increase much greater than we can conceive that any possible exertions of mankind could make it.

Taking the population of the world at any number, a thousand millions, for instance, the human species would increase in the ratio of—1, 2, 4, 8, 16, 32, 64, 128, 256, 512, etc. and subsistence as—1, 2, 3, 4, 5, 6, 7, 8, 9, 10, etc. In two centuries and a quarter, the population would be to the means of subsistence as 512 to 10; in three centuries as 4,096 to 13; and in two thousand years the difference would be almost incalculable, though the produce in that time would have increased to an immense extent.

No limits whatever are placed to the productions of the earth; they may increase forever and be greater than any assignable quantity; yet still the power of population being a power of a superior order, the increase of the human species can only be kept commensurate to the increase of the means of subsistence by the constant operation of the strong law of necessity acting as a check upon the greater power.

The effects of this check remain now to be considered.

Among plants and animals the view of the subject is simple. They are all impelled by a powerful instinct to the increase of their species, and this instinct is interrupted by no reasoning or doubts about providing for their offspring. Wherever therefore there is liberty, the power of increase is exerted; and the superabundant effects are repressed afterwards by want of room and nourishment, which is common to animals and plants, and among animals, by becoming the prey of others.

The effects of this check on man are more complicated.

Impelled to the increase of his species by an equally powerful instinct, reason interrupts his career and asks him whether he may not bring beings into the world for whom he cannot provide the means of subsistence. In a state of equality, this would be the simple question. In the present state of society, other considerations occur. Will he not lower his rank in life? Will he not subject himself to greater difficulties than he at present feels? Will he not be obliged to labour harder? And if he has a large family, will his utmost exertions enable him to support them? May he not see his offspring in rags and misery, and clamouring for bread that he cannot give them? And may he not be reduced to the grating necessity of forfeiting his independence, and of being obliged to the sparing hand of charity for support? . . .

The theory on which the truth of this position depends appears to me so extremely clear that I feel at a loss to conjecture what part of it can be denied.

That population cannot increase without the means of subsistence is a proposition so evident that it needs no illustration.

That population does invariably increase where there are the means of subsistence, the history of every people that have ever existed will abundantly prove.

And that the superior power of population cannot be checked without producing misery or vice, the ample portion of these too bitter ingredients in the cup of human life and the continuance of the physical causes that seem to have produced them bear too convincing a testimony.

Population Growth, Resource Consumption, and a Sustainable World: Joint Statement by the Royal Society of London and the U.S. National Academy of Sciences (February 1992)

This statement was issued in advance of the UN conference on the environment held in Rio de Janeiro in June 1992. It points to the environmental burden imposed on the Earth by "each additional human being," and the indisputable fact that "the recent expansion of the human population" has accelerated the "pace of environmental change." Science and technology have a role to play in meeting the challenges posed by this change, but equally important are global policies to promote, among other things, a "more rapid stabilization of world population."

World population is growing at the unprecedented rate of almost 100 million people every year, and human activities are producing major changes in the global environment. If current predictions of population prove accurate and patterns of human activity on the planet remain unchanged, science and technology may not be able to prevent either irreversible degradation of the environment or continued poverty for much of the world. The following joint statement, prepared by the Officers of the Royal Society of London and the U.S. National Academy of Sciences, reflects the judgment of a group of scientists knowledgeable about the historic contributions of science and technology to economic growth and environmental protection. It also reflects the shared view that sustainable development implies a future in which life is improved worldwide through economic development, where local environments and the biosphere are protected, and science is mobilized to create new opportunities for human progress . . . .

World Population

In its 1991 report on world population, the United Nations Population Fund (UNFPA) states that population growth is even faster than forecast in its report of 1984. Assuming nevertheless that there will in the future be substantial and sustained falls in fertility rates, the global population is expected in the UN's mid-range projection to rise from 5.4 billion in 1991 to 10 billion in 2050. This rapid rise may be unavoidable; considerably larger rises must be expected if fertility rates do not stabilize at the replacement level of about 2.1 children per woman. At present, about 95 percent of this growth is in the less developed countries (LDCs); the percentage of global population that live in the LDCs is projected to increase from 77 percent in 1990 to 84 percent in 2020.

The Environment

Although there is a relationship between population, economic activity, and the environment, it is not simple. Most of the environmental changes during the twentieth century have been a product of the efforts of humans to secure improved standards of food, clothing, shelter, comfort, and recreation. Both developed and developing countries have contributed to environmental degradation. Developed countries, with 85 percent of the world's gross national product and 23 percent of its population, account for the majority of mineral and fossil-fuel consumption. One issue alone, the increases in atmospheric carbon dioxide, has the potential for altering global climate with significant consequences for all countries. The prosperity and technology of the developed countries, however, give them the greater possibilities and the greater responsibility for addressing environmental problems.

In the developing countries the resource consumption per capita is lower, but the rapidly growing population and the pressure to develop their economies are leading to substantial and increasing damage to the local environment. This damage comes by direct pollution from energy use and other industrial activities, as well as by activities such as clearing forests and inappropriate agricultural practices.

The Reality of the Problem

Scientific and technological innovations, such as in agriculture, have been able to overcome many pessimistic predictions about resource constraints affecting human welfare. Nevertheless, the present patterns of human activity accentuated by population growth should make even those most optimistic about future scientific progress pause and reconsider the wisdom of ignoring these threats to our planet. Unrestrained resource consumption for energy production and other uses, especially if the developing world strives to achieve living standards based on the same levels of consumption as the developed world, could lead to catastrophic outcomes for the global environment.

Some of the environmental changes may produce irreversible damage to the earth's capacity to sustain life. Many species have already disappeared, and many more are destined to do so. Man's own prospects for achieving satisfactory living standards are threatened by environmental deterioration, especially in the poorest countries where economic activities are most heavily dependent upon the quality of natural resources.

If they are forced to deal with their environmental and resource problems alone, the LDCs face overwhelming challenges.

They generate only 15 percent of the world's GNP, and have a net cash outflow of tens of billions of dollars per year. Over 1 billion people live in absolute poverty, and 600 million on the margin of starvation. And the LDCs have only 6–7 percent of the world's active scientists and engineers, a situation that makes it very difficult for them to participate fully in global or regional schemes to manage their own environment.

In places where resources are administered effectively, population growth does not inevitably imply deterioration in the quality of the environment. Nevertheless, each additional human being requires natural resources for sustenance, each produces by-products that become part of the ecosystem, and each pursues economic and other activities that affect the natural world. While the impact of population growth varies from place to place and from one environmental domain to another, the overall pace of environmental changes has unquestionably been accelerated by the recent expansion of the human population.

International Action

There is an urgent need to address economic activity, population growth, and environmental protection as interrelated issues. The forthcoming UN Conference on Environment and Development, to be held in Brazil, should consider human activities and population growth, in both the developing and developed worlds, as crucial components affecting the sustainability of human society. Effective family planning, combined with continued economic and social development in the LDCs, will help stabilize fertility rates at lower levels and reduce stresses to the global environment. At the same time, greater attention in the developed countries to conservation, recycling, substitution and efficient use of energy, and a concerted program to start mitigating further buildup of greenhouse gases will help to ease the threat to the global environment.

Unlike many other steps that could be taken to reduce the rate of environmental changes, reductions in rates of population growth can be accomplished through voluntary measures. Surveys in the developing world repeatedly reveal large amounts of unwanted childbearing. By providing people with the means to control their own fertility, family planning programs have major possibilities to reduce rates of population growth and hence to arrest environmental degradation. Also, unlike many other potential interventions that are typically specific to a particular problem, a reduction in the rate of population growth would affect many dimensions of environmental changes. Its importance is easily underestimated if attention is focused on one problem at a time.

The Contributions of Science

What are the relevant topics to which scientific research can make mitigating contributions? These include: development of new generations of safe, easy to use, and effective contraceptive agents and devices; development of environmentally benign alternative energy sources; improvements in agricultural production and food processing; further research in plant and animal genetic varieties; further research in biotechnology relating to plants, animals, and preservation of the environment; and improvements in public health, especially through development of effective drugs and vaccines for malaria, hepatitis, AIDS, and other infectious diseases causing immense human burdens. Also needed is research on topics such as: improved land-use practices to prevent ecological degradation, loss of topsoil, and desertification of grasslands; better institutional measures to protect watersheds and groundwater; new technologies for waste disposal, environmental remediation, and pollution control; new materials that reduce pollution and the use of hazardous substances during their life cycle; and more effective regulatory tools that use market forces to protect the environment.

Greater attention also needs to be given to understanding the nature and dimension of the world's biodiversity. Although we depend directly on biodiversity for sustainable productivity, we cannot even estimate the numbers of species of organisms—plants, animals, fungi, and microorganisms—to an order of magnitude. We do know, however, that the current rate of reduction in biodiversity is unparalleled over the past 65 million years. The loss of biodiversity is one of the fastest moving aspects of global change, is irreversible, and has serious consequences for the human prospect in the future.

What are the limits of scientific contributions to the solution of resource and environmental problems? Scientific research and technological innovation can undoubtedly mitigate these stresses and facilitate a less destructive adaptation of a growing population to its environment. Yet, it is not prudent to rely on science and technology alone to solve problems created by rapid population growth, wasteful resource consumption, and harmful human practices.

Conclusions

The application of science and technology to global problems is a key component of providing a decent standard of living for a majority of the human race. Science and technology have an especially important role to play in developing countries in helping them to manage their resources effectively and to participate fully in worldwide initiatives for common benefit. Capabilities in science and technology must be strengthened in LDCs as a matter of urgency through joint initiatives from the developed and developing worlds. But science and technology alone are not enough. Global policies are urgently needed to promote more rapid economic development throughout the world, more environmentally benign patterns of human activity, and a more rapid stabilization of world population.

The future of our planet is in the balance. Sustainable development can be achieved, but only if irreversible degradation of the environment can be halted in time. The next 30 years may be crucial.

Warning to Humanity, November 18, 1992

Later in the same year as the joint statement from the Royal Society and the National Academy of Sciences (see previous item), the Union of Concerned Scientists issued its own statement. It was more ominous in tone and content than the earlier statement, cautioning that if there were not a "great change in our stewardship of the earth," the unavoidable consequence would be "vast human misery" and a planet "irretrievably mutilated." Blunt language was used to warn developed countries of the harmful effects of their "overconsumption" and pollution, and to warn the developing countries of the environmental damage, poverty, and unrest that they will experience if their populations "go unchecked." The statement was signed by over 1,500 scientists, including half of the living Nobel laureates in the sciences.

Introduction

Human beings and the natural world are on a collision course. Human activities inflict harsh and often irreversible damage on the environment and on critical resources. If not checked, many of our current practices put at serious risk the future that we wish for human society and the plant and animal kingdoms, and may so alter the living world that it will be unable to sustain life in the manner that we know. Fundamental changes are urgent if we are to avoid the collision our present course will bring about.

The Environment:

The environment is suffering critical stress;

The Atmosphere

Stratospheric ozone depletion threatens us with enhanced ultraviolet radiation at the earth's surface, which can be damaging or lethal to many life forms. Air pollution near ground level, and acid precipitation, are already causing widespread injury to humans, forests and crops.

Water Resources

Heedless exploitation of depletable groundwater supplies endangers food production and other essential human systems. Heavy demands on the world's surface waters have resulted in serious shortages in some 80 countries, containing 40% of the world's population. Pollution of rivers, lakes and groundwater further limits the supply.

Oceans

Destructive pressure on the oceans is severe, particularly in the coastal regions which produce most of the world's food fish. The total marine catch is now at or above the estimated maximum sustainable yield. Some fisheries have already shown signs of collapse. Rivers carrying heavy burdens of eroded soil into the seas also carry industrial, municipal, agricultural, and livestock waste—some of it toxic.

Soil

Loss of soil productivity, which is causing extensive land abandonment, is a widespread by-product of current practices in agriculture and animal husbandry. Since 1945, 11% of the earth's vegetated surface has been degraded—an area larger than India and China combined—and per capita food production in many parts of the world is decreasing.

Forests

Tropical rain forests, as well as tropical and temperate dry forests, are being destroyed rapidly. At present rates, some critical forest types will be gone in a few years and most of the tropical rain forest will be gone before the end of the next century. With them will go large numbers of plant and animal species.

Living Species

The irreversible loss of species, which by 2100 may reach one-third of all species now living, is especially serious. We are losing the potential they hold for providing medicinal and other benefits, and the contribution that genetic diversity of life-forms gives to the robustness of the world's biological systems and to the astonishing beauty of the earth itself.

Much of this damage is irreversible on a scale of centuries or permanent. Other processes appear to pose additional threats. Increasing levels of gases in the atmosphere from human activities, including carbon dioxide released from fossil fuel burning and from deforestation, may alter climate on a global scale. Predictions of global warming are still uncertain—with projected effects ranging from tolerable to very severe—but the potential risks are very great.

Our massive tampering with the world's interdependent web of life—coupled with the environmental damage inflicted by deforestation, species loss, and climate change—could trigger widespread adverse effects, including unpredictable collapses of critical biological systems whose interactions and dynamics we only imperfectly understand.

Uncertainty over the extent of these effects cannot excuse complacency or delay in facing the threat.

Population

The earth is finite. Its ability to absorb wastes and destructive effluent is finite. Its ability to provide food and energy is finite. Its ability to provide for growing numbers of people is finite. And we are fast approaching many of the earth's limits. Current economic practices which damage the environment, in both developed and underdeveloped nations, cannot be continued without the risk that vital global systems will be damaged beyond repair.

Pressures resulting from unrestrained population growth put demands on the natural world that can overwhelm any efforts to achieve a sustainable future. If we are to halt the destruction of our environment, we must accept limits to that growth. A World Bank estimate indicates that world population will not stabilize at less than 12.4 billion, while the United Nations concludes that the eventual total could reach 14 billion, a near tripling of today's 5.4 billion. But, even at this moment, one person in five lives in absolute poverty without enough to eat, and one in ten suffers serious malnutrition.

No more than one or a few decades remain before the chance to avert the threats we now confront will be lost and the prospects for humanity immeasurably diminished.

Warning

We the undersigned, senior members of the world's scientific community, hereby warn all humanity of what lies ahead. A great change in our stewardship of the earth and the life on it, is required, if vast human misery is to be avoided and our global home on this planet is not to be irretrievably mutilated.

What we must do

Five inextricably linked areas must be addressed simultaneously:

1. We must bring environmentally damaging activities under control to restore and protect the integrity of the earth's systems we depend on.

   We must, for example, move away from fossil fuels to more benign, inexhaustible energy sources to cut greenhouse gas emissions and the pollution of our air and water. Priority must be given to the development of energy sources matched to third world needs—small scale and relatively easy to implement.

We must halt deforestation, injury to and loss of agricultural land, and the loss of terrestrial and marine plant and animal species.

2. We must manage resources crucial to human welfare more effectively.

    We must give high priority to efficient use of energy, water, and other materials, including expansion of conservation and recycling.

3. We must stabilize population. This will be possible only if all nations recognize that it requires improved social and economic conditions, and the adoption of effective, voluntary family planning.

4. We must reduce and eventually eliminate poverty.

5. We must ensure sexual equality, and guarantee women control over their own reproductive decisions.

The developed nations are the largest polluters in the world today. They must greatly reduce their overconsumption, if we are to reduce pressures on resources and the global environment. The developed nations have the obligation to provide aid and support to developing nations, because only the developed nations have the financial resources and the technical skills for these tasks.

Acting on this recognition is not altruism, but enlightened self-interest: whether industrialized or not, we all have but one lifeboat. No nation can escape from injury when global biological systems are damaged. No nation can escape from conflicts over increasingly scarce resources. In addition, environmental and economic instabilities will cause mass migrations with incalculable consequences for developed and undeveloped nations alike.

Developing nations must realize that environmental damage is one of the gravest threats they face, and that attempts to blunt it will be overwhelmed if their populations go unchecked. The greatest peril is to become trapped in spirals of environmental decline, poverty, and unrest, leading to social, economic and environmental collapse.

Success in this global endeavor will require a great reduction in violence and war. Resources now devoted to the preparation and conduct of war—amounting to over $1 trillion annually—will be badly needed in the new tasks and should be diverted to the new challenges.

A new ethic is required—a new attitude towards discharging our responsibility for caring for ourselves and for the earth. We must recognize the earth's limited capacity to provide for us. We must recognize its fragility. We must no longer allow it to be ravaged. This ethic must motivate a great movement, convince reluctant leaders and reluctant governments and reluctant peoples themselves to effect the needed changes.

The scientists issuing this warning hope that our message will reach and affect people everywhere.

We need the help of many.

We require the help of the world community of scientists—natural, social, economic, political;

We require the help of the world's business and industrial leaders;

We require the help of the world's religious leaders; and

We require the help of the world's peoples.

We call on all to join us in this task.

National Security Study Memorandum 200 (December 10, 1974)

Subject: Implications of Worldwide Population Growth for U.S. Security and Overseas Interests

The "population-bomb" worries of the 1960s set off alarm bells not only among thoughtful citizens but also at the highest levels of the U.S. government. In early 1974, at President Nixon's direction, the National Security Council undertook an analysis of the impact of global population trends on America's national security. The aim was to assess the impact of continued rapid growth of world population over the coming quarter-century. The final report of nearly 200 pages, known as NSSM 200, was submitted in December 1974 to Nixon's successor, President Ford; it remained a classified document until 1989. Typically for the time period, it expressed great worry about impending "massive famines." Other possible risks from population growth abroad included chronic unemployment, food riots, sectarian violence, revolutions, and counterrevolutionary coups. U.S. assis-

tance, the analysts suggested, might enable less developed countries to lower their population growth rates. The following excerpts are from the executive summary of the report.

World Demographic Trends

1. World population growth since World War II is quantitatively and qualitatively different from any previous epoch in human history. The rapid reduction in death rates, unmatched by corresponding birth rate reductions, has brought total growth rates close to 2 percent a year, compared with about 1 percent before World War II, under 0.5 percent in 1750–1900, and far lower rates before 1750. The effect is to double the world's population in 35 years instead of 100 years. Almost 80 million are now being added each year, compared with 10 million in 1900.

2. The second new feature of population trends is the sharp differentiation between rich and poor countries. Since 1950, population in the former group has been growing at 0 to 1.5 percent per year, and in the latter at 2.0 to 3.5 percent (doubling in 20 to 35 years). Some of the highest rates of increase are in areas already densely populated and with a weak resource base. . . .

Adequacy of World Food Supplies

5. Growing populations will have a serious impact on the need for food, especially in the poorest, fastest growing LDCs. While under normal weather conditions and assuming food production growth in line with recent trends, total world agricultural production could expand faster than population, there will nevertheless be serious problems in food distribution and financing, making shortages, even at today's poor nutrition levels, probable in many of the larger, more populous LDC regions. Even today 10 to 20 million people die each year due, directly or indirectly, to malnutrition. Even more serious is the consequence of major crop failures which are likely to occur from time to time.

6. The most serious consequence for the short and middle term is the possibility of massive famines in certain parts of the world, especially the poorest regions. World needs for food rise by 2-1/2 percent or more per year (making a modest allowance for improved diets and nutrition) at a time when readily available fertilizer and well-watered land is already largely being uti-

lized. Therefore, additions to food production must come mainly from higher yields. Countries with large population growth cannot afford constantly growing imports, but for them to raise food output steadily by 2 to 4 percent over the next generation or two is a formidable challenge. Capital and foreign exchange requirements for intensive agriculture are heavy, and are aggravated by energy cost increases and fertilizer scarcities and price rises. The institutional, technical, and economic problems of transforming traditional agriculture are also very difficult to overcome.

7. In addition, in some overpopulated regions, rapid population growth presses on a fragile environment in ways that threaten longer-term food production: through cultivation of marginal lands, overgrazing, desertification, deforestation, and soil erosion, with consequent destruction of land and pollution of water, rapid siltation of reservoirs, and impairment of inland and coastal fisheries.

Minerals and Fuel

8. Rapid population growth is not in itself a major factor in pressure on depletable resources (fossil fuels and other minerals), since demand for them depends more on levels of industrial output than on numbers of people. On the other hand, the world is increasingly dependent on mineral supplies from developing countries, and if rapid population frustrates their prospects for economic development and social progress, the resulting instability may undermine the conditions for expanded output and sustained flows of such resources.

9. There will be serious problems for some of the poorest LDCs with rapid population growth. They will increasingly find it difficult to pay for needed raw materials and energy. Fertilizer, vital for their own agricultural production, will be difficult to obtain for the next few years. Imports for fuel and other materials will cause grave problems which could impinge on the U.S., both through the need to supply greater financial support and in LDC efforts to obtain better terms of trade through higher prices for exports. . . .

Economic Development and Population Growth

10. Rapid population growth creates a severe drag on rates of economic development otherwise attainable, sometimes to the

point of preventing any increase in per capita incomes. In addition to the overall impact on per capita incomes, rapid population growth seriously affects a vast range of other aspects of the quality of life important to social and economic progress in the LDCs. . . .

15. The universal objective of increasing the world's standard of living dictates that economic growth outpace population growth. In many high population growth areas of the world, the largest proportion of GNP is consumed, with only a small amount saved. Thus, a small proportion of GNP is available for investment—the "engine" of economic growth. Most experts agree that, with fairly constant costs per acceptor, expenditures on effective family planning services are generally one of the most cost effective investments for an LDC country seeking to improve overall welfare and per capita economic growth. We cannot wait for overall modernization and development to produce lower fertility rates naturally since this will undoubtedly take many decades in most developing countries, during which time rapid population growth will tend to slow development and widen even more the gap between rich and poor.

Political Effects of Population Factors

19. The political consequences of current population factors in the LDCs—rapid growth, internal migration, high percentages of young people, slow improvement in living standards, urban concentrations, and pressures for foreign migration—are damaging to the internal stability and international relations of countries in whose advancement the U.S. is interested, thus creating political or even national security problems for the U.S. In a broader sense, there is a major risk of severe damage to world economic, political, and ecological systems and, as these systems begin to fail, to our humanitarian values.

20. The pace of internal migration from countryside to overswollen cities is greatly intensified by rapid population growth. Enormous burdens are placed on LDC governments for public administration, sanitation, education, police, and other services, and urban slum dwellers (though apparently not recent migrants) may serve as a volatile, violent force which threatens political stability.

21. Adverse socio-economic conditions generated by these and related factors may contribute to high and increasing levels

of child abandonment, juvenile delinquency, chronic and growing underemployment and unemployment, petty thievery, organized brigandry, food riots, separatist movements, communal massacres, revolutionary actions and counter-revolutionary coups. Such conditions also detract from the environment needed to attract the foreign capital vital to increasing levels of economic growth in these areas. If these conditions result in expropriation of foreign interests, such action, from an economic viewpoint, is not in the best interests of either the investing country or the host government.

22. In international relations, population factors are crucial in, and often determinants of, violent conflicts in developing areas. Conflicts that are regarded in primarily political terms often have demographic roots. Recognition of these relationships appears crucial to any understanding or prevention of such hostilities.

General Goals and Requirements for Dealing with Rapid Population Growth

23. The central question for world population policy in the year 1974 is whether mankind is to remain on a track toward an ultimate population of 12 to 15 billion—implying a five- to sevenfold increase in almost all the underdeveloped world outside of China—or whether (despite the momentum of population growth) it can be switched over to the course of earliest feasible population stability—implying ultimate totals of 8 to 9 billions and not more than a three or four-fold increase in any major region.

24. What are the stakes? We do not know whether technological developments will make it possible to feed over 8, much less 12 billion people in the 21st century. We cannot be entirely certain that climatic changes in the coming decade will not create great difficulties in feeding a growing population, especially people in the LDCs who live under increasingly marginal and more vulnerable conditions. There exists at least the possibility that present developments point toward Malthusian conditions for many regions of the world.

25. But even if survival for these much larger numbers is possible, it will in all likelihood be bare survival, with all efforts going in the good years to provide minimum nutrition, and utter

dependence in the bad years on emergency rescue efforts from the less populated and richer countries of the world. In the shorter run—between now and the year 2000—the difference between the two courses can be some perceptible material gain in the crowded poor regions, and some improvement in the relative distribution of intra-country per capita income between rich and poor, as against permanent poverty and the widening of income gaps. A much more vigorous effort to slow population growth can also mean a very great difference between enormous tragedies of malnutrition and starvation as against only serious chronic conditions.

Policy Recommendations

26. There is no single approach which will "solve" the population problem. The complex social and economic factors involved call for a comprehensive strategy with both bilateral and multilateral elements. At the same time actions and programs must be tailored to specific countries and groups. Above all, LDCs themselves must play the most important role to achieve success.

27. Coordination among the bilateral donors and multilateral organizations is vital to any effort to moderate population growth. Each kind of effort will be needed for worldwide results. . . .

29. While specific goals in this area are difficult to state, our aim should be for the world to achieve a replacement level of fertility (a two-child family on the average) by about the year 2000. This will require the present 2 percent growth rate to decline to 1.7 percent within a decade and to 1.1 percent by 2000. Compared to the U.N. medium projection, this goal would result in 500 million fewer people in 2000 and about 3 billion fewer in 2050. Attainment of this goal will require greatly intensified population programs. A basis for developing national population growth control targets to achieve this world target is contained in the World Population Plan of Action.

30. The World Population Plan of Action is not self-enforcing and will require vigorous efforts by interested countries, U.N. agencies and other international bodies to make it effective. U.S. leadership is essential. The strategy must include the following elements and actions:

. . . Concentration on key countries. Assistance for population moderation should give primary emphasis to the largest and fastest growing developing countries where there is special U.S. political and strategic interest. Those countries are: India, Bangladesh, Pakistan, Nigeria, Mexico, Indonesia, Brazil, the Philippines, Thailand, Egypt, Turkey, Ethiopia and Colombia. Together, they account for 47 percent of the world's current population increase. . . .

For its own merits and consistent with the recommendations of the World Population Plan of Action, priority should be given in the general aid program to selective development policies in sectors offering the greatest promise of increased motivation for smaller family size. In many cases pilot programs and experimental research will be needed as guidance for later efforts on a larger scale. The preferential sectors include:

- Providing minimal levels of education, especially for women;
- Reducing infant mortality, including through simple low-cost health care networks;
- Expanding wage employment, especially for women;
- Developing alternatives to children as a source of old age security;
- Increasing income of the poorest, especially in rural areas, including providing privately owned farms;
- Education of new generations on the desirability of smaller families. . . .

World Population Prospects: The 2004 Revision—Highlights

Every two years, the UN Population Division issues a new set of global population projections to the year 2050. The projections nearly always are considered "front-page news" by the major media. In 2002, for example, much notice was taken of the fact that the United Nations lowered its estimate of midcentury population from 9.3 billion (the 2000 projection) to 8.9 billion, a decrease of 400 million. In 2004, by contrast, the projection was lifted from 8.9 to 9.1 billion. Of the many interesting points made in the summary below, one that stands out is the fact that by the year 2050 the developed countries as a whole will be losing 1 million people per year, while the developing countries will be gaining 35 million.

The key findings from the 2004 Revision can be summarized as follows:

1. By July 2005, the world [had] 6.5 billion inhabitants, 380 million more than in 2000 or a gain of 76 million annually. Despite the declining fertility levels projected over 2005–2050, the world population is expected to reach 9.1 billion according to the medium variant and will still be adding 34 million persons annually by mid-century.

2. Today, 95 percent of all population growth is absorbed by the developing world and 5 percent by the developed world. By 2050, according to the medium variant, the population of the more developed countries as a whole would be declining slowly by about 1 million persons a year and that of the developing world would be adding 35 million annually, 22 million of whom would be absorbed by the least developed countries.

3. Future population growth is highly dependent on the path that future fertility takes. In the medium variant, fertility is projected to decline from 2.6 children per woman today to slightly over 2 children per woman in 2050. If fertility were to remain about half a child above the levels projected in the medium variant, world population would reach 10.6 billion by 2050. A fertility path half a child below the medium would lead to a population of 7.6 billion by mid-century. That is, at the world level, continued population growth until 2050 is inevitable even if the decline of fertility accelerates.

4. Because of its low and declining rate of growth, the population of developed countries as a whole is expected to remain virtually unchanged between 2005 and 2050, at about 1.2 billion. In contrast, the population of the 50 least developed countries is projected to more than double, passing from 0.8 billion in 2005 to 1.7 billion in 2050. Growth in the rest of the developing world is also projected to be robust, though less rapid, with its population rising from 4.5 billion to 6.1 billion between 2005 and 2050.

5. Very rapid population growth is expected to prevail in a number of developing countries, the majority of which are least developed. Between 2005 and 2050, the population is projected to at least triple in Afghanistan, Burkina Faso, Burundi, Chad, Congo, the Democratic Republic of Congo, the Democratic Republic of Timor-Leste, Guinea-Bissau, Liberia, Mali, Niger and Uganda.

6. The population of 51 countries or areas, including Germany, Italy, Japan, the Baltic States and most of the successor

states of the former Soviet Union, is expected to be lower in 2050 than in 2005.

7. During 2005–2050, nine countries are expected to account for half of the world's projected population increase: India, Pakistan, Nigeria, the Democratic Republic of Congo, Bangladesh, Uganda, the United States of America, Ethiopia and China, listed according to the size of their contribution to population growth during that period.

8. In 2000–2005, fertility at the world level stood at 2.65 children per woman, about half the level it had in 1950–1955 (5 children per women). In the medium variant, global fertility is projected to decline further to 2.05 children per woman by 2045–2050. Average world levels result from quite different trends by major development group. In developed countries as a whole fertility is currently 1.56 children per woman and is projected to increase slowly to 1.84 children per woman in 2045–2050. In the least developed countries, fertility is 5 children per woman and is expected to drop by about half, to 2.57 children per woman by 2045–2050. In the rest of the developing world, fertility is already moderately low at 2.58 children per woman and is expected to decline further to 1.92 children per woman by mid-century, thus nearly converging to the fertility levels by then typical of the developed world. Realization of the fertility declines projected is contingent on access to family planning, especially in the least developed countries.

9. In 2000–2005, fertility remains above 5 children per woman in 35 of the 148 developing countries, 30 of which are least developed countries, while the pace of decline in several countries of sub-Saharan Africa and South-central Asia has been slower than anticipated. Overall, the countries with high fertility account for 10 percent of the world population. In contrast, fertility has reached below-replacement levels in 23 developing countries accounting for 25 percent of the world population. This group includes China whose fertility during 2000–2005 is estimated at 1.7 children per woman.

10. Fertility levels in the 44 developed countries, which account for 19 percent of the world population, are currently very low. All except Albania have fertility below replacement level and 15, mostly located in Southern and Eastern Europe, have reached levels of fertility unprecedented in human history (below 1.3 children per woman). Since 1990–1995, fertility decline has been the rule among most developed countries. The few in-

creases recorded, such as those in Belgium, France, Germany, the Netherlands and the United States, have been small.

11. Global life expectancy at birth, which is estimated to have risen from 47 years in 1950–1955 to 65 years in 2000–2005, is expected to keep on rising to reach 75 years in 2045–2050. In the more developed regions, the projected increase is from 76 years today to 82 years by mid-century. Among the least developed countries, where life expectancy today is 51 years, it is expected to be 67 years in 2045–2050. Because many of these countries are highly affected by the HIV/AIDS epidemic, the projected increase in life expectancy is dependent on the implementation of effective programs to prevent and treat HIV infection. In the rest of the developing world, under similar conditions, life expectancy is projected to rise from 66 years today to 76 years by mid-century.

12. Mortality in Eastern Europe has been increasing since the late 1980s. In 2000–2005 life expectancy in the region, at 67.9 years, was lower than it had been in 1960–1965 (68.6 years). The Russian Federation and the Ukraine are particularly affected by rises in mortality resulting partly from the spread of HIV.

13. Twenty-five years into the HIV/AIDS epidemic, the impact of the disease is evident in terms of increased morbidity and mortality and slower population growth. In Southern Africa, the region with the highest HIV/AIDS prevalence of the disease, life expectancy has fallen from 62 years in 1990–1995 to 48 years in 2000–2005, and is projected to decrease further to 43 years over the next decade before a slow recovery starts. As a consequence, population growth in the region is expected to stall between 2005 and 2020. In Botswana, Lesotho and Swaziland, the population is projected to decrease as deaths outnumber births. In most of the other developing countries affected by the epidemic, population growth will continue to be positive because their moderate or high fertility more than counterbalances the rise in mortality.

14. The primary consequence of fertility decline, especially if combined with increases in life expectancy, is population ageing, whereby the share of older persons in a population grows relative to that of younger persons. Globally, the number of persons aged 60 years or over is expected almost to triple, increasing from 672 million in 2005 to nearly 1.9 billion by 2050. Whereas 6 out of every 10 of those older persons live today in developing countries, by 2050, 8 out of every 10 will do so. An even more marked increase is expected in the number of the oldest-old (persons

aged 80 years or over): from 86 million in 2005 to 394 million in 2050. In developing countries, the rise will be from 42 million to 278 million, implying that by 2050 most oldest-old will live in the developing world.

15. In developed countries, 20 percent of today's population is aged 60 years or over and by 2050 that proportion is projected to be 32 percent. The elderly population in developed countries has already surpassed the number of children (persons aged 0–14) and by 2050 there will be 2 elderly persons for every child. In the developing world, the proportion of the population aged 60 or over is expected to rise from 8 percent in 2005 to close to 20 percent by 2050.

16. Increases in the median age, the age at which 50 percent of the population is older and 50 percent younger than that age, are indicative of population ageing. Today, just 11 developed countries have a median age above 40 years. By 2050, there will be 90 countries in that group, 46 in the developing world. Population aging, which is becoming a pervasive reality in developed countries, is also inevitable in the developing world and will occur faster in developing countries.

17. Countries where fertility remains high and has declined only moderately will experience the slowest population ageing. By 2050, about one in five countries is still projected to have a median age equal [to] or less than 30 years. The youngest populations will be found in least developed countries, 11 of which are projected to have median ages equal to or less than 23 years in 2050, including Afghanistan, Angola, Burundi, Chad, the Democratic Republic of Congo, Equatorial Guinea, Guinea-Bissau, Liberia, Mali, Niger, and Uganda.

18. During 2005–2050, the net number of international migrants to more developed regions is projected to be 98 million or an average of 2.2 million annually. The same number will leave the less developed regions. For the developed world, such a level of net migration will largely offset the expected excess of deaths over births during 2005–2050, which amounts to a loss of 73 million people. For the developing world, the 98 million emigrants represent scarcely less than 4 percent of expected population growth.

19. Over the period 2000–2005, 74 countries were net receivers of migrants. In 64 of these countries, the net migration projected reinforces population growth, and in 7 countries, it reverses the trend of population decline (Austria, Croatia, Germany, Greece, Italy, Slovakia and Slovenia). In three countries,

the migration slows down population decline but does not reverse it (Czech Republic, Hungary and the Russian Federation).

20. In terms of annual averages for the period 2005–2050, the major net receivers of international migrants are projected to be the United States (1.1 million annually), Germany (202,000), Canada (200,000), the United Kingdom (130,000), Italy (120,000) and Australia (100,000). The major countries of net emigration are projected to be China (–327,000 annually), Mexico (–293,000), India (–241,000), the Philippines (–180,000), Indonesia (–164,000), Pakistan (–154,000) and the Ukraine (–100,000).

Census Bureau Projects Doubling of Nation's Population by 2100

Like the United Nations Population Division, the United States Census Bureau issues long-range population projections. Before January 2000, however, the Census Bureau had never projected U.S. population levels to the end of the twenty-first century. What they announced were numbers that raised some eyebrows! The "middle" or maximum-likelihood forecast put U.S. population in 100 years at 571 million, or almost twice the current population.

The nation's resident population could more than double in this century, according to national population projections to the year 2100 released today by the Commerce Department's Census Bureau.

According to the projections, the nation's resident population, 273 million on July 1, 1999, is projected to reach 404 million in 2050 and 571 million in 2100. These results are based on middle-level assumptions regarding population growth during the century.

"Even though childbearing levels in the United States remain quite close to the level needed only to replace the population, the increasing number of potential parents and continued migration from abroad would be sufficient to add nearly 300 million people during the next century," said Census Bureau analyst Frederick W. Hollmann. "Because the Hispanic and Asian and Pacific Islander populations in the U.S. are younger than the nation as a whole and because they continue to receive international migrants, these populations will become increasingly prominent."

The data also show lowest and highest alternative projections. The lowest series projects population growth to 314 million in 2050 and then a decline to 283 million in 2100. The highest projects 553 million people in 2050 and 1.2 billion in 2100.

The projections do not take into account possible future changes in the way people report their race and ethnicity, and, because of the length of time covered and other uncertainties, they are considered less reliable for the latter part of the century.

According to the middle series projections, the Hispanic population (of any race) would triple from 31.4 million in 1999 to 98.2 million in 2050. By 2005, Hispanics may become the nation's largest minority group. The percentage of Hispanics in the total population could rise from 12 percent in 1999 to 24 percent in 2050.

The Asian and Pacific Islander population, meanwhile, would more than triple, from 10.9 million in 1999 to 37.6 million in 2050. Its percentage of the total population would rise from 4 percent now to 9 percent in 2050.

According to the projections, the non-Hispanic White and African-American populations would increase more slowly than the other groups. The non-Hispanic White population would rise from 196.1 million in 1999 to 213.0 million in 2050, a 9 percent increase. Its share of the total population would decline, however, from 72 percent in 1999 to 53 percent in 2050.

The African-American population, according to the projections, would rise from 34.9 million in 1999 to 59.2 million in 2050, a 70-percent increase; under this scenario, the African-American share of the total population would increase slightly, from 13 percent to 15 percent.

Between 1999 and 2050, the total number of foreign-born would more than double, increasing from 26.0 million to 53.8 million. The proportion of the nation's population that is foreign-born may rise from 10 percent in 1999 to 13 percent in 2050.

The population age 65 and over would grow from 34.6 million in 1999 to 82.0 million in 2050, a 137-percent increase. The projections also show an especially rapid surge in the elderly population as the surviving "baby boomers" pass age 65; in the year 2011, baby boomers (those born between 1946 and 1964) will begin turning 65. Between 2011 and 2030, the number of elderly would rise from 40.4 million (13 percent of the population) to 70.3 million (20 percent of the population).

TABLE 7.1
Total U.S. Resident Population (millions):
Middle, Lowest, and Highest series, 1999–2100

Year	Lowest	Middle	Highest
1999	272.7	272.8	273.0
2025	308.2	337.8	380.4
2050	313.5	403.7	552.8
2075	304.0	480.5	809.2
2100	282.7	571.0	1,182.4

Source: Population Projections Program, Population Division, U.S. Census Bureau.

The projections show that the number of children under 18 would increase from 70.2 million in 1999 to 95.7 million in 2050. However, their share of the nation's population would decline slowly, falling from 26 percent in 1999 to 24 percent in 2050.

The projections are based on assumptions about future childbearing, mortality, and migration. The level of childbearing among women for the middle series is assumed to remain close to present levels, with differences by race and Hispanic origin diminishing over time. Mortality is assumed to decline gradually with less variation by race and Hispanic origin than at present. International migration is assumed to vary over time and decrease generally relative to the size of the population.

This is the first time that the Census Bureau has projected the population to 2100 and the first time it includes information on the foreign-born population. The projections are presented by age, sex, race, and Hispanic origin.

World Population to 2300

There is something rather extraordinary about any forecast relating to human behavior that extends three centuries *into the future. Accurate predictions can be made of astronomical events hundreds and even thousands of years in advance of their occurrence, but of course human beings are far more unpredictable, individually and collectively, than inanimate celestial objects! Yet demographers at the United Nations in 2003 tackled the challenge of making truly long-*

*range population projections—300-year projections—for the first time
ever. They did it for the benefit of "environmental scientists, policy
makers and others who assess the long-term implications of demographic trends."*

Long-range population projections are reported to 2300, covering twice as long a period as ever covered in previous UN projections. These projections are not done by major area and for selected large countries (China and India), as was the previous
practice, but for all countries of the world, providing greater
detail.

In these projections, world population peaks at 9.22 billion in
2075. Population therefore grows slightly beyond the level of 8.92
billion projected for 2050 in the *2002 Revision,* on which these projections are based. However, after reaching its maximum, world
population declines slightly and then resumes increasing, slowly,
to reach a level of 8.97 billion by 2300, not much different from
the projected 2050 figure.

This pattern of rise, decline, and rise again results from assumptions about future trends in vital rates: that, country by
country, fertility will fall below replacement level—though in
some cases not for decades—and eventually return to replacement; and that, country by country, life expectancy will eventually follow a path of uninterrupted but slowing increase. With alternative assumptions about fertility, long-range trends could be
quite different. With long-range total fertility 0.3 children above
replacement, projected world population in 2300 is four times as
large as the main projection; with total fertility 0.2 children below
replacement, world population in 2300 is one-quarter of the main
projection.

Regions and countries will follow similar demographic
paths in the long run, given similar assumptions for different
countries about long-range vital rate trends. However, because
initial assumptions differ, and because this gives rise to slight
variations in trends, countries and regions will not be exactly
alike, even by 2300. In fact, what are today considered more developed and less developed regions will still be demographically
distinguishable, with regard, for instance, to life expectancies and
proportions at advanced ages. In addition, regions and countries
will go through critical stages of growth—zero growth, subreplacement fertility, a return to positive growth—at different
points in the future, giving rise to a global demographic map

with areas that shrink and stretch at different times in the next three centuries.

Europe and Africa will be particularly out of phase. Europe will hit its low point in growth in 2050, Africa not till 80 years later, after all other major areas. From 2000 to 2100, Europe's share of world population is cut in half, 12.0 to 5.9 percent, while Africa's almost doubles, from 13.1 to 24.9 percent. While shares of world population for major areas will rise and fall over the following two centuries, the distribution by 2300 will resemble that in 2100.

Smaller regions within continents exhibit divergent patterns. For instance:

Three African regions—Eastern Africa, Middle Africa, and Western Africa—will grow unusually fast in comparison to every other region through 2100, even though total fertility will be close to replacement by 2050.

Southern Africa is seeing a decline in life expectancy to a lower level than anywhere else, but life expectancy will rebound, rise quite rapidly, and overtake other African regions.

Asian regions will grow fastest to the west, slowest to the east, but in every case with growth rates, at least up to 2100, below Eastern, Middle, and Western Africa. By 2100, Asia, instead of being four-and-a half times as populous as Africa, will be only 2.2 times as populous.

Latin America and the Caribbean is the most homogenous major area, with most of its regions following relatively parallel fertility and life expectancy paths.

Northern America is unusual as the only region that will not experience negative growth, mainly due to projected migration up to 2050. (No migration is incorporated in projections beyond that date.)

Europe, like Asia, will experience higher growth to the west, lower growth to the east. Eastern Europe stands out with low life expectancy, and even in the long run does not catch up with other regions.

Growth patterns depend on assumptions about vital rates. Total fertility is assumed to decline, at a varying pace dictated by country circumstances, to a below-replacement level of 1.85 children per woman. Countries already at this level or below, and other countries when they reach it, eventually return to replacement over a period of a century and stay at replacement indefinitely. All countries are projected to have reached replacement fertility by 2175, but past fertility trends continue to affect population trends for another 50 years.

Life expectancy is assumed to rise continuously, with no upper limit, though at a slowing pace dictated by recent country trends. By 2100, life expectancy is expected to vary across countries from 66 to 97 years, and by 2300 from 87 to 106 years. Rising life expectancy will produce small but continuing population growth by the end of the projections ranging from 0.03 to 0.07 percent annually.

Growth patterns affect the balance between population and land. Density, in people per square kilometer of land, will continue to be especially variable in Oceania, where by 2100 it will range from 504 persons per sq. km. in Micronesia to 3.6 persons per sq. km. in Australia/New Zealand. Some large countries in South-central Asia will also be unusually dense by 2100, with India having 491 persons per sq. km., Pakistan 530 persons per sq. km., and Bangladesh 1,997 persons per sq. km.

These populations pressing on the land will be old by current standards. Where the world median age in 2000 is 26 years, by 2100 it will be 44 years, and by 2300, 48 years. Before they reach the point where those over 40 are half the population, countries go through a period labeled here the demographic window, when the proportion of children and youth under 15 years falls below 30 percent and the proportion of people 65 years and older is still below 15 percent. For a 30–40 year period, the proportion of the population in between, of working age, is particularly prominent in the population. Europe entered the demographic window before 1950 and is now leaving it and entering a third age when older people are particularly prominent in the age distribution. Much of Africa will not enter the demographic window until 2045 or later.

Beyond the demographic window, population ageing becomes a predominant demographic feature. Between 2100 and 2300, the proportion of world population 65 years and older will increase by one-third (from 24 to 32 percent); the proportion 80 years and older will double (from 8.5 to 17 percent); and the proportion 100 years and older will increase nine times (from 0.2 to 1.8 percent). Assuming that the retirement age worldwide in 2000 is 65 years, people retire on average only two weeks short of their life expectancy. Assuming that retirement age stays unchanged, by 2300 people will retire 31 years short of their life expectancy.

Program of Action of the International Conference on Population and Development, Cairo, 1994

Three international conferences on population have been held under the auspices of the United Nations—at Bucharest (1974), Mexico City (1984), and Cairo (1994). The 1994 conference was officially titled International Conference on Population and Development, or ICPD. More clearly than in 1974 or 1984, the Cairo conference situated population policymaking within a broader context of all-round human development. Governments were urged to take the necessary steps to ensure the provision of reproductive health services to all their citizens, to broaden opportunities for women, and to equalize educational opportunities for girls and boys. There was an implicit recognition that high fertility rates, where they still occur, are unlikely to be reduced, or reduced sufficiently to ease population pressures, until women achieve a fuller measure of empowerment in their personal and social lives. Much behind-the-scenes negotiating was needed to achieve a final consensus on this document, with Dr. Nafis Sadik, head of the UNFPA and secretary-general of the ICPD, playing an important mediating role.

Chapter 1 Preamble

. . . 1.3. The world population is currently estimated at 5.6 billion. While the rate of growth is on the decline, absolute increments have been increasing, currently exceeding 86 million persons per annum. Annual population increments are likely to remain above 86 million until the year 2015.

1.4. During the remaining six years of this critical decade, the world's nations by their actions or inactions will choose from among a range of alternative demographic futures. The low, medium and high variants of the United Nations population projections for the coming 20 years range from a low of 7.1 billion people to the medium variant of 7.5 billion and a high of 7.8 billion. The difference of 720 million people in the short span of 20 years exceeds the current population of the African continent. Further into the future, the projections diverge even more significantly. By the year 2050, the United Nations projections range from 7.9 billion to the medium variant of 9.8 billion and a high of 11.9 billion. Implementation of the goals and objectives contained in the present 20-year Program of Action, which address[es] many of the fundamental population, health, education and development challenges facing the entire human community, would result in world population growth during this period and beyond at levels below the United Nations medium projection. . . .

1.8. Over the past 20 years, many parts of the world have undergone remarkable demographic, social, economic, environmental and political change. Many countries have made substantial progress in expanding access to reproductive health care and lowering birth rates, as well as in lowering death rates and raising education and income levels, including the educational and economic status of women. While the advances of the past two decades in areas such as increased use of contraception, decreased maternal mortality, implemented sustainable development plans and projects and enhanced educational programs provide a basis for optimism about successful implementation of the present Program of Action, much remains to be accomplished. The world as a whole has changed in ways that create important new opportunities for addressing population and development issues. Among the most significant are the major shifts in attitude among the world's people and their leaders in regard to reproductive health, family planning and population growth, resulting, *inter alia*, in the new comprehensive concept of reproductive health, including family planning and sexual health, as defined in the present Program of Action. A particularly encouraging trend has been the strengthening of political commitment to population-related policies and family-planning programs by many Governments. In this regard, sustained economic growth in the context of sustainable development will enhance the ability of countries to meet the pressures of expected population growth; will facilitate the demographic transition in countries where there is an imbalance between demographic rates and social, economic and environmental goals; and will permit the balance and integration of the population dimension into other development-related policies.

1.9. The population and development objectives and actions of the present Program of Action will collectively address the critical challenges and interrelationships between population and sustained economic growth in the context of sustainable development. In order to do so, adequate mobilization of resources at the national and international levels will be required as well as new and additional resources to the developing countries from all available funding mechanisms, including multilateral, bilateral and private sources. Financial resources are also required to strengthen the capacity of national, regional, subregional and international institutions to implement this Program of Action. . . .

1.11. Intensified efforts are needed in the coming 5, 10 and 20 years, in a range of population and development activities, bearing in mind the crucial contribution that early stabilization of the world population would make towards the achievement of sustainable development. The present Program of Action addresses all those issues, and more, in a comprehensive and integrated framework designed to improve the quality of life of the current world population and its future generations. The recommendations for action are made in a spirit of consensus and international cooperation, recognizing that the formulation and implementation of population-related policies is the responsibility of each country and should take into account the economic, social and environmental diversity of conditions in each country, with full respect for the various religious and ethical values, cultural backgrounds and philosophical convictions of its people, as well as the shared but differentiated responsibilities of all the world's people for a common future. . . .

1.13. Many of the quantitative and qualitative goals of the present Program of Action clearly require additional resources, some of which could become available from a reordering of priorities at the individual, national and international levels. However, none of the actions required—nor all of them combined—is expensive in the context of either current global development or military expenditures. A few would require little or no additional financial resources, in that they involve change in lifestyles, social norms or government policies that can be largely brought about and sustained through greater citizen action and political leadership. But to meet the resource needs of those actions that do require increased expenditures over the next two decades, additional commitments will be required on the part of both developing and developed countries. This will be particularly difficult in the case of some developing countries and some countries with economies in transition that are experiencing extreme resource constraints.

Chapter 2 Principles

... *Principle 4.* Advancing gender equality and equity and the empowerment of women, and the elimination of all kinds of violence against women, and ensuring women's ability to control their own fertility, are cornerstones of population- and development-related programs. The human rights of women and the girl child are an inalienable, integral and indivisible part of universal human rights. The full and equal participation of women in civil, cultural, economic, political and social life, at the national, regional and international levels, and the eradication of all forms of discrimination on grounds of sex, are priority objectives of the international community.

Principle 5. Population-related goals and policies are integral parts of cultural, economic and social development, the principal aim of which is to improve the quality of life of all people.

Principle 6. Sustainable development as a means to ensure human well-being, equitably shared by all people today and in the future, requires that the interrelationships between population, resources, the environment and development should be fully recognized, properly managed and brought into harmonious, dynamic balance. To achieve sustainable development and a higher quality of life for all people, States should reduce and eliminate unsustainable patterns of production and consumption and promote appropriate policies, including population-related policies, in order to meet the needs of current generations without compromising the ability of future generations to meet their own needs. ...

Principle 8. Everyone has the right to the enjoyment of the highest attainable standard of physical and mental health. States should take all appropriate measures to ensure, on a basis of equality of men and women, universal access to health-care services, including those related to reproductive health care, which includes family planning and sexual health. Reproductive health-care programs should provide the widest range of services without any form of coercion. All couples and individuals have the basic right to decide freely and responsibly the number and spacing of their children and to have the information, education and means to do so. ...

Principle 10. Everyone has the right to education, which shall be directed to the full development of human resources, and human dignity and potential, with particular attention to women and the girl child. Education should be designed to respect human rights and fundamental freedoms, including those relating to population and development. The best interests of the child shall be the guiding principle of those responsible for his or her education and guidance; that responsibility lies in the first place with the parents.

Chapter 3 Interrelationships between Population, Sustained Economic Growth and Sustainable Development

. . . 3.14. Efforts to slow down population growth, to reduce poverty, to achieve economic progress, to improve environmental protection, and to reduce unsustainable consumption and production patterns are mutually reinforcing. Slower population growth has in many countries bought more time to adjust to future population increases. This has increased those countries' ability to attack poverty, protect and repair the environment, and build the base for future sustainable development. Even the difference of a single decade in the transition to stabilization levels of fertility can have a considerable positive impact on quality of life.

3.15. Sustained economic growth within the context of sustainable development is essential to eradicate poverty. Eradication of poverty will contribute to slowing population growth and to achieving early population stabilization. Investments in fields important to the eradication of poverty, such as basic education, sanitation, drinking water, housing, adequate food supply and infrastructure for rapidly growing populations, continue to strain already weak economies and limit development options. The unusually high number of young people, a consequence of high fertility rates, requires that productive jobs be created for a continually growing labor force under conditions of already widespread unemployment. The numbers of elderly requiring public support will also increase rapidly in the future. Sustained economic growth in the context of sustainable development will be necessary to accommodate those pressures.

Chapter 4 Gender Equality, Equity and Empowerment of Women

. . . 4.1. The empowerment and autonomy of women and the improvement of their political, social, economic and health status is a highly important end in itself. In addition, it is essential for the achievement of sustainable development. The full participation and partnership of both women and men is required in productive and reproductive life, including shared responsibilities for the care and nurturing of children and maintenance of the household. In all parts of the world, women are facing threats to their lives, health and well-being as a result of being overburdened with work and of their lack of power and influence. In most regions of the world, women receive less formal education than men, and at the same time, women's own knowledge, abilities and coping mechanisms often go unrecognized. The power relations that impede women's attainment of healthy and fulfilling lives operate at many levels of society, from the most personal to the highly public. Achieving change requires policy and program actions that will improve women's access to secure livelihoods and economic resources, alleviate their extreme responsibilities with regard to housework, remove legal impediments to their participation in public life, and raise social awareness through effective programs of education and mass communication. In addition, improving the status of women also enhances their decision-making capacity at all levels in all spheres of life, especially in the area of sexuality and reproduction. This, in turn, is essential for the long-term success of population programs. Experience shows that population and development programs are most effective when steps have simultaneously been taken to improve the status of women. . . .

Chapter 7 Reproductive Rights and Reproductive Health

. . . 7.12. The aim of family-planning programs must be to enable couples and individuals to decide freely and responsibly the number and spacing of their children and to have the information and means to do so and to ensure informed choices and make available a full range of safe and effective methods. The success of population education and family-planning programs in a variety of settings demonstrates that informed individuals everywhere can and will act responsibly in the light of their own needs and those of their families and communities. The principle of informed free choice is essential to the long-term success of family-planning programs. Any form of coercion has no part to play. In every society there are many social and economic incentives and disincentives that affect individual decisions about child-bearing and family size. Over the past century, many Governments have experimented with such schemes, including specific incentives and disincentives, in order to lower or raise fertility. Most such schemes have had only marginal impact on fertility and in some cases have been counterproductive. Governmental goals for family planning should be defined in terms of unmet needs for information and services. Demographic goals, while legitimately the subject of government development strategies, should not be imposed on family-planning providers in the form of targets or quotas for the recruitment of clients.

7.13. Over the past three decades, the increasing availability of safer methods of modern contraception, although still in some respects inadequate, has permitted greater opportunities for individual choice and responsible decision-making in matters of reproduction throughout much of the world. Currently, about 55 percent of couples in developing regions use some method of family planning. This figure represents nearly a fivefold increase since the 1960s. Family-planning programs have contributed considerably to the decline in average fertility rates for developing countries, from about six to seven children per woman in the 1960s to about three to four children at present. However, the full range of modern family-planning methods still remains unavailable to at least 350 million couples worldwide, many of whom say they want to space or prevent another pregnancy. Survey data suggest that approximately 120 million additional women worldwide would be currently using a modern family-planning method if more accurate information and affordable services were easily available, and if partners, extended families and the community were more supportive. . . .

7.16. All countries should, over the next several years, assess the extent of national unmet need for good-quality family-planning services and its integration in the reproductive health context, paying particular attention to the most vulnerable and underserved groups in the population. All countries should take steps to meet the family-planning needs of their populations as soon as possible and should, in all cases by the year 2015, seek to provide universal access to a full range of safe and reliable family-planning methods and to related reproductive health services which are not against the law. The aim should be to assist couples and individuals to achieve their reproductive goals and give them the full opportunity to exercise the right to have children by choice.

World Population Policies 2003

The study of world population takes on an additional dimension when one goes beyond the facts and figures and asks how they are viewed by the public—and by governments. Is population growth regarded as too rapid? Too slow? Are fertility rates satisfactory? If not, have policies been implemented to correct the problem? The United Nations periodically queries the governments of the world on these questions and then releases its findings. Some of the main conclusions of the 2003 survey are presented below:

1. Population Size and Growth

Continued high rates of population growth remain an issue of policy concern for many countries of the developing world. In 2003, 54 percent of countries in the less developed regions considered their rate of population growth to be too high . . . Countries that viewed population growth as too high encompassed most of Africa (77 percent) and over half of the islands of Oceania (56 percent). More than one-third of countries in Asia (36 percent) and Latin America and the Caribbean (36 percent) viewed their population growth rate as too high.

To a great extent, concerns with the detrimental consequences of high population growth translate into policy interventions. Fifty-one percent of the Governments of developing countries and 67 percent of the Governments of the least developed countries have policies aimed at reducing population growth . . . One of the most significant population policy developments of the second half of the 1990s is the continued rise in the number of African Governments that report policies aimed at reducing the rapid growth of their population: 72 percent in

2003, up from 60 percent in 1996, 39 percent in 1986, and 25 percent in 1976.

In the developed world, a declining share of countries are satisfied with their level of population growth. Only half of countries report they are satisfied with their rate of population growth, down from 82 percent in 1986 and 71 percent in 1996 . . .

Nearly all the [developed] countries which declare their growth rate to be unsatisfactory view them as too low. One-half of developed countries do not have policies aimed at influencing population growth . . . The share of developed countries that express concern with low rates of population growth has increased rapidly to 48 percent in 2003 from 27 percent in 1996. Consequently, the proportion of developed countries that have policies aimed at raising the growth of their population has climbed from 23 percent in 1996 to 38 percent in 2003.

2. Population Age Structure

An inevitable consequence of the demographic transition and the shift to lower fertility and mortality has been the evolution in the age structure of world population. Many societies, especially in the more developed regions, have already attained older population age structures than have ever been seen in the past. Many developing countries in the midst of the demographic transition are experiencing rapid shifts in the relative numbers of children, working-age population and older persons.

Once only limited to developed countries, concerns with the consequences of population ageing have spread to many developing countries as well. As of 2003, 56 percent of reporting countries view population ageing as a major concern, and 43 percent as a minor concern . . . Although concerns with population ageing are much more pronounced among developed countries, where three-quarters of Governments consider it a major concern, a number of Governments in developing countries are becoming concerned by this demographic phenomenon, as well. Almost one-half of developing countries expressed major concern over population ageing in 2003.

As regards the working-age population, almost three-quarters (71 percent) of reporting countries viewed the size of the population in the ages 15–59 years as a major concern . . . Developed and developing countries differ in terms of the nature of the concern. Whereas developed countries are concerned that the size of the working-age population is too small, thus creating labor shortages, most developing countries feel that the working-age population is too large, posing problems of high unemployment.

3. Fertility and Family Planning

The percentage of countries that are satisfied with the level of fertility continues to decline . . . However, this global comparison masks a marked difference between the more developed regions and the less developed regions. In the more developed regions, 58 percent of countries find their fertility levels to be too low and none indicate that fertility is too high. The opposite is true in the less developed regions, where 58 percent of countries indicate too high a fertility level, whereas only 8 percent indicate too low. By 2003, only 37 percent of countries said that the present level of fertility was satisfactory. Twice as many countries in the world consider their fertility level too high (43 percent) as too low (20 percent).

Among the group of least developed countries, 78 percent said fertility was too high. This latter percentage has been rising steadily since 1976. In that year, only 31 percent of the least developed countries thought their fertility was too high. By 1986, the percentage had risen to 54 percent, and since 1996 it has remained at 78 percent.

The persistence of low fertility has become a concern for more countries in recent years, particularly, as noted above, in the more developed regions where fertility has fallen to 1.6 children per woman for the period 2000–2005. In 2003, 58 percent of the countries in the more developed regions considered fertility to be too low, up from 21 percent in 1976. Of the 39 countries that considered fertility too low in 2003, 27 were in Europe and nine were in Asia . . .

There is a notable correspondence between the percentage of countries that considered fertility to be too high and those that had implemented policies to lower it. Eighty-four countries (43 percent of the total) considered fertility to be too high, and 83 countries had policies to lower fertility . . . This represents a greater convergence between Governments' views and policies than was previously seen. In 1976, for example, 55 countries stated that fertility was too high, but only 40 countries had policies to lower fertility.

Of the 39 countries that considered fertility to be too low in 2003, seven had not implemented policies aimed at raising it. These countries were: Bosnia and Herzegovina, Germany, Italy, Norway, Portugal, Spain and Switzerland. By contrast, only five of 84 countries that considered fertility too high had failed to adopt fertility-reduction policies. The five countries with high fertility but without fertility policies were geographically diverse: Afghanistan, Djibouti, Guinea-Bissau, Paraguay and Sao Tome and Principe.

Governments' views and policies with regard to the use of contraceptive methods have changed considerably during the last quarter-century. The practice of limiting access to contraceptives has nearly vanished. By 2003, 93 percent of all countries supported the provision of contraceptive methods either directly (through Government facilities) or indirectly (through support of nongovernmental sources) . . . In 1976, almost three-fourths of Governments were providing such support. Direct support for contraceptive methods is considerably more pervasive among developing countries, where 85 percent of Governments are providing such support. Among the developed countries, less than one-half provide contraceptives directly. This reflects the partial withdrawal of the State from the provision of health and welfare services and the growing prominence of nongovernmental organizations and the private sector in the delivery of reproductive health services. Thirteen countries around the world provide no support.

Adolescent fertility is a concern for Governments, particularly in the less developed regions. Early childbearing entails a risk of maternal death that is much greater than average, while the children of young mothers have higher levels of morbidity and mortality. In 2003, 61 percent of countries in the less developed regions and 63 percent of the least developed countries viewed it as a major concern . . . In more developed regions, it was a major concern for one-third of the countries and a minor concern for 48 percent. Some 80 percent of the world's Governments now have programs in place to address adolescent fertility . . . , up from 60 percent in 1996.

United Nations Principles for Older Persons

Decade by decade, the world's population is getting grayer. Issues concerning the elderly will therefore require more attention in years to come. Individuals will have to make financial and lifestyle decisions based on longer time horizons than ever before. Pension systems will be strained to the limit. Governments will confront extraordinary demands on their tax revenues to fund programs for seniors. And conflicts among generations over the allocation of social resources may be difficult to avoid. The final two documents give a sense of how the international community has begun coming to grips with the aging issue. The UN document excerpted below was adopted by the General Assembly on December 16, 1991.

The General Assembly . . .

In pursuance of the International Plan of Action on Ageing, adopted by the World Assembly on Ageing [Madrid] and endorsed by the General Assembly in its resolution 37/51 of 3 December 1982,

Appreciating the tremendous diversity in the situation of older persons, not only between countries but within countries and between individuals, which requires a variety of policy responses,

Aware that in all countries, individuals are reaching an advanced age in greater numbers and in better health than ever before,

Aware of the scientific research disproving many stereotypes about inevitable and irreversible declines with age,

Convinced that in a world characterized by an increasing number and proportion of older persons, opportunities must be provided for willing and capable older persons to participate in and contribute to the ongoing activities of society,

Mindful that the strains on family life in both developed and developing countries require support for those providing care to frail older persons,

Bearing in mind the standards already set by the International Plan of Action on Ageing and the conventions, recommendations and resolutions of the International Labor Organization, the World Health Organization and other United Nations entities,

Encourages Governments to incorporate the following principles into their national programs whenever possible:

Independence

1. Older persons should have access to adequate food, water, shelter, clothing and health care through the provision of income, family and community support and self-help.

2. Older persons should have the opportunity to work or to have access to other income-generating opportunities.

3. Older persons should be able to participate in determining when and at what pace withdrawal from the labor force takes place.

4. Older persons should have access to appropriate educational and training programs.

5. Older persons should be able to live in environments that are safe and adaptable to personal preferences and changing capacities.

6. Older persons should be able to reside at home for as long as possible.

Participation

7. Older persons should remain integrated in society, participate actively in the formulation and implementation of policies that directly affect their well-being and share their knowledge and skills with younger generations.

8. Older persons should be able to seek and develop opportunities for service to the community and to serve as volunteers in positions appropriate to their interests and capabilities.

9. Older persons should be able to form movements or associations of older persons.

Care

10. Older persons should benefit from family and community care and protection in accordance with each society's system of cultural values.

11. Older persons should have access to health care to help them to maintain or regain the optimum level of physical, mental and emotional well-being and to prevent or delay the onset of illness.

12. Older persons should have access to social and legal services to enhance their autonomy, protection and care.

13. Older persons should be able to utilize appropriate levels of institutional care providing protection, rehabilitation and social and mental stimulation in a humane and secure environment.

14. Older persons should be able to enjoy human rights and fundamental freedoms when residing in any shelter, care or treatment facility, including full respect for their dignity, beliefs, needs and privacy and for the right to make decisions about their care and the quality of their lives.

Self-fulfillment

15. Older persons should be able to pursue opportunities for the full development of their potential.

16. Older persons should have access to the educational, cultural, spiritual and recreational resources of society.

Dignity

17. Older persons should be able to live in dignity and security and be free of exploitation and physical or mental abuse.

18. Older persons should be treated fairly regardless of age, gender, racial or ethnic background, disability or other status, and be valued independently of their economic contribution.

Madrid International Plan of Action on Ageing, 2002

In 1982, the first World Assembly on Ageing was held in Vienna and resulted in adoption of an International Plan of Action on Ageing. The second World Assembly on Ageing was convened in 2002 in Madrid. The Plan of Action approved by the delegates was ratified on December 18, 2002, by the UN General Assembly. It is a lengthy document, listing many issues, objectives, and actions to be taken. The introduction, reproduced here, conveys all the main concerns.

1. The twentieth century saw a revolution in longevity. Average life expectancy at birth has increased by 20 years since 1950 to

66 years and is expected to extend a further 10 years by 2050. This demographic triumph and the fast growth of the population in the first half of the twenty-first century mean that the number of persons over 60 will increase from about 600 million in 2000 to almost 2 billion in 2050 and the proportion of persons defined as older is projected to increase globally from 10 percent in 1998 to 15 percent in 2025. The increase will be greatest and most rapid in developing countries where the older population is expected to quadruple during the next 50 years. In Asia and Latin America, the proportion of persons classified as older will increase from 8 to 15 percent between 1998 and 2025, although in Africa the proportion is only expected to grow from 5 to 6 percent during the period but then doubling by 2050. In sub-Saharan Africa, where the struggle with the HIV/AIDS pandemic and with economic and social hardship continues, the percentage will reach half that level. In Europe and North America, between 1998 and 2025 the proportion of persons classified as older will increase from 20 to 28 percent and 16 to 26 percent, respectively. Such a global demographic transformation has profound consequences for every aspect of individual, community, national and international life. Every facet of humanity will evolve: social, economic, political, cultural, psychological and spiritual.

2. The remarkable demographic transition under way will result in the old and the young representing an equal share of the world's population by mid-century. Globally, the proportion of persons aged 60 years and older is expected to double between 2000 and 2050, from 10 to 21 percent, whereas the proportion of children is projected to drop by a third, from 30 to 21 percent. In certain developed countries and countries with economies in transition, the number of older persons already exceeds the number of children and birth rates have fallen below replacement levels. In some developed countries, the number of older persons will be more than twice that of children by 2050. In developed countries the average of 71 men per 100 women is expected to increase to 78. In the less developed regions, older women do not outnumber older men to the same extent as in the developed regions, since gender differences in life expectancy are generally smaller. Current sex ratios in developing countries average 88 men per 100 women among those 60 and older, and are projected to change slightly to 87 by mid-century.

3. Population ageing is poised to become a major issue in developing countries, which are projected to age swiftly in the first

half of the twenty-first century. The proportion of older persons is expected to rise from 8 to 19 percent by 2050, while that of children will fall from 33 to 22 percent. This demographic shift presents a major resource challenge. Though developed countries have been able to age gradually, they face challenges resulting from the relationship between ageing and unemployment and sustainability of pension systems, while developing countries face the challenge of simultaneous development and population ageing.

4. There are other major demographic differences between developed and developing countries. While today the overwhelming proportion of older persons in developed countries live in areas classified as urban, the majority of older persons in developing countries live in rural areas. Demographic projections suggest that, by 2025, 82 percent of the population of developed countries will live in urban areas, while less than half of the population of developing countries will live there. In developing countries, the proportion of older persons in rural areas is higher than in urban areas. Although further study is needed on the relationship between ageing and urbanization, the trends suggest that in the future in rural areas of many developing countries there will be a larger population of older persons.

5. Significant differences also exist between developed and developing countries in terms of the kinds of households in which older persons live. In developing countries a large proportion of older persons live in multigenerational households. These differences imply that policy actions will be different in developing and developed countries.

6. The fastest growing group of the older population is the oldest old, that is, those who are 80 old years or more. In 2000, the oldest old numbered 70 million and their numbers are projected to increase to more than five times that over the next 50 years.

7. Older women outnumber older men, increasingly so as age increases. The situation of older women everywhere must be a priority for policy action. Recognizing the differential impact of ageing on women and men is integral to ensuring full equality between women and men and to the development of effective and efficient measures to address the issue. It is therefore critical to ensure the integration of a gender perspective into all policies, programs and legislation.

8. It is essential to integrate the evolving process of global ageing within the larger process of development. Policies on age-

ing deserve close examination from the developmental perspective of a broader life course and a society-wide view, taking into account recent global initiatives and the guiding principles set down by major United Nations conferences and summits.

9. The International Plan of Action on Ageing, 2002 calls for changes in attitudes, policies and practices at all levels in all sectors so that the enormous potential of ageing in the twenty-first century may be fulfilled. Many older persons do age with security and dignity, and also empower themselves to participate within their families and communities. The aim of the International Plan of Action is to ensure that persons everywhere are able to age with security and dignity and to continue to participate in their societies as citizens with full rights. While recognizing that the foundation for a healthy and enriching old age is laid early in life, the Plan is intended to be a practical tool to assist policy makers to focus on the key priorities associated with individual and population ageing. The common features of the nature of ageing and the challenges it presents are acknowledged and specific recommendations are designed to be adapted to the great diversity of circumstances in each country. The Plan recognizes the many different stages of development and the transitions that are taking place in various regions, as well as the interdependence of all countries in a globalizing world.

10. A society for all ages, which was the theme for the 1999 International Year of Older Persons, contained four dimensions: individual lifelong development; multigenerational relationships; the interrelationship between population ageing and development; and the situation of older persons. The International Year helped to advance awareness, research, and policy action worldwide, including efforts to integrate the issue of ageing in all sectors and foster opportunities integral to all phases of life.

11. The major United Nations conferences and summits and special sessions of the General Assembly and review follow-up processes have set goals, objectives and commitments at all levels intended to improve the economic and social conditions of everyone. These provide the context in which the specific contributions and concerns of older persons must be placed. Implementing their provisions would enable older persons to contribute fully and benefit equally from development. There are a number of central themes running through the International Plan of Action on Ageing, 2002 linked to these goals, objectives, and commitments, which include:

(a) The full realization of all human rights and fundamental freedoms of all older persons;

(b) The achievement of secure ageing, which involves reaffirming the goal of eradicating poverty in old age and building on the United Nations Principles for Older Persons;

(c) Empowerment of older persons to fully and effectively participate in the economic, political and social lives of their societies, including through income-generating and voluntary work;

(d) Provision of opportunities for individual development, self-fulfillment and well-being throughout life as well as in late life, through, for example, access to lifelong learning and participation in the community while recognizing that older persons are not one homogenous group;

(e) Ensuring the full enjoyment of economic, social and cultural rights, and civil and political rights of persons and the elimination of all forms of violence and discrimination against older persons;

(f) Commitment to gender equality among older persons through, inter alia, elimination of gender-based discrimination;

(g) Recognition of the crucial importance of families, intergenerational interdependence, solidarity and reciprocity for social development;

(h) Provision of health care, support, and social protection for older persons, including preventive and rehabilitative health care;

(i) Facilitating partnership between all levels of government, civil society, the private sector, and older persons themselves in translating the International Plan of Action into practical action;

(j) Harnessing of scientific research and expertise and realizing the potential of technology to focus on, inter alia, the individual, social and health implications of ageing, in particular in developing countries;

(k) Recognition of the situation of ageing indigenous persons, their unique circumstances and the need to seek means to give them an effective voice in decisions directly affecting them.

12. The promotion and protection of all human rights and fundamental freedoms, including the right to development, is essential for the creation of an inclusive society for all ages in which older persons participate fully and without discrimination and on the basis of equality. Combating discrimination based on age

and promoting the dignity of older persons is fundamental to ensuring the respect that older persons deserve. Promotion and protection of all human rights and fundamental freedoms is important in order to achieve a society for all ages. In this, the reciprocal relationship between and among generations must be nurtured, emphasized, and encouraged through a comprehensive and effective dialogue.

13. The recommendations for action are organized according to three priority directions: older persons and development; advancing health and well-being into old age; and ensuring enabling and supportive environments. The extent to which the lives of older persons are secure is strongly influenced by progress in these three directions. The priority directions are designed to guide policy formulation and implementation towards the specific goal of successful adjustment to an ageing world, in which success is measured in terms of social development, the improvement for older persons in quality of life and in the sustainability of the various systems, formal and informal, that underpin the quality of well-being throughout the life course.

14. Mainstreaming ageing into global agendas is essential. A concerted effort is required to move towards a wide and equitable approach to policy integration. The task is to link ageing to other frameworks for social and economic development and human rights. Whereas specific policies will vary according to country and region, population ageing is a universal force that has the power to shape the future as much as globalization. It is essential to recognize the ability of older persons to contribute to society by taking the lead not only in their own betterment but also in that of society as a whole. Forward thinking calls us to embrace the potential of the ageing population as a basis for future development.

References

General Assembly, United Nations. 1991. "United Nations Principles for Older Persons," Resolution 46/91, adopted December 16, 1991.

Kendall, Henry. 1992. "World Scientists' Warning to Humanity." Cambridge, MA: Union of Concerned Scientists. Accessible at http://www.ucsusa.org/ucs/about/page.cfm?pageID=1009

Madrid International Plan of Action on Ageing. 2002. In *Report of the Second World Assembly on Ageing, Madrid, 8–12 April, 2002.* New York: United Nations.

Malthus, Thomas Robert. 1993 [1798]. *An Essay on the Principle of Population.* Edited by Geoffrey Gilbert. New York: Oxford University Press.

National Academy of Sciences and Royal Society of London. 1992. Joint Statement: "Population Growth, Resource Consumption, and a Sustainable World."

Population Division of the Department of Economic and Social Affairs, United Nations Secretariat. 1995. *Programme of Action Adopted at the International Conference on Population and Development, Cairo, 5–13 September 1994.*

Population Division of the Department of Economic and Social Affairs, United Nations Secretariat. 2004. *World Population Policies 2003: Highlights.* New York: United Nations.

Population Division of the Department of Economic and Social Affairs, United Nations Secretariat. 2004. *World Population in 2300: Proceedings of the United Nations Expert Meeting on World Population in 2300.* New York: United Nations.

Population Division of the Department of Economic and Social Affairs, United Nations Secretariat. 2005. *World Population Prospects: The 2004 Revision: Highlights.* New York: United Nations.

U.S. Bureau of the Census. 2000. "Census Bureau Projects Doubling of Nation's Population by 2100." Press release, January 13, 2000.

U.S. National Security Council. 1974. *National Security Study Memorandum 200: Implications of Worldwide Population Growth for U.S. Security and Overseas Interests.* Washington, DC. NSC classified document (declassified 7/3/89).

8

Directory of Organizations

M any organizations, both public and private, have an interest in population. The purpose of some is simply to collect and disseminate accurate information—for example, the Population Reference Bureau and the U.S. Census Bureau. Other organizations serve an informational function but also have an agenda they seek to promote; this would describe an agency such as the United Nations Population Fund, or UNFPA. And finally, there are organizations, such as Population Connection, Negative Population Growth, and the Population Research Institute, whose reason for being is almost entirely to advance a cause or an agenda. When you consider all the agencies, institutes, and organizations that have a research or policy connection to population, the number reaches well into the hundreds, if not thousands. It would be impossible to list all such organizations here—and fortunately it isn't necessary, since most of those chosen for inclusion have, on their websites, a "links" feature that will quickly generate a large number of related websites. The usual caveat applies: websites are not eternal. For various reasons they are sometimes relocated or renamed or simply disappear.

Carrying Capacity Network (CCN)
2000 P Street, NW, Suite 310
Washington, DC 20036
(202) 296-4548
Fax: (202) 296-4609

carryingcapacity@covad.net
http://www.carryingcapacity.org

Carrying Capacity Network is one of a number of advocacy organizations seeking to educate the public and influence policymakers in the direction of slower population growth. It focuses squarely on *U.S.* population. On its board of advisors are the biodiversity expert Thomas Lovejoy, the alternative energy expert L. Hunter Lovins, the Cornell population expert David Pimentel, and other environmental activists. Among their stated goals are "national revitalization, immigration reduction, economic sustainability, and resource conservation," but the immigration goal seems to outrank the others. CCN subscribes to the view, often associated with ecologist Paul Ehrlich, that citizens of the industrially advanced nations have a much more damaging impact, per capita, on the environment than those in less industrialized nations—hence the need to slow population growth in the United States. Given current demographic patterns, this leads CCN to advocate, at least in the short run, a strict moratorium on further immigration above the 100,000 rate per year.

Publications: CCN posts an "Action Alert" to its website every month or two; these tend to relate mainly to immigration bills proposed or pending in Congress. CCN also sells a number of booklets (originally "Network Bulletins") for $3 each, with titles such as "Is Immigration an Environmental Issue?" Various articles on population, conservation, and sustainability can be downloaded from the website.

Center for Migration Studies (CMS)
209 Flagg Place
Staten Island, NY 10304-1199
(718) 351-8800
Fax: (718) 667-4598
offices @cmsny.org
http://www.cmsny.org

Founded in 1964 and incorporated in 1969, the Center for Migration Studies (CMS) is a nonprofit educational institute devoted to the study of migration. It is one of six such centers worldwide that comprise the Federation of Centers for Migration Studies. Scalabrini was an Italian Catholic prelate (1839–1905) who worked with and for migrants and became known as the "apostle of migrants." Several religious orders devoted to the assistance of migrants have been named after him. The main but not exclusive focus of CMS is on immigration into the United States, and this includes the special needs of refugees. Each year CMS helps organize a legal conference on immigrant and refugee policy held in Washington, D.C.

Publications: CMS publishes the quarterly *International Migration Review*, considered to be the leading journal in the field; it covers all aspects of human mobility. Also published by CMS is a bimonthly magazine, *Migration World*, which is directed to those who are "socially and pastorally involved with immigrants and refugees," and a number of books on migrant history and issues. A free biannual newsletter, *CMS Newsletter*, reports on recent or upcoming activities, publications, and conferences.

Centre for Development and Population Activities (CEDPA)
1400 16th Street, NW, Suite 100
Washington, DC 20036
(202) 667-1142
Fax: (202) 332-4496
cmail@cedpa.org
http://www.cedpa.org/index.html

The Centre for Development and Population Activities (CEDPA) is dedicated to empowering and improving the lives of women and girls worldwide. It aims to ensure that women's priorities are taken fully into account in policy discussions and development planning. To that end, it partners with hundreds of women's organizations around the world, the largest number of which are in Africa, though it is also well represented in Central America and the Caribbean region. Established in 1975, CEDPA has been engaged for decades in capacity-building, leadership training, and the advocacy of gender equity. Many of its alumnae played influential roles in the Cairo conference of 1994 (ICPD). It has been active in specific programs such as AIDS prevention, girls' education, and raising women's political awareness. It takes a strong interest in women's health, especially their reproductive health. CEDPA headquarters are in Washington, D.C., and it operates offices in seven countries, including India, Nigeria, and South Africa.

Publications: CEDPA makes available a wide range of materials in print form and online: training manuals, special-topics booklets, newsletters, and brief reports. The offerings are most extensive in the first two categories. Most publications tend to be rather narrowly focused. A typical booklet might be entitled "Improving Girls' Lives in Egypt: A Decade of Progress."

Committee on Population
The National Academy of Sciences
500 Fifth Street, NW, W1108
Washington, DC 20001
(202) 334-3187
Fax: (202) 334-3829
http://www7.nationalacademies.org/cpop

Little noticed by the public or media—and perhaps preferring it that way—the Committee on Population was created in 1983 by the National Academy of Sciences (NAS), with a mandate to apply demographic science to a range of public-policy issues. There are presently only eleven members of the Committee, all scholars at major universities or research institutes in the United States and abroad. The Committee has issued several influential reports over the years on such topics as the effects of rapid population growth, the link (if any) between population growth and economic development, and the demographic situation of sub-Saharan Africa. In recent years, it has organized panels and workshops on aging, fertility, health, data collection, and population projection. At all times, the work of the Committee is supposed to be guided by a spirit of scientific impartiality. Funding for the Committee's activities comes from government agencies and several private foundations, such as the Rockefeller and the Andrew W. Mellon Foundations.

Publications: In the past several years, the Committee has issued around four new reports per year. Two titles from 2003 were *Cities Transformed: Demographic Change and Its Implications in the Developing World* and *Offspring: Human Fertility Behavior in Biodemographic Perspective*. The reports may be ordered online in hard copy or PDF format, and individual PDF chapters may also be ordered at a discount.

Federation for American Immigration Reform (FAIR)
1666 Connecticut Avenue, NW, Suite 400
Washington, DC 20009

(202) 328-7004
Fax: (202) 387-3447
info@fairus.org
http://www.fairus.org

Given the importance of immigration to current and future levels of U.S. population, it makes sense to become acquainted with national organizations that have an interest in the issue. FAIR is not diffident about where it stands on immigration: it wants *less* of it. FAIR seeks to reduce and then eliminate illegal immigration. It would also have the United States cut legal immigration to more "traditional" levels—it suggests 300,000 annually. A nonprofit, nonpartisan organization with a nationwide membership of over 70,000, FAIR tries to influence public policy in various ways, running ads during political campaigns, testifying in Congress, making its spokespersons available for interviews in the media, doing grassroots organizing, and even litigating in court. The organization was founded in 1978. Its national advisory board includes former Colorado governor Richard Lamm and John Tanton, founder of FAIR and a former president of Zero Population Growth.

Publications: FAIR publishes a monthly newsletter called *Immigration Report*. The more frequently updated e-zine called the *Stein Report*—FAIR's president is Dan Stein—offers current news stories and headlines about (mainly illegal) immigration, with an option for readers to respond online. There are links to many other organizations with an interest in reforming/curbing immigration. The research materials at the website include a page called "Immigration in Your Backyard," which offers an opportunity to pick any state and find out how immigration is impacting it. Bear in mind, however, that FAIR makes no pretense of "giving both sides" of the issue: it is firmly opposed to the continuation of what it calls "mass migration" into the United States.

International Center for Migration, Ethnicity and Citizenship (ICMEC)
65 Fifth Avenue, Room 227
New York, NY 10003
(212) 229-5399
Fax: (212) 989-0504

icmec@newschool.edu
http://www.newschool.edu/icmec

The International Center for Migration, Ethnicity and Citizenship (ICMEC) was founded in 1993 at the New School for Social Research—since renamed the New School University—in New York City. It is devoted to scholarly research on the causes of large-scale international migration and on the most appropriate policy responses. ICMEC provides a forum for debate and reflection on migration matters by scholars, public officials, journalists, and members of the NGO community. Although it takes a strong interest in the *causes* of heavy migration flows, such as the breakup of multiethnic societies and the instabilities attending the end of the Cold War, it is equally interested in the reception given newcomers in the host countries. The Center sponsors, and often collaborates with others in sponsoring, seminars, roundtable discussions, conferences, and symposia on policy issues related to migration, ethnicity, and citizenship.

Publications: The Center has issued a series of working papers that can be ordered for a small fee; most can also be downloaded.

International Organization for Migration (IOM)
17 Route des Morillons
CH-1211 Geneva 19
Switzerland
Tel: +41-22-7179111
Fax: +41-22-7986150
info@iom.int
http://www.iom.int

The mission statement of the International Organization for Migration (IOM) declares its commitment to the principle that "humane and orderly migration benefits migrants and society." Closely allied to the United Nations since its founding in 1951, this intergovernmental body assists refugees and internally displaced persons all over the world. By now it has helped over 12 million people, including Kurds in northern Iraq, East Timorese refugees, and displaced Sudanese in the Darfur region. Assistance can take the form of moving threatened people from their homeland to safer places abroad, repatriating people who had earlier fled their homelands, or simply assisting people who have lost food and shelter where they are. Headquartered in Geneva,

Switzerland, the IOM has offices and operations on every continent. It gives technical assistance to governments facing migration challenges, tries to encourage economic and social development through migration, and upholds the dignity and welfare of migrants—of which, by one recent estimate, there are 185 million around the world. The IOM website offers online information on a variety of migration issues, such as trafficking in migrants, migrant rights, migration-relevant reports and resolutions of the United Nations, and reference information.

Publications: The biennial *World Migration Report* is the IOM's flagship publication; it aims to provide a comprehensive picture of global migration trends. Various other books, surveys, and studies on migration are listed on the IOM website and in their extensive catalog (running to fifty-two pages in 2005). Titles such as *Migrant Transfers as a Development Tool: The Case of Somaliland* (2003) are probably more technical than a general reader would want or need. But others, like *The Human Rights of Migrants* (2001), would interest many students of migration. The IOM also publishes a quarterly journal, *International Migration,* which tackles both theoretical and empirical migration issues from the perspectives of economists, political scientists, demographers, sociologists, and others. A quarterly bulletin (essentially a newsletter) called *Migration* reports on current IOM activities around the world.

International Planned Parenthood Federation (IPPF)
Regent's College
Inner Circle, Regent's Park
London NW1 4NS
United Kingdom
Tel +44 (0)20 7487 7900
Fax +44 (0)20 7487 7950
E-mail info@ippf.org

The International Planned Parenthood Federation (IPPF) is an umbrella for 149 member organizations—like Planned Parenthood Federation of America—that operate in a total of 183 countries. It claims to be the "largest sexual and reproductive health agency in the world." One of the IPPF's founders in 1952 was the birth-control pioneer Margaret Sanger, who served as president of the organization until 1959. Currently, the IPPF operates within a strategic framework based on five A's: adolescents,

AIDS, abortion, access, and advocacy. It tries to secure for young people the right to information about sexuality and reproduction; it works to integrate HIV/AIDS prevention and treatment services into regular reproductive health programs; it seeks to secure women's right to choose, both through lobbying for legal protection of that right and through provision of high-quality abortion services; it tries to ensure access to reproductive health information and services, especially for women who are vulnerable and marginalized (for example, the young and the poor); and it lobbies and advocates for support of reproductive freedoms around the world.

Publications: The IPPF itself issues only a few PDF documents relating to topics such as HIV/AIDS and medical aspects of reproductive health care. A more complete listing of e-publications, press releases, print publications, and other tools may be found at the website of IPPF/WHR; naturally, these deal mainly with the Western Hemisphere Region (WHR).

National Audubon Society
700 Broadway
New York, NY 10003
(212) 979-3000
Fax: (212) 979-3188
http://www.audubon.org/

The great bird artist, John J. Audubon (1785–1851), wrote a first-hand account of what it was like to have the sky darkened for hours by vast numbers of passenger pigeons flying overhead. A few decades after his death, this bird, once the most numerous in North America, was on the verge of extinction (the last one died in 1914). The national organization bearing Audubon's name was founded in 1905 with a mission to "conserve birds, other wildlife, and their habitats." For the last quarter-century the Audubon Society has considered human population a conservation issue, and it has advocated for increased family planning, among other measures, to slow the loss of critical habitats around the globe. It participates in the "Planet" campaign to increase U.S. public awareness of international family planning along with partners like Save the Children, Planned Parenthood, and Population Action International.

Publications: The Society does not issue any publications that regularly focus on the population issue, but its website offers half a dozen online topical "fact sheets" concerning population and the environment, as well as the visually attractive sixteen-page report, *Population and Habitat: Making the Connection.*

National Wildlife Federation (NWF)
11100 Wildlife Center Drive
Reston, VA 20190-5362
(800) 822-9919
http://www.nwf.org

Like the National Audubon Society—and unlike the Sierra Club—the National Wildlife Federation (NWF) has opted to keep addressing population as an environmental issue. (None of the three organizations currently has an official position on immigration levels into the United States.) Founded in 1936, the NWF has four million members and supporters. Its annual budget, in the range of $100 million, exceeds those of Audubon and Sierra. While population per se is not NWF's highest-priority issue, it does have the program category of Population and Environment. The NWF strongly supports international family planning. It wants the United States to fund such activities more fully and lift the restrictions presently placed on the funding. Making the connection between poverty and the overexploitation of natural resources, the NWF also pushes for more generous U.S. support of efforts to meet the Millennium Development Goals adopted at the United Nations in 2000. (In this drive it is joined by a conservation ally, the National Audubon Society.)

Publications: NWF's rich panoply of photogenic materials, in pamphlets, reports, calendars, and books, indirectly advances the message that wildlife at its best is endangered by the growth of human numbers. In addition, the Federation issues online fact sheets relating more directly to the population issue. These are found under the website heading Population and Environment. Also posted is a set of frequently asked questions on the subject of population and the current issue of *Crowds & Critters,* the newsletter of the Population and Environment program.

Negative Population Growth (NPG)
2861 Duke Street., Suite 36
Alexandria, VA 22314
(703) 370-9510
Fax: (703) 370-9514
npg@npg.org
http://www.npg.org

Founded in 1972, Negative Population Growth (NPG) is a membership organization of over 25,000 that calls itself "the leading voice in the population awareness movement." NPG is quite explicit about its long-term goal: to see the population of the United States *decline* to a level of 150 to 200 million, through voluntary incentives for smaller families and tighter immigration policies. By tighter immigration, NPG means 100,000 to 200,000 annually—at least a million below the current rate. NPG holds that a smaller national population would ensure less strain on ecosystems, less depletion of natural resources, and a better quality of life. Its website features a variety of NPG publications (some rather dated), population clocks for both the United States and the world, polling numbers for public attitudes about population, and links to other organizations concerned with population, immigration, and the environment.

Publications: NPG publishes a quarterly newsletter for its members and maintains a weekly population news listserve. Its website offers a number of special reports and position papers available for downloading.

Population Action International (PAI)
1300 Nineteenth Street, NW, Second Floor
Washington, DC 20036
(202) 557-3400
Fax: (202) 728-4177
pai@popact.org
http://www.populationaction.org

Population Action International (PAI) believes that "every person who wants reproductive health services should have access to them." A relatively small, privately funded organization, PAI seeks to build public support for policies and programs that can slow population growth, particularly in developing countries.

The policies advocated by PAI are generally in line with the "program of action" adopted by the International Conference on Population and Development (Cairo, 1994), such as universal access to family planning, improved health care for women, and more gender equality. PAI lobbies Congress both directly and indirectly to enlarge U.S. funding of international population efforts; it also interacts with the United Nations and other international agencies on matters related to population. It arranges seminars, briefings, and roundtables, and it maintains an informative website with links to like-minded organizations and downloadable policy briefs on various population issues. PAI was established in 1965 as the Population Crisis Committee. It is funded entirely by foundations (Rockefeller, Packard, Pew, Rasmussen, etc.) and individuals.

Publications: PAI publishes a variety of fact sheets, occasional papers, wall charts, and books, all listed on its website.

Population Communications International (PCI)
777 United Nations Plaza—5th Floor
44th Street at 1st Avenue
New York, NY 10017
(212) 687-3366
Fax: (212) 661-4188
info@population.org
http://www.population.org

For over twenty years, Population Communications International (PCI) has been producing country-specific soap operas, for both radio and television, which incorporate messages of positive decision-making in regard to sex, reproductive health, gender roles, and family planning. The overall purpose is to change behavior in ways that conform to the goals established at the Cairo conference in 1994 (International Conference on Population and Development). China, India, Pakistan, Brazil, and Tanzania are among the more than twenty-five countries on four continents where PCI has worked with local partner organizations to research and produce serial dramas. Local input and research are critical in tailoring the programs to the specific cultural values of each country. PCI also helps evaluate, systematically, the impact of its programs. A recent five-year study found that Tanzanians living in the areas to which a PCI radio drama was broadcast altered their sexual behavior in ways that were significantly helpful for HIV/AIDS prevention.

Publications: PCI's *Annual Report* has a great deal of information about the mission and recent accomplishments of the organization, and audio clips of several PCI productions can be accessed online.

Population Connection
1400 Sixteenth Street NW, Suite 320
Washington, DC 20036
(202) 332-2200
Toll free 1-800-POP-1956
Fax: (202) 332-2302
info@populationconnection.org
http://www.populationconnection.org

Population Connection, formerly known as Zero Population Growth (ZPG), promotes "progressive action" to achieve a sustainable balance between the planet's resources and its population. One of the founders of ZPG in 1968 was Paul Ehrlich, author of *The Population Bomb.* The organization remains, despite its re-branding in 2002, an exemplar of the traditional neo-Malthusian stance on world population—namely, one of intense concern about "overpopulation." Population Connection firmly supports the United Nations Population Fund, international family planning, women's right to choose, and every kind of voluntary effort to curb global overpopulation. It lobbies Congress and engages in publicity campaigns. Its Legislative Action Center allows one to find out how each elected federal officeholder voted on key population-related issues *and* to send an e-mail to any or all of them. Population education is a major priority of Population Connection, with extensive lesson plans and curricular materials for schools downloadable from the website. Most such materials relate to the K-12 grade levels, but the Campus Outreach Program also arranges presentations and workshops on college campuses.

Publications: Issued quarterly, *the reporter* (formerly *The ZPG Reporter*) covers various population issues in the news. The monthly *Campus Activist Update* is addressed to an audience of college-age activists. Both publications can be downloaded from the website.

Population Council
One Dag Hammarskjold Plaza
New York, NY 10017
(212) 339-0500
Fax: (212) 755-6052
pubinfo@popcouncil.org
http://www.popcouncil.org

For more than half a century, the Population Council has funded and conducted research on reproductive health, fertility regulation, and family planning. With a worldwide staff of over 550 and an annual budget of roughly $70 million, it is an institution of global influence. In developing countries, it collaborates with governments and nongovernmental organizations to enhance the quality of family-planning programs. It sponsors research in over fifty developing countries, in Asia, Africa, and Latin America. Through a program of awards, fellowships, training, and collaborations, it works to increase professional expertise in the developing nations. Although the Population Council sponsors and publishes research on family structure, gender relations, and other social-demographic issues, it is probably better known to the public for having developed the contraceptive device "Norplant" and several modern versions of the intrauterine device (IUD). In recent years, it has stepped into a void left by the major U.S. pharmaceutical companies and sponsored the introduction of the so-called abortion pill, RU 486. (The drug became available to American women in 2000 under the brand name Mifeprex.) The Council is also pursuing the development of other contraceptive techniques, such as patches and implants. External funding for the Population Council comes from governments, NGOs, corporations, individuals, and foundations. The Council was founded in 1952 by John D. Rockefeller III.

Publications: Population Briefs, published three times a year, is a research newsletter for population specialists, distributed at no charge, with coverage of demographic and reproductive news and updates on the achievements of Council-sponsored programs. *Studies in Family Planning* is a peer-reviewed quarterly journal with articles and commentary on family-planning programs in (mainly) Africa and Asia. *Population and Development Review* has been a leading quarterly journal of demography since 1975. Scholarly yet readable, it explores economic, political, and sociological aspects of population, present and past.

The Population Institute (PI)
107 Second Street, NE
Washington, DC 20002
(202) 544-3300
Fax: (202) 544-0068
web@populationinstitute.org
http://www.populationinstitute.org

The Population Institute (PI), established in 1969 and headed by the peripatetic Werner Fornos until his retirement in 2005, advocates and educates on the subject of population. It seeks to raise awareness—among students, the media, and legislators—of the need for a more sustainable pace of global population growth. PI strongly supports U.S. assistance to international family-planning programs. Its own funding comes from foundations, corporations, and individuals, but not from the government. As part of its effort to heighten awareness of the population issue, the Institute sponsors a variety of programs and campaigns, including its Educate America Campaign, World Population Awareness Week, Global Media Awards, and Future Leaders of the World Program. The Media Awards are given out annually to journals and journalists judged to have achieved excellence in their population reporting. The Institute boasts a network of 100,000 volunteers who work to support its aims.

Publications: The Population Institute publishes POPLINE, a bimonthly newspaper covering recent developments in the population field. It is distributed, at no charge, to legislators, the media, and activists. Educators may receive POPLINE at no cost; others pay $25. Also issued by the Institute is a *21st Century Monograph* series ($7.25 each) that focuses on the linkages between population and literacy, food, environment, health, and women's empowerment.

Population Reference Bureau (PRB)
1875 Connecticut Avenue, NW, Suite 520
Washington, DC 20009-5728
(202) 483-1100
Toll free 1-(800)-877-9881
Fax: (202) 328-3937
popref@prb.org
http://www.prb.org

Founded in 1929, the Population Reference Bureau (PRB) has a well-earned reputation for producing clear, accurate, and timely population information, both for the United States and the rest of the world. By describing itself as a nonprofit, *nonadvocacy* organization (emphasis added), PRB hints at one of the ways it differs from several other groups with the word "population" in their titles: it draws no policy conclusions from the data it presents. Nor does it do any lobbying to advance a political or social agenda. Its concern is only with the facts and their accurate dissemination. That lofty ideal does not prevent the PRB from being committed to research, education, and outreach, abroad and at home. Its professional staff monitors, and reports on, trends in population and a range of social issues that are linked to population, such as crime, aging, the status of minorities, and the environment. PRB provides technical services to governments and nongovernmental organizations. It runs seminars, training courses, and briefings to assist various audiences in understanding population issues. It is a resource for the print and broadcast media, and its comprehensive library makes it a valuable resource for scholars and researchers as well. PRB takes an active interest in education, making available a wide array of curricular materials to teachers, especially at the middle and high school levels.

Publications: PRB publishes the highly useful *World Population Data Sheet (WPDS)* in wall-poster format. For every country and region of the world the *WPDS* presents the most recent data on the birthrate, death rate, life expectancy, total fertility rate, population projections (to the years 2025 and 2050), and much more. On a less frequent basis, PRB also has issued several other data sheets, on topics ranging from "women of our world" to "the world's youth." The quarterly *Population Bulletin* covers various population-related topics in depth; they can be either U.S.-oriented or international in scope. *Population Today* is the PRB newsletter. *PRB Reports on America,* published occasionally, deal with important U.S. population issues and their impact on society.

Population Research Institute (PRI)
1190 Progress Drive, Suite 2D
P.O. Box 1559
Front Royal, VA 22630
(540) 622-5240

Fax: (540) 622-2728
pri@pop.org
Web: www.pop.org

The Population Research Institute (PRI) is a conservative pro-life organization that seeks to debunk the "myth" of overpopulation, while "defending human life" and stopping "human rights abuses" committed in the name of family planning. It is not to be confused with the identically named Institute at Pennsylvania State University, which is a purely academic entity offering graduate training in demography. The PRI in Virginia was founded in 1989 by Paul Marx, a Benedictine priest. It came to prominence a few years ago by leveling accusations that the UNFPA was complicit in Chinese population-policy abuses, accusations that became the ostensible basis for President Bush's cutoff of U.S. financial support to that UN agency.

Publications: The bimonthly *PRI Review* offers articles that are written in op-ed style, many by PRI president Steven Mosher and many on the evils of abortion, Chinese population policy, and feminism. The *PRI Weekly Briefing* is much the same.

United Nations Population Division (UNPD)
2 United Nations Plaza, Rm. DC2-1950
New York, NY 10017
(212) 963-3179
Fax (212) 963-2147

Within the United Nations' Department of Economic and Social Affairs, the Population Division (UNPD) has a broad charge: to keep tabs on population developments and trends around the world—and keep the rest of us informed. Its functions are perhaps best described as scientific and administrative, unlike the UNFPA (see next entry), which operates in a more practical and policy-implementing mode. The public knows the UNPD mainly through its various demographic publications, like its well-publicized population projections. But it also renders support services to the General Assembly and other elements of the UN system, supports governments around the world with timely data collection and assistance in building up their own statistical capabilities, and keeps track of global progress toward achieving the aims of the ICPD Program of Action (Cairo, 1994). Longtime director Joseph Chamie retired in 2004; the new director is Hania Zlotnik.

Publications: This is the place to go for timely and authoritative accounts of global demographics. Most UNPD publications are available online as well as in hard copy. The following is just a sampling of what the UNPD publishes periodically: *World Population Prospects: The 2004 Revision, World Population to 2300, World Fertility Report, World Population Policies, World Contraceptive Use,* and *Population and HIV/AIDS 2005* (wall chart). UNPD also manages the website for POPIN, the UN population information network, which is a sort of electronic clearinghouse of demographic information from around the world.

United Nations Population Fund (UNFPA)
220 East 42nd Street
New York, NY 10017
(212) 297-5000
Fax: (212) 370-0201
hq@unfpa.org
http://www.unfpa.org

A UN agency created in 1969, the UNFPA is the world's largest multilateral source of funding for family-planning programs. Its mission is to ensure that "every pregnancy is wanted, every birth is safe, and every young person is free of HIV/AIDS." That is its mandate under the Program of Action adopted in 1994 at the International Conference on Population and Development (ICPD), held in Cairo. The UNFPA works toward the goals of lower maternal and child mortality, universal access to primary education for children of both sexes, and universal access to reproductive health care, especially for women. It offers technical and financial assistance to developing countries as they design and implement their own national population programs. UNFPA funding comes from contributions of governments that are separate from their normal UN dues. The United States was a key supporter of the UNFPA at its inception. In recent years, domestic political considerations have caused that support to waver. Congress regularly authorizes a contribution, but since 2002 the Bush administration has held back the funds. The Netherlands currently provides more funding than any other nation.

Publications: From 1978 onward, the annual *State of World Population* has presented in-depth reports on selected population issues, such as urbanization, adolescent health and rights, the environment, and poverty. The 2004 report was subtitled *The Cairo Con-*

sensus at Ten: Population, Reproductive Health and the Global Effort to End Poverty. The *Annual Report* of the UNFPA is a good place to learn more about what the Fund does and where; its thirty-six pages can be read online.

United States Agency for International Development (USAID)
Ronald Reagan Building
Washington, DC 20523-1000
(202) 712-0000
Fax (202) 216-3524
pinquiries@usaid.gov
www.usaid.gov

Since its creation in 1961, USAID has been the main conduit for American technical and financial assistance to foreign countries. Its mission includes helping countries recover from natural disasters, helping them develop out of poverty, and facilitating their transition to democracy. In 1967, Congress specifically mandated that AID provide funds for family-planning efforts abroad. Two years later, President Nixon strongly endorsed U.S. funding of such programs, and they have had steady support in Congress ever since. Levels of funding have varied, however. The highest AID appropriation for family planning came in 1996, at $542 million. In all recent years President Bush has budgeted $425 million for this program within AID. Most observers consider the United States a leader in supporting international family planning, though less so today than in the past. AID's overall goal for these programs is to assist couples in having the number of children they want, with enough spacing—ideally three to five years—to maintain the health of both mother and children. The Agency has recently been working to integrate its programs in family planning, child and maternal health, and HIV/AIDS prevention.

Publications: The USAID Office of Population and Reproductive Health has placed a few items of interest on the AID website: a timeline, a list of the Agency's achievements in family planning, and FAQs. A handy listing of the restrictions Congress has placed on USAID-funded activities is given at http://www.usaid.gov/our_work/global_health/pop/mcpolicy.html.

United States Census Bureau
International Programs Center
Washington, DC 20233-8800
Fax: (301) 457-3034
ipc@census.gov
http://www.census.gov/ipc/www

Anyone who thinks the job of the U.S. Census Bureau is limited to counting Americans every ten years should think again. It's true that the Bureau has long produced population estimates for virtually every locality in the United States, from the states and counties to metropolitan areas and Puerto Rican *municipios*. (It also produces tremendous quantities of data on U.S. income, poverty, health, and education.) But probably of most interest to those studying world population is the International Programs Center, or IPC, where a wealth of demographic information on all the world's countries and regions can be obtained either in print or online. Much of this information is free; the rest is available at modest cost either from the Bureau itself (Atlanta office) or from the Government Printing Office in Washington. At the heart of the IPC's data-gathering work is something called the International Data Base (IDB), a computerized data bank covering demographic and socioeconomic indicators for 227 countries and areas of the world. Online, one can tap into this statistical storehouse in creative ways, such as ordering up a customized table on infant mortality rates, male and female, in the less developed countries from 1985 to 2005. Information is also available on fertility rates, migration, marital status, family planning, literacy, and labor force activity for most nations, and in many cases the data extend back to 1950. There is an option for downloading the data to one's own computer.

Publications: The IPC issues a multitude of technical reports and papers, many on an occasional basis, all indexed at the website. Their main publication, however, is the *Global Population Profile,* which comes out biennially. The most recent is for 2002.

Worldwatch Institute
1776 Massachusetts Avenue, NW
Washington, DC 20036-1904
(202) 452-1999

Fax: (202) 296-7365
worldwatch@worldwatch.org
www.worldwatch.org

Worldwatch is one of the best-known environmentalist organizations in the world. Founded in 1974 by Lester Brown and located in the nation's capital, its mission is to work for a society that is "environmentally sustainable" and "socially just." Global population has been a focus of interest all along, but in keeping with the new paradigm that has emerged in the past decade, Worldwatch now addresses the population issue within a broader context of concerns about gender equity, health, the environment, and sustainability. Worldwatch monitors a number of global environmental "threats," from topsoil erosion to greenhouse gases. Its core research staff of fourteen turns out "cutting-edge analysis" of these developments on a regular basis and in so readable a form that it routinely finds its way into mainstream media outlets. Worldwatch is supported financially by such foundations as Ford, Hewlett, MacArthur, Rockefeller, and Packard.

Publications: The institute's flagship publication is *State of the World,* published annually since 1984. Each year Worldwatch identifies and analyzes in depth an issue (in 2005, global security) of importance for a sustainable future. Another report published annually by Worldwatch is *Vital Signs,* which, since 1992, has laid out a variety of key trends for the economy and environment both graphically and in text. Other publications include the bimonthly magazine *World Watch,* a series of *Worldwatch Papers* (over 150 titles; $7 each), and a small number of environmental books. News "briefs" and "releases" and issue "alerts" also pour forth continuously from the Institute.

9

Selected Print and Nonprint Resources

This chapter offers an extensive listing of resources on world population issues, ranging from standard reference works to videos and websites. In a time when Internet search engines are loaded with billions of words and *trillions* of data bits, one's first impulse in looking for answers to a population-related question is to go online. That is not necessarily a bad idea. Some of the websites listed below are extraordinarily useful. But there are many *print* resources, too, that can provide quick answers to questions and sometimes much fuller explorations of issues than will be found at the typical website. A well-stocked university or public library ought to have most of the works listed below. Print resources have been arranged in two categories: monographs and yearbooks/handbooks/data sheets. In the first category are books that deal with population history and policy, population debates, migration, resource limits, trends for the future, and personal reflections. In the second category are works that normally are published on an annual or biennial schedule to reflect the latest population data. At this writing, all the books or booklets listed are in print; the ISBN numbers are for paperback editions whenever that is an option.

Monographs

Barry, John M. *The Great Influenza: The Epic Story of the Deadliest Plague in History.* New York: Penguin, 2005. 560 pages. ISBN 0-14303-448-0.

It is now going on a century since the influenza pandemic of 1918 killed at least 50 million people, and today only AIDS rivals the flu as an ongoing global infectious threat (bioterrorism aside). The story of the 1918 pandemic has been told before, and well. What Barry adds to earlier accounts is a closer attention to U.S. political, institutional, and personal details that help us see the full historical significance of what happened. The flu took a global toll, but much of the story is appropriately told through an American lens: the disease originated at an army camp in Kansas; it was spread to Europe by American troops (World War I); it was U.S. government officials who insisted that the troops be sent overseas despite warnings of the risks of disease spread; and the U.S. medical establishment made a heroic but unsuccessful attempt to contain, and decode the mystery of, the disease. There are more succinct accounts of the 1918 pandemic than Barry's but none more gripping.

Borjas, George J. *Heaven's Door: Immigration Policy and the American Economy.* Princeton, NJ: Princeton University Press, 1999. 288 pages. ISBN 0-691-08896-9.

This book has been much praised, and deservedly so, for the clarity it brings to the issue of U.S. immigration policy. Borjas, who as a boy in the early 1960s was a refugee from Castro's Cuba and who now teaches public policy at Harvard's Kennedy School of Government, takes a clear-eyed view of the costs and benefits of immigration to various concerned parties—native-born Americans, immigrants themselves, and those left behind in the sending countries. He insists that the facts about immigration, in themselves, tell us nothing about the direction in which we should go with policy. We must first answer some important questions about whose interests we rank highest and what kinds of changes we are willing to tolerate in the slicing of the economic pie as a result of immigration. Borjas argues that the current wave of immigrants (around a million a year) is massive enough that we are justified in calling this era the "Second Great Migration" in U.S. history. What troubles Borjas and others are the declining education levels and skills of the recent arrivals, which intensify competition for low-skill, low-wage jobs in the United States and thus harm the least-skilled native workers. In its current pattern, he argues, immigration is tending to shift income away from native workers toward business owners and consumers. The kind of immigration reform he proposes would favor the entry of skilled workers and lower the overall annual quota of immigration to about half a million.

Bouvier, Leon F., and Jane T. Bertrand. *World Population: Challenges for the 21st Century.* Santa Ana, CA: Seven Locks Press, 1999. 214 pages. ISBN 0-929765-66-4.

The basic plan of this book is to review demographic patterns and shifts that occurred in the late twentieth century and then assess their probable impact on populations in the twenty-first century. But in execution the book turns out to be a loosely organized set of reflections and speculations on population, presented in a lively, engaging prose style, and tilted toward a U.S. readership. The authors, professors at Old Dominion and Johns Hopkins Universities, respectively, are alert to the long-term consequences of low fertility in the developed nations and high fertility in the rest of the world. The most notable effect of this fertility differential will be mounting immigration pressure on the developed nations. (Bouvier has written on this subject before.) For the United States, the recommended policy is twofold: first, *resist* the rising immigration pressures and hold the numbers of immigrants to more manageable, or assimilable, levels; and second, do what it takes to ensure that those who immigrate are given the fullest opportunity to advance themselves socially and economically into the mainstream of American life. Encouraging lower birthrates in the developing countries is the other side of the policy. The authors strongly favor generous funding for such efforts.

Bowden, Rob. *An Overcrowded World?* 21st Century Debates series. Chicago: Raintree, 2002. 64 pages. ISBN 0739848720.

This short introduction to the topic of world population might fit very well into a middle school unit on global issues. It lays out the optimistic view that population will continue to grow at rates that are sustainable *and* the pessimistic view that population is already beyond the planet's carrying capacity. The discussion is lively and accessible enough to convince young readers that population is an important issue for their futures.

Brown, Lester R., Gary Gardner, and Brian Halweil. *Beyond Malthus: Nineteen Dimensions of the Population Challenge.* New York: W. W. Norton, 1999. 167 pages. ISBN 0-393-31906-7.

This study from the Worldwatch Institute echoes some themes from two earlier Worldwatch books, *Full House* and *Who Will Feed China?* Even though worldwide population growth has slowed, it certainly has not become a nonissue. In the years ahead, we can expect difficulties with each of the following dimensions of human well-being: grain production, freshwater supplies, biodiversity, energy, oceanic fish catches, meat production, infectious diseases, cropland acreage, forests, climate change, materials for construction and other uses, urbanization, protected wildlife areas, and waste disposal, as well as the more socially defined issues of jobs, housing, education, internal and international conflict, and income levels. Given the long list of topics covered here, and the relatively short length of the book, truly in-depth analysis can hardly be expected. But important questions are raised, and for those who want to dig deeper, there are footnotes to be followed up.

Caplow, Theodore, Louis Hicks, and Ben J. Wattenberg. *The First Measured Century: An Illustrated Guide to Trends in America, 1900–2000.* Washington, DC: American Enterprise Institute Press, 2001. 308 pages. ISBN 0-84474138-8.

This book presents a host of demographic, economic, and social trends for the United States across the twentieth century using a format of a short essay on one page and a related graph on the other. Of the fifteen chapters, at least three are directly relevant to the study (or teaching) of U.S. population trends: "Population," "Family," and "Health." To give a sense of the breadth of coverage, the "Population" chapter includes the following topics: total population, population growth rate, life expectancy, changing age structure, centenarians, geographic distribution, urban-rural breakdown, national origins of immigrants, proportion of foreign-born and minorities in the total U.S. population, and ethnic composition of the ten largest U.S. cities. A subject index and footnote section will be useful to many readers. One of the authors, Ben J. Wattenberg of the American Enterprise Institute, has built a reputation as an acute observer of American and world population trends. His 1987 book *The Birth Dearth* was one of the first efforts to outline the social and political consequences of declining fertility in the West.

Castles, Stephen, and Mark J. Miller. *The Age of Migration: International Population Movements in the Modern World.* 3rd ed. New York: Guilford Press, 2003. 338 pages. ISBN 0-57230-900-8.

This book, by an Australian sociologist and an American political scientist, offers a good all-around treatment of the international migration process, stressing the way that migration creates (or enlarges) ethnic minorities in the countries of destination, and thus alters both the social and political dynamic within those countries. Other broad tendencies of recent years include the globalization and acceleration of migration: more and more countries are becoming involved, at higher rates of migratory flow. Also observable, say the authors, is a kind of flexibility of reasons for migrating, so that a particular flow, or "chain," that begins for one reason (say, for political asylum) can sustain itself for quite different reasons (economic advancement, for example, or family reunification). These reasons can greatly complicate the task of governments in formulating migration policy. There is a chapter on the history of international migration before 1945, another on migration *since* 1945, and an interesting chapter comparing the migration experiences of Germany and Australia. What does not get much attention here (nor in most other books in this field) is migration *within* the developing world.

Cohen, Joel. *How Many People Can the Earth Support?* New York: W. W. Norton & Company, 1995. 542 pages. ISBN 0-393-31495-2.

This study of the Earth's carrying capacity has become a modern classic. Cohen tackles the title question with gusto but also with the care and precision of a man schooled in the rigors of the scientific method. He demonstrates that there are many ways to speculate about the maximum human population of our planet and many ways to translate those speculations into hard numbers. Cohen has examined every approach thoroughly; his book is packed with data, graphs, analysis, and quotations. Yet he retains a healthy skepticism about the entire exercise, as evident in his Law of Prediction, which states: "The more confidence someone places in an unconditional prediction of what will happen in human affairs, the less confidence you should place in that prediction" (p. 134). The key conclusion of the book is captured in the title of the penultimate chapter: "Entering the Zone." It opens with these sobering words: "The human population of the Earth now travels in the zone where a substantial fraction of scholars have estimated upper limits on human population size" (p. 367). Cohen's work is unlikely to be superseded any time soon.

Cook, Noble David. *Born to Die: Disease and New World Conquest (1492–1650)*. Cambridge: Cambridge University Press, 1998. 272 pages. ISBN 0-521-62730-3.

One of the most interesting (if saddening) ways to learn about demographic processes is to study historical episodes of drastic population decline. A particularly striking case, vividly rendered in *Born to Die*, is that of European contact with the indigenous peoples of the Western Hemisphere. Europeans arrived in waves, beginning in 1492, and made it clear wherever they went, from the Hudson Bay to the southernmost tip of South America, that they intended to subdue local Amerindian populations—by force if necessary. But all too often, force was not needed because the infectious diseases brought in by the "conquerors" effectively did the conquering. The Aztecs, Incas, and other indigenous peoples could not resist what they had never been exposed to: smallpox, typhus, measles, influenza, malaria, yellow fever, and plague. The resulting pandemics and depopulation almost defy comprehension. Cook knows his subject well, having written on it several times before.

Diamond, Jared. *Collapse: How Societies Choose to Fail or Succeed*. New York: Viking, 2005. 576 pages. ISBN 0-670-03337-5.

Jared Diamond, a professor of physiology at UCLA, wrote about the rise of civilizations in his Pulitzer Prize-winning *Guns, Germs, and Steel* (1996). In what might be considered a sequel, Diamond turns his attention in *Collapse* to the decline—sometimes mysterious and haunting—of certain societies in the past. An overarching theme is the human capacity to ignore environmental limits, even when doing so puts at risk the very survival of the tribe, colony, or nation. Rapid population growth, though never the sole factor in a societal collapse, plays a supporting role in a number of them. Chapter 10, "Malthus in Africa: Rwanda's Genocide," is a case in point. The conventional account of the 1994 genocide in Rwanda puts the blame for mass murder on ethnic hatreds between Hutus and Tutsis, fanned by power-hungry political extremists. Diamond looks deeper and finds a country that, by the early 1990s, had a population density higher in some regions than Bangladesh, the world's most densely populated agricultural nation. Growing land scarcity fueled widespread property disputes and formed the backdrop for rising levels of societal violence. Other chapters explore the demise of the Anasazi and Maya, the prehistoric Polynesians on Easter Island, and Viking colonists in Greenland, among others. Diamond draws some disturbing parallels between past and present societies, yet reveals himself late in the book as a "cautious optimist."

Eberstadt, Nicholas. *Prosperous Paupers and Other Population Problems.* New Brunswick, NJ: Transaction Publishers, 2000. 272 pages. ISBN 1-56000-423-1.

Eberstadt has been writing on global *de*population since 1997. In this book he explores the full implications of a continued trend toward lower fertility around the world, which could spell a rapid graying of populations, significant shifts in the population shares of countries and continents, changes in the workforce, potential crises in the support of the elderly, and a transformation in the traditional idea of the family. Many people in the future may have no siblings, aunts, uncles, cousins, nieces, or nephews, but only direct ancestors and single offspring. Eberstadt likes to take the demographic road "less traveled by"; the eleven essays in this volume, ten of them revised or reprinted from other places, constitute an alternative take on many of the major population issues of the day. Few of them will win approval from population activists or the "global [population] policy apparatus," which, in Eberstadt's view, is reflexively antinatalist.

Evans, Lloyd T. *Feeding the Ten Billion: Plants and Population Growth.* Cambridge: Cambridge University Press, 1998. 247 pages. ISBN 0-521-64685-5.

The author, a distinguished plant physiologist, wrote this book in part to update the sort of question Malthus was posing two centuries ago. How will we manage to feed the population we expect to have by the middle of the twenty-first century? (The United Nations now expects slightly more than *nine* rather than ten billion people, but the question is still there.) Getting to the answer involves a long journey through centuries of scientific discoveries and developments. Fortunately, Evans has a knack for making science palatable. Among his conclusions: we will need to depend on agricultural research just as much in the future as we have in the past, and the bulk of the increased food production of the coming half-century will need to be achieved in Asia and Africa.

Homer-Dixon, Thomas F. *Environment, Scarcity, and Violence.* Princeton, NJ: Princeton University Press, 2001. 272 pages. ISBN 0-691-08979-5.

Thomas Homer-Dixon, a political scientist at the University of Toronto, fears that one version of the Malthusian nightmare—too many people, resulting in human dislocation, distress, and even death—may have begun to be realized in several parts of the world. Homer-Dixon's version links population growth to rising pressures on renewable resources such as forests, freshwater supplies, and croplands, and ultimately, in the presence of other kinds of social and political stress, to the outbreak of violence. Societies with stable governments, educated citizens, and efficient markets have often been able to overcome resource pressures with innovations. But when those advantages are lacking, one sees the breakdown of civil order, whether in the form of ethnic conflict, urban disorders, or insurrection. Homer-Dixon's theorizing is never crude and never without empirical support. (His examples are drawn from Mexico, Africa, and other places.) The threats he identifies appear substantial, especially in light of the dependence half the world's people place on local renewable resources for their well-being. The book's extensive footnotes and bibliography will allow readers to pursue this important topic in several directions.

Huggins, Laura E., and Hanna Skandera. *Population Puzzle: Boom or Bust?* Stanford, CA: Hoover Institution Press, 2004. 425 pages. ISBN 0-8179-4532-6.

Just about every controversial or near-controversial aspect of world population gets some coverage in this reader. Topics include basic theory (from Malthus onward), ethics, hunger, natural resources, pollution, energy, quality of life, mortality and fertility trends, migration, and demographic prediction. The selected readings are comprehensive and well-chosen. Some are a bit dated, and most are relatively short, but that does not keep this from being a satisfying introduction to the range of intellectual and policy challenges arising from population.

Isbister, John. *The Immigration Debate: Remaking America.* West Hartford, CT: Kumarian Press, 1996. 262 pages. ISBN 1-56549-053-3.

Slightly dated, this book still offers one of the best introductions to the subject of immigration into the United States. Isbister, an economist at the University of California, Santa Cruz, addresses the economic, political, historical, and moral aspects of immigration in prose that is clear enough for any general reader. One issue he focuses on is whether the labor market skills of recent immigrants have deteriorated in comparison with earlier immigrants. This issue has been hotly debated by professional economists and, as the author makes clear, remains unsettled. An interesting final chapter rehearses the ethical arguments both for and against an open border policy. Overall, Isbister sees more long-term rewards than risks—though he concedes the risks—in maintaining the current high rate of immigration into the United States.

Jain, Anrudh K. (ed). *Do Population Policies Matter? Fertility and Politics in Egypt, India, Kenya, and Mexico.* New York: The Population Council, 1998. 203 pages. ISBN 0-87834-091-2.

This volume explores in depth the political and historical contexts within which population policies in four countries have been formulated, implemented, and evaluated. For anyone who may naively have thought that a country's transition from high to low fertility was a simple process, these essays will prove eye-opening. Many stakeholders have an input into the design of population programs, be they women's groups, NGOs, government bureaucracies, donor countries, religious leaders, academics and other policy elites, the media, or the medical establishment. The authors of these four case studies are mainly sociologists and economists. Anrudh Jain, of the Population Council in New York, provides an overview chapter on "population policies that matter" and a short concluding chapter on the future of population policies.

Lee, James Z., and Wang Feng. *One Quarter of Humanity: Malthusian Mythology and Chinese Realities, 1700–2000.* Cambridge, MA: Harvard University Press, 2001. 268 pages. ISBN 0-674-00709-3.

From as early as the eighteenth century, Western observers have believed that Chinese demographic behavior differed from that of Europeans. One sees this, for example, in the writings of the economists Adam Smith and Thomas Malthus. Lee and Feng's book makes clear that, while Malthus and others got many details wrong, their assertion of *distinctive* Chinese population practices was fundamentally correct. From 1700 to the present, Chinese strategies for regulating population have included high rates of abortion and female infanticide, low male rates of marriage, low fertility within marriage, and high rates of adoption. Given China's status as the world's most populous nation, and given the controversy over its one-child policy, this book should be of interest to many readers.

Livi-Bacci, Massimo. *A Concise History of World Population.* 3rd ed. Malden, MA: Blackwell Publishers, 2001. 251 pages. ISBN 0-631-22335-5.

This selective survey of the theory, biology, history, and policy of world population comes from one of Europe's leading demographers. Livi-Bacci builds an analytical framework within which human populations are seen as making compromises between forces of constraint and forces of choice. *Constraining* factors include climate, disease, limited food and energy supplies, and environmental quality; the *choices* for man include flexible strategies of marriage and reproduction, defenses against disease, and migration from less to more favorable locations. This conceptual framework comes to life in chapters that explore historical episodes of demographic expansion and decline, as well as contemporary examples of population dynamics. Some of the graphs are tricky enough to challenge the uninitiated, but the main lines of argument are clear enough even without graphs. In its discussion of the current world situation, the book lingers much longer on India and China than Africa, which serves to remind us that Livi-Bacci has written a *concise,* not a *complete,* account of world population. A fourth edition is planned.

Longman, Phillip. *The Empty Cradle: How Falling Birthrates Threaten World Prosperity and What to Do about It.* New York: Basic Books, 2004. 240 pages. ISBN 0-465-05050-6.

This well-written book touches upon some important policy aspects of the new demographic reality we face—slowing population growth rates. One assumes it was the publisher who insisted on the silly subtitle with which this volume is burdened. Longman does offer plenty of information about the population slowdown, but his emphasis is not so much on "world prosperity" as it is on the threats to *U.S.* prosperity. (One chapter is devoted to demographic trends in China, Russia, and Europe.) Longman is attentive to the rising cost of childrearing in the United States, as well as the huge fiscal challenge Americans will face in coming decades with growing numbers of elderly who will be living years longer than in the past. He makes the novel suggestion that Social Security taxes be reduced or eliminated for couples who bear children in sufficient numbers. His rationale is that people who have children already bear the major cost of raising to adulthood the next generation of Social Security taxpayers, and they should not have to pay twice. He also has recommendations on how to keep the senior population healthier and therefore less costly to the health care system. Longman, a senior fellow at the New America Foundation, writes widely on demographic issues.

Malthus, Thomas R. *An Essay on the Principle of Population* [1798]. Edited by Geoffrey Gilbert. New York: Oxford University Press, 1999. 172 pages. ISBN 0-19-283747-8.

This is where most population controversies got their start. Malthus laid out the basic questions in their starkest terms: How quickly can populations grow? How fast can food supplies be increased? And what forces will constrain population within the available stock of resources? The picture Malthus painted in 1798 was fairly grim (famine, pestilence, war) but not without hints of a humane way out of the dilemma. He understood that humankind's capacity for altering behavior in light of probable future consequences makes us different from other animals. He also understood the importance of government policies, for good or ill, in influencing people's reproductive choices. This essay is required reading for anyone who wants to see how the terms of the ongoing population debate were set two centuries ago. There are other paperback editions on the market, but this one features an up-to-date editorial introduction, a list of suggested readings, the original text as it appeared in 1798, a set of explanatory notes, and a topical index.

McKibben, Bill. *Maybe One: A Case for Smaller Families.* New York: Plume, 1999. 254 pages. ISBN 0-452-28092-3.

A few years ago McKibben wrote a rueful book called *The End of Nature*, in which he examined the irreversible impact human beings are having on the natural world. There is no longer any corner of the planet so remote as to be able to escape the effects of human activity. Nothing is truly "natural" (untainted by humanity) any more, including the climate. *Maybe One* can be seen as a companion volume, or even a logical sequel, to the earlier book. What, after all, could make more sense to anyone deeply committed to preserving the wondrous diversity of creation than a deliberate restraint on childbearing? Essentially, this is a book about how and why an intelligent, thoughtful couple (the McKibbens) chose to have only one child. It explores the varied reasons for that personal decision as well as the social and economic consequences to be anticipated—not all of them positive—if *many* people made the same decision. Although McKibben is careful not to insist that the one-child idea is right for everyone, he will leave most readers convinced that the choice he and his wife made was an honorable one and that, with the environment in its present condition, there is a great deal to be said for it.

O Grada, Cormac. *Black '47 and Beyond: The Great Irish Famine in History, Economy, and Memory.* Princeton, NJ: Princeton University Press, 2000. 320 pages. ISBN 0-691-07015-6.

One cannot claim a good understanding of the dynamics of world population, past and present, without giving some attention to the millions of lives that have, as Malthus put it, been "mowed down by the scythe of famine." History knows no famine more famous, or traumatic to the nation involved, than the Great Irish Famine of the 1840s, brought on by the failure of the all-important potato crop. The human cost to Ireland was one-eighth of its population dead and a huge further loss through emigration. Much has been written about all this, including an earlier study by O Grada, but this book offers a fresh look at every aspect of the famine. The author compares the severity of the Irish famine to some of the notable famines of the twentieth century, assesses the predictability (or unpredictability) of this famine, examines its agonizingly lengthy course, asks how adequate or inadequate was the English response, and finds A. K.

Sen's theory of famines—that they are the result of inadequate entitlements—only partially useful in explaining the Irish catastrophe.

Peterson, Peter G. *Gray Dawn: How the Coming Age Wave Will Transform America—and the World.* New York: Three Rivers Press, 2000. 320 pages. ISBN 0812990692.

Almost everywhere in the world, populations on average are growing older—markedly so in Europe and Japan. Peter Peterson's book takes a hard look at the difficulties this "graying" of the age structure will pose and some possible ways to mitigate them. The main problem is that workers are choosing to leave the labor force earlier than they used to, are living *longer* than they used to, and are saving less than they need to. How, then, will they be able to afford a long, comfortable retirement? Solutions such as reduced pension benefits to the elderly, higher ages for receiving state pensions (like Social Security), or higher taxes on the working generation will be, to say the least, unpopular: Maybe unacceptable. Peterson offers a number of proposals for dealing with the problem, for example, encouraging more saving by workers and later retirement ages. The author is a former chairman of Lehman Brothers.

Population. Opposing Viewpoints series. San Diego, CA: Greenhaven Press, 2005. 186 pages. ISBN 0-7377-2952-X.

The Opposing Viewpoints series has long been a mainstay of college classrooms where discussion and debate are fostered. Students are presented with short essays on both sides of controversial issues so that they can exercise their own critical thinking and decide for themselves which side has the stronger argument. Two of the main issues explored in the newly released "Population" volume are the rapid aging of people in the developed parts of the world and the environmental costs of population growth.

Rostow, Walt W. *The Great Population Spike and After: Reflections on the 21st Century.* New York: Oxford University Press, 1998. 228 pages. ISBN 0-19-511691-7.

This book is not *mainly* about population, but it illustrates how the assumptions we make about population can be fundamental to how we envision our economic future. Its author, the late Walt Rostow, was a student of economic growth for decades. Here he asks whether the demographic trends we see around us in the world today, particularly the slowdown toward zero and even negative population growth in the industrialized nations, are moving us toward economic stagnation or whether economic growth is destined to continue. His answers are mostly optimistic. He sees no reason why revolutionary technological advances should not continue to occur, as they have been, with some regularity, since the eighteenth century. The population-focused reader can easily skim through Rostow's concluding speculations on the subject of U.S. international responsibilities in the complicated world we are entering.

Sen, Amartya K. *Development as Freedom.* New York: Knopf/ Anchor, 2000. 384 pages. ISBN 0-385-72027-0.

Everything the Nobel Prize-winning economist Amartya Sen writes on the subject of population and poverty is worth reading. This book is not *primarily* about population, but two chapters deal explicitly and lucidly with it. Chapter 7, Famines and Other Crises, restates what Sen has been arguing for many years (see especially his 1981 book, *Poverty and Famines*), that famines are not a simple matter of excess population in relation to food production. The Malthusian perspective is simplistic, for it ignores the fact that "the ability to acquire food has to be *earned*" (p. 162, emphasis Sen's). Thus, it is a lack of earnings or other monetary entitlements that put people at risk of hunger or starvation, and this becomes the key not only to explaining but to preventing famine. Chapter 9, Population, Food and Freedom, finds the global food-production picture fairly encouraging and argues strongly against any form of coercion in family-planning programs. Coercion can be less effective than its advocates believe, ethical issues aside. Sen is no fan of China's one-child policy, but he strongly admires what has been accomplished in the southern Indian state of Kerala, in terms of lowered fertility, higher literacy, and the empowerment of women.

Sen, Gita, Adrienne Germain, and Lincoln C. Chen (eds.). *Population Policies Reconsidered: Health, Empowerment, and Rights.* Cambridge, MA: Harvard University Press, 1994. 280 pages. ISBN 0-674-69003-6.

Population policy as it was once conceived is dead. Notions of population *control*, with explicit goals, targets, or quotas, have been abandoned in most countries. At the international level, as seen at the Cairo International Conference on Population and Development in 1994, and at the academic and intellectual level, the new paradigm stresses women's health and empowerment. Less is heard about demographic issues, more about upholding human rights. Women's perspectives are being voiced, almost for the first time, in discussions about population. The new approach gets a vigorous airing in this volume of seventeen essays, written and co-written by thirty scholars, activists, and practitioners from various fields. All are committed to rethinking the subject of population. This affordable paperback puts readers on the "cutting edge" of that effort. The prose—academically dense in places—is punctuated with boxes, figures, and tables. One of the editors, Gita Sen, has earned a reputation as a leading international women's rights activist; she co-founded and remains active in Development Alternatives with Women for a New Era (DAWN), a network of advocates for women's causes in the developing world.

Simon, Julian. *The Ultimate Resource 2.* Princeton, NJ: Princeton University Press, 1998. 778 pages. ISBN 0-691-00381-5.

When Julian Simon published the earlier edition of this book (as *The Ultimate Resource*) in 1981, it was met with considerable skepticism by environmental activists and most academic demographers. Economists were more favorably impressed, and the business media, for example, *The Wall Street Journal* and *Fortune* magazine, unanimously so. That, essentially, is where things stand two and a half decades later. Simon's optimistic views about the long-term impact of population on the economy and environment—most notably, his view that natural resources are *not* becoming scarcer over time—got an extensive hearing during the 1980s and 1990s. They are not as easily dismissed today as they once were. The "ultimate resource" in the Simon worldview is human ingenuity, something that increases with human numbers. Population growth *can* pose short-term scarcity problems, but over time new solutions are found, and ultimately people live better than before. Simon delights in confounding and refuting his "Malthusian" opponents with humor, statistics, and a crisp prose style. The book, despite its length, is not a scholarly tome.

Rather, it is a collection of thematically linked essays, many of them keyed to provocative questions like "Are Humans Causing Species Holocaust?" and "Do Humans Breed Like Flies?"

Teitelbaum, Michael S., and Jay Winter. *A Question of Numbers: High Migration, Low Fertility, and the Politics of National Identity.* New York: Hill and Wang, 1998. 290 pages. ISBN 0-8090-7781-7.

This book examines how the combination of declining fertility and rising immigration—trends that became entrenched during the period 1965–1995—now affect not only the demography but the very sense of national identity of the industrialized nations in Europe and North America. The result in one country after another has been, at best, heated debate and political skirmishing, at worst, violence directed against immigrant minorities. The book presents case studies of Germany, France, Britain, Yugoslavia, the former Soviet Union, Romania, Canada, and the United States. It also takes up the issues of refuge- and asylum-seeking migration and Islamic fundamentalism as factors affecting Western attitudes toward immigrants from Muslim nations. One cannot read this book without concluding that "population politics" is going to be with us for a long time to come.

Tobias, Michael. *World War III: Population and the Biosphere at the End of the Millennium.* New York: Continuum Publishing Company, 1998. 296 pages. ISBN 0-8264-1085-5.

Michael Tobias has traveled the world, taking in the sights and smells of overpopulation, overconsumption, and environmental devastation, and this book is the result. There are chapters on China, India, Indonesia, and Africa, in each case detailing the environmental disruption and degradation occurring in part because of expanding human numbers. The so-called developed nations do not escape his scorn. In a chapter titled The Price of Development, Japan, the United States, the Netherlands, and Italy are among the nations found to have paid a terrible environmental price for their material progress. Tobias is prone to slip into rhetorical overdrive, as when he bemoans the "mindless vandalism wreaked by humans on the scale of a planetary cancer" (p. 203). But he also has a keen eye for the telling detail, a genuine passion for nature in all of its splendid—and tenuous—

diversity, and a proselytizer's determination to open readers' eyes to the problem and the solution, both of which are *us*.

Wattenberg, Ben J. *Fewer: How the New Demography of Depopulation Will Shape Our Future.* Chicago: Ivan R. Dee, 2005. 256 pages. ISBN 1-56663-673-6.

In 1987, Ben Wattenberg warned, in *The Birth Dearth*, of an impending slowdown and even shrinkage of population among the Western nations, something he feared would produce a loss of Western influence on the global scene. *Fewer* is best viewed, perhaps, as an update of the earlier book. The data are fresh, the charts redrawn, the core message much the same. Wattenberg, a senior fellow at the American Enterprise Institute in Washington, D.C., combines an abiding interest in population trends with an unapologetically neoconservative outlook on economic and geopolitical matters. His style can be digressive and almost glib, but like most smart, opinionated people, he holds your interest. (For many years Wattenberg has hosted "Think Tank," a PBS talk show in Washington, D.C.) A point that is likely to stick in the reader's mind is that the United Nations recently lowered its expectation of how low the fertility rate is headed in most countries by mid-century from 2.1 to 1.85, that is, from replacement to *subreplacement* level! Wattenberg rightly considers this "big news" (p. 16). Still, it is difficult to share the depopulation concerns of authors like Longman, Peterson, and Wattenberg when nearly everyone agrees that the world is on course to *add* at least two and maybe three billion people by 2050.

Weeks, John R. *Population: An Introduction to Concepts and Issues.* 9th ed. Belmont, CA: Wadsworth Publishing Company, 2004. 675 pages. ISBN 0-534-62769-2.

This clear and comprehensive treatment of demography (the study of population) sets the standard for college textbooks on the subject. Weeks, a demographer at San Diego State University, has a knack for expressing complex ideas in relatively straightforward (sometimes funny and folksy) ways. The graphs, tables, and maps are well-chosen and clearly explained, and the data are as timely as circumstances will allow. There are chapters on the basic demographic processes—mortality, fertility, migration—as well as on population structure and characteristics; population, development, and the environment; population policy; and demographics, which is the term for practical applications of population data in business, social, and political planning. Throughout the text, Canada and Mexico are brought into the discussion as nations to which the U.S. population experience can be compared. Readers of the present volume are especially directed to Chapter 2, Global Population Trends. At the ends of chapters are Suggested Readings and Websites of Interest.

Handbooks, Yearbooks, and Data Sheets

Haupt, Arthur, and Thomas T. Kane. *The Population Reference Bureau's Population Handbook*, 5th ed. Washington, DC: Population Reference Bureau, 2004. 68 pages. ISBN 0-917136-12-8.

This useful little handbook features short chapters on all the standard demographic concepts and measures: age and sex composition, fertility, mortality, morbidity, nuptiality, migration, race and ethnicity, households and families, urbanization, and population change. Examples are given for all the main concepts, and they are drawn from every part of the world. The contrasts can be most instructive; for example, 55.3 percent of births in Sweden were outside marriage in 1999, while in Greece that proportion was only 4.0 percent (p. 20). Chapter 12, Population Change, is a marvelous crash course in demography, all packed into seven pages! A fairly complete glossary of technical terms is provided in the appendix, and there is a listing of equivalent English, Spanish, and French demographic terms. The handbook is downloadable from the PRB website at no cost.

Population Reference Bureau. *The 2005 World Population Data Sheet*. Washington, DC: Population Reference Bureau, 2005. ISSN 0085-8315.

Published annually in a wall-chart format, the *World Population Data Sheet* is an extraordinary resource for anyone interested in world population issues. For every country in the world, it gives the essential demographic statistics: population, birth- and death rates, rate of natural increase, infant mortality rate, total fertility rate, percentage "young" and "old," life expectancy, percentage of adults with HIV/AIDS, contraceptive use, Gross National Income (GNI) per capita, and more. Data are also given in aggregated form for the world, the more developed countries, the less developed countries, and the various regions, for example, Northern Africa, Eastern Africa, Middle Africa, and Southern Africa. There is no handier source of world population information than this data sheet.

United Nations Population Division. *World Population Policies 2003*. New York: United Nations. 450 pages. ISBN 9211513936.

Every two years, the United Nations issues a volume detailing the population policies of the nearly 200 nations of the world. Its purpose is to make clear what governments are doing, and what their attitudes are, on the whole range of population-related variables, such as fertility, mortality, aging, migration, and spatial distribution of people. For those interested in the *policy* aspects of population, this volume is indispensable. Earlier volumes in the series were titled *National Population Policies* and, before 1998, *Global Review and Inventory of Population Policies*.

United Nations Population Division. *World Population Prospects: The 2004 Revision*. New York: United Nations, 2005. *Vol. I: Comprehensive Tables*, *Vol. II: Sex and Age Distribution of the World Population*, and *Vol. III: Analytical Report* (all forthcoming).

Since 1951 the United Nations' Population Division has issued world population projections every few years. (The intervals have been as long as six years, as short as two.) As might be expected, these estimates are the most widely referred to of any such attempts to forecast the world's demographic future. Low-, medium-, and high-fertility paths to the population of 2050 are presented, so people may decide for themselves which forecast seems most plausible. The media and the public generally confine their attention to the "medium" estimate; some specialists, however, believe that recent declines in fertility around the world have been so unexpectedly large that more attention should be given to the United Nations' low-fertility estimate. Volume I offers detailed demographic projections for each country, region, and the whole world, to the year 2050. Volume II gives age and sex distributions for countries and regions back to 1950 and, on an estimated basis, forward to 2050 (on low-, medium-, and high-fertility assumptions). Volume III reports some of the technical demographic reasoning that lies behind the estimates and projections of the first two volumes. The highlights of the 2004 revision will be found in Chapter 7.

United Nations Population Fund (UNFPA). *State of World Population 2005: The Promise of Equality: Gender Equity, Reproductive Health and the Millennium Development Goals.* New York: United Nations, 2005. 120 pages. ISBN 0897147502.

Each year the UNFPA issues a report highlighting what it considers the major population challenges the world faces. In 2004, the theme was "The Cairo Consensus at Ten: Population, Reproductive Health and the Global Effort to End Poverty." In 2003 it was "Making 1 Billion Count: Investing in Adolescents' Health and Rights." In its 2005 report, the UNFPA sought to reconnect the ideas of reproductive freedom and health to the Millennium Development Goals (MDGs) that the United Nations adopted in 2000. The fundamental priorities and commitments of the UNFPA are those of the international community as enunciated at the Cairo conference (ICPD) in 1994. They are not necessarily those of the U.S. government, which, since 2001, has often appeared out of step with the rest of the world in these matters. The amount of *new* information in these reports from one year to the next is not large, but graphs, tables, and footnote references do get updated.

U.S. Bureau of the Census. *Global Population Profile: 2002.* Washington, DC: U.S. Government Printing Office, 2004. 226 pages. ISBN 1-59610-035-4.

The International Programs Center (IPC) of the U.S. Census Bureau prepares its own estimates and projections of world population, country by country, that do not necessarily coincide with those prepared by the United Nations. The differences are normally not large and need not be explained in detail here. The heart of the *Global Population Profile* consists of tables of population data by region and country. There are tables of total population given by decade back to 1950 and forward to 2050. Birth, death, and natural increase rates are also given for every country in 2002, and there is an age-group breakdown by country, for example, number aged 0–4, 5–9, 10–14. (At older ages, the age ranges widen, for example, 20–44, 45–64.) A special chapter addresses the AIDS pandemic in the twenty-first century; another looks at contraceptive prevalence in developing countries. This publication seems designed to be as much an educational tool as a data source book. It includes (brief) discussions of the history of world population, the main forces determining future population growth, trends in life expectancy, the demographic effects of migration, and much more.

U.S. Bureau of the Census. *Statistical Abstract of the United States 2004–2005: The National Data Book.* Washington, DC: U.S. Government Printing Office, 2004–2005. 1006 pages. ISBN 0-16-072331-0.

Issued annually by the Census Bureau since 1878 and now offered in both print and CD-ROM formats, the *Statistical Abstract* provides a wealth of demographic information for the United States. Sections 1 (Population) and 2 (Vital Statistics) contain ninety pages of detailed statistics, covering everything from the most basic—total U.S. population by year—to the most specific, if not arcane, such as Death Rates from Malignant Neoplasms by Race, Sex, and Age: 1950 to 2000. Vital statistics are presented in great detail: births, deaths, marriage, divorce, all categorized by the appropriate qualifiers, such as race, age, sex, and cause. The 1,000-plus fine-print pages of this volume fully justify the subtitle, "The National Data Book."

Nonprint Resources

Population Websites

The Internet has become a kind of electronic almanac, offering information (and sometimes *mis*information) on every topic imaginable. The subject of population is, for the most part, well served by the Internet. Numerous reliable and up-to-date Internet sites allow one to explore population issues in depth. Some are oriented to the environmental aspects of population, some to the family-planning aspects; some deal with population policy, and some are simply places to obtain demographic data. A number of websites offer several of these features at one location. Because so many sites provide links to other population-related websites, the following is a selective list.

Those sites that are data-oriented generally provide not only global population data but more detailed statistics by country, and often for the past and the projected future as well as the present. Some sites offer their data in multiple formats: downloadable files, wall charts, booklets, and CD-ROMs. Hardly anyone but a professional demographer requires data on a CD-ROM, so that particular resource is not covered here.

Alan Guttmacher Institute
http://www.agi-usa.org

This is the premier site for information on reproductive health, including contraception, pregnancy and birth, sexually transmitted diseases, and the law and public policy relating to reproduction. The Institute is often the source of news stories in the mainstream media.

Carrying Capacity Network
http://www.carryingcapacity.org

This site invites one to think of overpopulation as a U.S. national issue. Its policy orientation is toward the limitation of further immigration into the United States.

Center for Immigration Studies
http://www.cis.org

Immigration is a key part of the population picture for a number of countries; for the United States it has become critical to present and future population trends. This website takes a decidedly unenthusiastic view of immigration's impact on the United States. The site offers many studies of individual immigration issues both online or in print.

Family Planning Association of India
http://fpaindia.org

This website provides an example of the vital family-planning work being done around the world by nongovernmental organizations. More examples can be reached through links at the International Planned Parenthood Federation (IPPF) website.

The Hunger Site
http://www.thehungersite.com

The Hunger Site allows visitors to click on a button and make a free donation of staple food *every day* to hungry people overseas. The site is commercially sponsored (and cluttered with ads, which of course pay for the free food donations). It does not attempt to make an analytical connection between hunger and population, but it could provoke interesting discussions about possible reasons for hunger. There is a link to teacher resources.

International Planned Parenthood Association
http://www.ippf.org

Comparable to the Alan Guttmacher Institute in its concerns but with more of an international and program orientation, the IPPF is another good source of information on reproductive health. There are links to all the member organizations that compose the IPPF.

International Programs Center of U.S. Bureau of the Census
http://www.census.gov/ipc/www

This is perhaps the single best place to get reliable information about world population. The IPC and its predecessor agencies have been collecting and processing international demographic data for over fifty years. The site has a world population clock, an international database (IDB) with current and historical data on national populations, a feature that permits one to view and print population pyramids for individual countries, and projections of future population trends by Census Bureau experts.

Migration News
http://migration.ucdavis.edu/mn

Started in 1993 by Philip Martin at the University of California, Davis, this site summarizes worldwide migration news, month by month, and offers an archive of past issues. It also provides links to other immigration sites. The coverage of Canadian and rural migration issues is noteworthy.

Negative Population Growth
http://www.npg.org

Negative Population Growth (NPG) has been worrying about overpopulation for several decades. Its website currently emphasizes *U.S.* problems, such as urban sprawl and deteriorating quality of life, caused (allegedly) by too rapid population growth and exacerbated by immigration. NPG offers a population news listserve and an Internet Forum Series of occasional papers at its site.

Population Communications International
http://www.population.org

Population Communications International (PCI) is an organization that uses the media, especially TV and radio soap operas, to deliver messages about safe and responsible sexual behavior. Its website provides interesting, up-to-date information about this new approach, including a multimedia section that lists several PCI-produced programs, both video and audio, with sample clips available for easy downloading.

Population Connection
http://www.populationconnection.org

Population Connection, the renamed old Zero Population Growth (ZPG), is dedicated to the study—and containment—of world population growth. It has resources for teachers, advocates, campus activists, and journalists. Teachers will find the materials quite helpful since they include classroom games, role-playing simulations, and other learning materials (some bilingual), as well as a quarterly newsletter for teachers. The Take Action section highlights federal legislation of interest to those concerned about population issues.

The Population Council
http://www.popcouncil.org

The Population Council is the world's foremost organization devoted to reproductive health research. Its website provides an overview of the worldwide research that it sponsors and conducts in all areas related human reproduction. Beyond the usual topics of contraception, abortion, sexually transmitted diseases, and gender and family dynamics, the Population Council also sponsors research on more social-scientific aspects of demography, for example, aging, experimental health programs, population and the environment, and urban health and poverty. Many papers and reports are available for downloading at the website.

Population Institute
http://www.populationinstitute.org

At this website one may order booklets on population subjects (for a fee) and see the most recent issue of the Institute's bimonthly newsletter *Popline.*

Population Reference Bureau
http://www.prb.org

This site may offer the most complete and objective coverage of population issues on the Web. It is a splendid resource for students and teachers alike (the Educators link supplies a number of curricular suggestions for teachers). The site offers online versions of the *World Population Data Sheet* and the *Population Bulletin* series, as well as press releases, a demographic glossary, and various reports focused mainly on U.S. population topics. There is a Graphics Bank of population-related charts and images suitable for PowerPoint presentations.

Sierra Club
http://www.sierraclub.org

Although bitterly divided by internal battles over U.S. immigration policy a few years ago, the Sierra Club has not distanced itself from the subject of population. Its website offers, under "Our Priority Campaigns," reports, fact sheets, and brochures on population, as well as a listserve and suggestions on how to get involved as an activist on population issues.

United Nations Population Fund
http://www.unfpa.org

This website gives access to online versions of the publications of the UN Population Fund, of which there are many, including the annual *State of World Population.* The strong emphasis at the UNFPA is on the empowerment of women. That is in line with the deliberations and Program of Action finalized at the 1994 International Conference on Population and Development in Cairo.

United Nations Population Information Network (POPIN)
http://www.un.org/popin/

Suppose you would like to find the latest United Nations data on world marriage patterns, or world fertility patterns, or projections of world population to the year 2300. POPIN is the web entry point for UN population information, and it would be the handiest starting point for locating such data. It also offers Cyber-SchoolBus, with curricular materials (K–12) and suggestions on a wide range of global issues including world hunger.

World Health Organization
http://www.who.int/whosis

The World Health Organization (WHO) Statistical Information System site is the place to go for authoritative information on the extent and impact of diseases worldwide (including HIV/AIDS), mortality rates, and everything health-related. It has enormous depth of coverage on health issues and, as a bonus, has links to world population estimates and projections, including those of the United Nations.

Worldwatch Institute
http://www.worldwatch.org

The Worldwatch website provides access to many of the organization's studies, Worldwatch Papers, and *World Watch* magazine articles. The well-known annual *State of the World* report often features a chapter on, or related to, population trends. Two online features are worth noting: "China Watch" has news updates and analysis of Chinese environmental issues, and "Worldwatch University" offers a variety of educational resources to college students and their faculty. Worldwatch is one of the most respected sources of information on population, resources, and the environment.

Videos

Many videotapes/DVDs on the topic of population are now available. These can be fine classroom supplements or jumping-off points for group discussions and other meetings centered on global issues. The arrival of the six-billionth inhabitant of the planet late in 1999 stimulated interest in the production of this kind of video, as did the convening of the International Conference on Population and Development in Cairo in 1994. Several of the videos reviewed below take note of the bicentennial of the publication of Malthus's *Essay on Population* (1798), although only one is devoted exclusively to Malthus and his ideas. The oldest video reviewed is "Dodging Doomsday" (1992), which has become a minor classic by now. Other videos date from 1994 or later and are available from the source indicated.

Baby Crash: Causes and Consequences of Declining Birthrates
Date: 2002
Length: 46 minutes
Price: $149.95 (purchase, VHS or DVD-R)
Source: Films for the Humanities and Sciences

This video brings into sharp focus the many issues surrounding the trend in industrialized countries toward unprecedented, low fertility rates. A number of demographic experts are featured in short comments about this phenomenon, but the real emphasis is on young couples, married and unmarried, in Canada, Sweden, Italy, and Japan. We get to know them by name and learn how they think about the issue of childbearing and childrearing. Young women in Japan, for example, are seen to enjoy "freedom to the absolute limit" with good incomes, the comforts of their parents' homes, and no family responsibilities of their own. Major attention is placed on a Swedish couple and an Italian couple: the Swedes have two children and no easy time raising them, but at least their government offers significant financial aid to them, while the Italians, whose government offers almost nothing to parents, are childless. A key message seems to be that *women* will determine what happens next. They are walking a "fine line between career ambitions and diapers," and if denied the assistance needed to combine the two, they will probably choose the former! Suitable for all ages from middle school up.

Crisis Control: Stemming the Spread of HIV/AIDS
Date: 2004
Length: 26 minutes
Price: $195 (purchase, VHS or DVD), $45 (rental)
Source: Bullfrog Films

This video is no. 13 in an impressive series of short films on the subject of how the UN Millennium Development Goals are being met—and in some cases *not* met—by the global community. Produced by the Television Trust for the Environment (TVE) with funding from several European governments, international agencies, and private foundations, the programs were all originally shown on BBC World in their *Life* series 4. (TVE is based in London.) This one concerns a huge imponderable in the world population equation: AIDS. Projections of national populations all over the world are sensitive to assumptions made about the spread or control of this epidemic disease. The video focuses on two countries, Ukraine and Zambia. Ukraine has a fairly low AIDS mortality rate currently but a high rate of HIV *infection*, making it a crisis waiting to happen unless preventive actions are taken. The crisis has long since arrived in Zambia, where AIDS has been a deadly presence for twenty years. It has created orphans by the hundreds of thousands; it has killed thousands of teachers, nurses, and engineers. Until quite recently, there was little hope of being able to afford the anti-retroviral drugs that can hold AIDS at bay. As with "Reel to Real," the twenty-second video in this series (see below), there is an excellent web page linked to "Crisis Control." Suitable for grades 7–12 and older.

Decade of Decision
Date: 1994
Length: 14 minutes
Price: $95 (purchase), $20 (rental)
Source: Bullfrog Films

Narrated by newscaster Walter Cronkite and produced by Population Action International, this succinct video makes the case that the "brakes" must be put on population "momentum" during the decade of the 1990s [now past]. It poses the population issue in standard Ehrlichian terms: in the poorer parts of the world, human numbers are increasing too rapidly; in the richer parts, per capita consumption is rising too rapidly. The main policy emphasis is placed on the provision of family-planning services to those who presently lack access to them. A study guide is available. Suitable for ages 12 to adult.

Dodging Doomsday: Life Beyond Malthus
Date: 1992
Length: 51 minutes
Price: $129.95 (purchase, VHS or DVD-R)
Source: Films for the Humanities and Sciences

This British (BBC) program features Paul Ehrlich as the persuasive spokesman for the "gloomsters" and Julian Simon as the cheerful and equally convincing spokesman for the "cornucopians." Other population experts weigh in on various aspects of population. A genuine radical, Maria Elena Hurtado, argues that "overpopulation" is a smokescreen for the problems created by unequal land distribution in many countries. Two key questions are central to this balanced and engaging video: is population growing too big for the Earth to sustain, and is population to blame for various social and environmental problems we currently face? It would be hard to find another video that raises as many population-linked issues—economic, environmental, and political—as "Dodging Doomsday."

Food or Famine?
Date: 1997
Length: 49 minutes each (two videos)
Price for both: $295 (purchase), $95 (rental)
Source: Filmakers Library

This two-part video tackles the issue of sustainable agriculture within a framework of concern to feed a growing global population. Experts seen on camera include Lester Brown of the Worldwatch Institute, David Pimentel of Cornell University, Ismail Serageldin, chairman of International Agricultural Research, and Miguel Altieri, University of California. Part 1 sets out the basic dilemma: modern "industrial" agriculture feeds billions of people but relies on pesticides, herbicides, and a process of plant selection and breeding that reduces botanical diversity. The cost of monoculture is seen not only in a loss of the natural diversity of plants and soil organisms but also in worrisome rates of soil erosion. Yet there are positive developments to be seen in places such as Chile, California, and Canada, where some groups of farmers are following more organic and sustainable methods of agriculture with excellent results. Part 2 raises the larger issues of global population trends, loss of cropland to urban sprawl, degradation of existing farmlands, limits to water supply, and the shift toward higher-protein foods, all of which give reason to be concerned about the future. As in Part 1, the strength of the video lies in the clear focus on important questions—and in the telling film footage, such as the Indian farmer who has just dynamited the bottom of his well, already 30 meters deep, to try to reach the receding water table. While these videos raise serious Malthusian-type questions about humanity's capacity to feed our rising numbers without doing irreparable damage to the ecology, numerous examples of positive, environmentally friendly approaches are offered. Narrated by David Suzuki, this pair of videos would be best appreciated by those of college age or older.

Future in the Cradle
Date: 1996
Length: 22 minutes
Price: $59.95 (purchase, VHS), discounts for some teachers
Source: The Video Project

This aptly titled video examines the world population issue through the lens of the International Conference on Population and Development (ICPD) held in 1994 in the "cradle of civilization," Cairo. Featured speakers include Nafis Sadik, secretary-general of the conference, Timothy Wirth, U.S. representative to the conference, Paul Ehrlich, the well-known Stanford environmentalist, and David Brower of the Sierra Club. An interesting aspect of the video is its attention to the domestic U.S. political dimension of international family-planning and the significant shift of U.S. policy in 1993 (*re*-shifted by Bush in 2001). The tilt of the program is clearly toward affirming the goals set at the Cairo conference, that is, making reproductive health services more widely available around the world, and expanding educational and other opportunities for girls and women. Suitable for ages 14 and up.

The Grandchild Gap: The Effects of Low BirthRates
Date: 1997
Length: 56 minutes
Price: $89.95 (purchase, VHS or DVD-R)
Source: Films for the Humanities and Sciences

"The Grandchild Gap" was one of the first population videos to depart from the standard focus of the genre on worrisome rates of increase in world population. This video explores instead the emerging problem of *low* birthrates in Europe, a few East Asian nations, and the United States. Ben Wattenberg, senior scholar at the American Enterprise Institute, narrates. Also frequently on camera are Samuel Preston, a demographer at the University of Pennsylvania, and Andrew Cherlin, a sociologist at Johns Hopkins University. But equally compelling on screen are the ordinary young Italians and Americans who explain why they are choosing to delay marriage and keep their number of children low. More poignant are the older people who express regret at not having any grandchildren yet, or even much *prospect* of grandchildren. All the relevant background statistics are presented along the way, including fertility rates and "ideal" family size figures. (People in low-fertility countries seem uniformly to *want* more children than they end up having.) One long-term economic effect of the "birth dearth" will be the serious problem of supporting a disproportionately large retired generation from the work efforts of—and taxes paid by—a smaller generation. Wattenberg asks whether government can do anything to solve the problem and gets little encouragement from his experts. Much larger tax credits for children might increase the number of children people choose to have, or, as one expert suggests, might simply change the timing of births. Immigration receives less attention than it deserves as a possible mitigating force, at least in the United States. This video should stimulate plenty of discussion in audiences of high school age and older.

The Human Tide
Date: 1995
Length: 37 minutes
Price: $295 (purchase), $65 (rental)
Source: Filmakers Library

This video, narrated by David Suzuki for the Canadian television series "The Nature of Things," conveys a sense of urgency, of time running out, on the issue of world population. That is its strength, and it has a formidable cast of guest experts to drive home the crisis message: Paul Ehrlich, Nafis Sadik of the UN Population Fund, Lester Brown of Worldwatch Institute, Sharon Camp of the Population Crisis Committee, and Stephen Lewis, former Canadian ambassador to the United Nations. The video's weakness lies in its attempt to cover every single aspect of world population; in thirty-seven minutes, that cannot be done. The issue that receives the fullest treatment is birth control—the adequate or inadequate access to it in various parts of the world, the cost, the different types and how research is expanding the range of choices, abortion, the politics of family planning (mainly a domestic U.S. concern but with worldwide implications), and the need many see for the developed countries to be generous in funding the efforts developing countries are making to rein in their population growth. A striking fact is that in Ethiopia the cost of a year's supply of condoms (the best contraceptive choice where AIDS is a serious threat) is about one-third of annual income. On questions like the role of economic development in lowering fertility, the threatened loss of species and biodiversity, and the emerging problem of environmental refugees, this video has less to say than many others. Suitable for high school, college, and adult audiences.

Jam Packed
Date: 1997
Length: 29 minutes
Price: $79.95 (VHS)
Source: The Video Project

There is an MTV-like energy to this video, which is clearly aimed at the teenage U.S. audience. It cuts back and forth among scenes of urban sprawl, African wildlife (threatened by human overpopulation), experts stressing the urgency of slowing population growth, and candid statements by an unmarried young mother about the life-burdening effects of her accidental pregnancy. Much more emphasis is placed on the benefits of deferring sexual activity until marriage and on the threat to the environment from a wasteful American lifestyle than on the family-planning needs of less developed nations. Population Communications International, which produced the video, prides itself on careful pre-production research. It undoubtedly has found that the most effective way to engage American teens in global population issues is through the "up-close-and-personal" approach taken here. Suitable for ages 12 and up.

The Legacy of Malthus
Date: 1994
Length: 52 minutes
Price: $150 (purchase, VHS); $75 (rental); discount for activists
Source: Bullfrog Films

The view that poverty is not a result of overpopulation but of a maldistribution of resources, within and among nations, informs this unusual video. The director, Deepa Dhanraj, quotes and then subverts the message of Malthus as well as those present-day agencies that seem to accept the Malthusian explanation of poverty (e.g., the Population Institute and the UNFPA). The destitution of nineteenth-century Scottish crofters is contrasted, through alternating segments, with that of poor villagers in India. In both cases, it is made clear that unequal access to the land is the real problem. There is no narration, leaving the viewer to draw his or her own conclusions. Marred by poor audio quality in the copy reviewed. Suitable for ages 17 to adult.

Mothers of Malappuram
Date: 1996
Length: 10 minutes
Price: $95 (purchase, VHS), $25 (rent)
Source: Bullfrog Films

One of a six-video series called "Not the Numbers Game," this brief film deals with the shift in the Indian government's population policy from a top-down emphasis on numbers and targets to a greater emphasis on women's empowerment. (The new approach conforms to the recommendations made at the ICPD conference in Cairo in 1994.) Raising female literacy has been a key to lowering fertility in Kerala, the southern Indian state featured here. Elsewhere in India, women are assuming positions of power in village *panchayat* assemblies, becoming "engines of social change." Improved health services are another part of the picture, since lower infant mortality rates lead to lower birthrates. An optimistic video with a clear message. Suitable for ages 15 to adult.

Paul Ehrlich and the Population Bomb
Date: 1996
Length: 60 minutes
Price: $149.95 (purchase, VHS or DVD-R)
Source: Films for the Humanities and Sciences

No one who has worried about world population at any time during the past thirty-five years could be unfamiliar with the name Paul Ehrlich. This video gives Ehrlich a chance to speak at length on the issue that has made him a sort of environmental celebrity. It takes him from a youthful science enthusiast—his mother recalls his early interest in butterflies—through college and a research stint working with Eskimos around Hudson Bay, to his lifelong partnership with wife Anne, and his long career of teaching and ecological research at Stanford University. Considerable attention is paid to the sensational *Population Bomb* of 1968, which earned Ehrlich a visit, and then dozens of revisits, to the *Johnny Carson Show*. (In one scene, he is shown briefly debating Ben Wattenberg on that program.) There is film footage of poverty and starvation in Africa and India, and of the contrasting affluence of American consumers. A fair hearing is given to Ehrlich's arch-foe, economist Julian Simon, who has argued at great length that life is getting better and better for most of the Earth's inhabitants, that it will continue to do so, and that a rising population is part of the reason why. Ehrlich's impatience with Simon, economists in general, and "creationists" is unmistakable in his salty comebacks to all of them. Suitable for high school and older audiences.

The Pill
Date: 2003
Length: 55 minutes
Price: $24.98 (VHS purchase)
Source: PBS

This engaging video, in the PBS "American Experience" series, tells the story of how a scientific breakthrough, the contraceptive pill, brought profound change to women's lives in the United States. Before FDA approval of the pill in 1960, married couples had few reliable—and no *convenient*—means of limiting their fertility. Margaret Sanger, who fearlessly championed women's reproductive rights for decades, believed this had to change. The video makes clear her central role in promoting the search for a simple pill to regulate fertility. Photographs and film footage bring to life not only Sanger, but also her friend Katharine McCormick, the aging heiress who underwrote the research and development costs of the pill, Gregory Pincus, the man in charge of the research, and Dr. John Rock, the respected gynecologist who supervised the medical trials of the pill. How the oral contraceptive altered sexual, social, career, and political perspectives is recounted by several articulate women whose lives it affected. Viewers might want to contemplate the interesting simultaneity of the pill's arrival with the close of the high-fertility period known as the baby boom. Coincidence? Suitable for high-school ages and upward.

Population Six Billion
Date: 1999
Length: 56 minutes
Price: $129.95 (purchase, VHS or DVD-R)
Source: Films for the Humanities and Sciences

This video opens with a recitation of bad demographic news. Rising global population poses serious problems in the areas of the environment, housing, migration, and water supplies; per capita food production is now falling; there is an expanding pool of unemployed workers around the world. Over 100 countries face a doubled or tripled population by the year 2050. Kofi Annan, secretary-general of the United Nations, warns of an overpopulated world. But then the focus shifts to three highly specific case studies of countries that have been facing rapid population growth and have been *doing* something to curb it. The three are Vietnam, Uganda, and Mexico. In all three, scenes of misery and destitution are intercut with scenes of sex education classes or private counseling sessions. In Vietnam, one learns that abortion is so common—costing less than $2—that it is relied upon as a form of birth control. (Vietnam does not offer sex education in its schools.) In Uganda, the issue of female genital mutilation is addressed in a forceful way. In Mexico, the empowerment of women is treated as a high priority in connection with family planning. The tone is low-key throughout, but some material is adult enough that the video seems inappropriate for audiences below college level.

Reel to Real: Holding Our Ground
Date: 2004
Length: 23 minutes
Price: $195 (purchase, VHS or DVD), $45 (rental)
Source: Bullfrog Films

This video, no. 22 in the Life 4 series (see "Crisis Control" above), focuses on the issue of reproductive health and rights—central concerns at the International Conference on Population and Development (ICPD) held in Cairo in 1994. It looks at four countries—the Philippines, Latvia, Japan, and India—and how well they have met the lofty goals established at the ICPD. In the Philippines, the government has failed to deliver the kinds of reproductive health services to women that were envisioned in

1994. In part this is due to blocking actions by the Roman Catholic Church. In Latvia, youth education on sexuality and reproduction is so inadequate that one-fifth of all women aged 15 to 25 have had abortions. The ICPD commitment to adolescent education and services is not fully met there. Japan has a perilously low fertility rate, in part (it is believed) because it fails to offer enough child care services, but progress is being made in the private and public sectors. In India the strong preference for sons is driving an epidemic of female-fetus abortions; so far, laws have not had much effect in limiting the problem. Thoraya Obaid, executive director of the UNFPA, is on camera several times, making her points clearly and forcefully. Suitable for grades 7–12, college, and adult.

Setting the Grass Roots on Fire: Norman Borlaug and Africa's Green Revolution
Date: 2000
Length: 56 minutes
Price: $295 (video), $75 (rental)
Source: Filmakers Library

Population may not be in the title of this video, but it is never far from the center of concern, since Norman Borlaug's motivation throughout a long career has been to avert hunger and famine through agricultural research. His initial plant-breeding successes came in Mexico, as recounted in the video, but the real proof of a historic food-production breakthrough came on the Indian subcontinent during the 1960s and 1970s. (Borlaug won the Nobel Peace Prize in 1970.) At a late stage of his career—indeed he had already retired, *twice*—Borlaug was asked to apply his Green Revolution methods to Africa, a continent facing immense and almost hopeless odds against being able to feed its growing numbers. Partly at the urging of former President Jimmy Carter, Borlaug accepted the challenge. The contrast seen here between starving, cadaverous Ethiopians and happy, well-nourished children at a later date, after the Sasakawa-Global 2000 (SG 2000) program has been fully implemented, is moving—and convincing. The only skeptical moment permitted to intrude into this firmly upbeat version of Borlaug's life story is a mild confrontation between the scientist and a critic who questions the environmental impact of chemical fertilizers. (The response: fertilizers *can* pollute waterways when they are overused, but in Africa that is very unlikely, given the low doses applied. And in any case, is pollution a worse problem than starvation?) Suitable for ages 14 and up.

Telling Stories, Saving Lives
Date: 2005
Length: 20 minutes
Price: no charge if $25 is donated to PCI
Source: Population Communications International (PCI)

This is an outreach and recruitment tool of Population Communications International. Beyond its self-promoting message, however, the program offers an interesting inside look at the planning, production, and theoretical underpinnings, as well as the positive impact, of the soap operas for which PCI has become famous. PCI stresses that its stories are locally researched, written, produced, and acted. Through both radio and television, these programs are reaching a wide audience. Seeing itself as an agent of change, PCI has developed partnerships with the World Health Organization, the United Nations Population Fund, the International Planned Parenthood Federation, and the National Wildlife Federation, among others. Suitable for middle-school ages to adult.

Was Malthus Right? Population and Resources in the 21st Century
Date: 1998
Length: 27 minutes
Price: $129.95 (purchase, VHS or DVD-R), $75 (rent)
Source: Films for the Humanities and Sciences

This edition of the PBS program "Think Tank" raises a variety of questions about the relevance of Thomas Malthus's *Essay on Population* in a world of 6 billion rather than the 1 billion of 1798. The roundtable discussion, hosted by Ben Wattenberg, of the American Enterprise Institute, a Washington, D.C., think tank, includes Paul Demeny, a distinguished scholar at the Population Council in New York; Max Singer, a co-founder of the Hudson Institute; and Walter Reid, of the World Resources Council in Washington. The exchange of ideas ranges across various topics, from the exact nature of Malthus's population theory to the debated links among population growth, resource depletion, and environmental degradation. Unlike most videos on population, this one consists of nothing but unrehearsed talk around a table. The intellectual level, especially by television standards, is high. Suitable for college audiences and adults.

World in the Balance
Date: 2004
Length: 120 minutes
Price: $19.95 (purchase)
Source: Shop WGBH

This two-part program that aired on PBS stations in April 2004 gives a selective introduction to global population issues, particularly (1) the divergent population trends in the developed and developing regions and (2) the question of how China will handle its environmental challenges in coming years. The first segment covers the divergence issue by focusing on Japan, India, and sub-Saharan Africa. Japan is in trouble with a birthrate that, in spite of cash baby bonuses offered by the government, remains alarmingly low. The other two countries are, in every sense, worlds apart from Japan. Wrenching personal stories illustrate the powerlessness and dire health risks most Indian and Kenyan women face when it comes to sex and childbearing. The consequences: high birthrates, high infant death rates, and high maternal death rates. The second program segment deals exclusively with China and the vast environmental implications of its billion-plus population and rapid rise to economic affluence. Little emphasis is placed on the one-child policy; if anything, it appears to be a new norm to which the Chinese, in cities anyway, have accommodated themselves. As one expects from productions of Boston's WGBH station, this program is intelligently written, thought-provoking, and consistently engaging. Suitable for middle schools and older.

World Population
Date: 2000
Length: 7 minutes
Price: $65
Source: The Video Project

The concept of this video is simple and stark: portray the history of world population with dots lighting up on a world map. Each dot represents a million people. At the starting date of A.D. 1 there are very few dots, clustered mainly in India and China. As the digital clock ticks away, the dots slowly multiply. The growth of population is almost imperceptible at first, but by the end it is visually dramatic, especially accompanied by the sound of a beating heart. Important epochs of world history, for example, India's Golden Age, the Mayan Empire, and the Crusades, are noted with icons in a lower corner of the frame. (A ten-page "activity guide" provides further details on these historical eras, as well as discussion questions.) At the end, when population trends have been extrapolated to the year 2030, a simple message is offered: the quality of our environment in the future will be determined by the decisions we make about both population and consumption. Suitable for ages 12 to adult.

World War III: The Population Explosion and Our Planet
Date: 1994
Length: 50 minutes
Price: $89 (purchase)
Source: The Video Project

Written, directed, and produced by Michael Tobias and based on a book of the same title, "World War III" is one of the most compelling videos on the issue of global population growth and its repercussions. It opens with some basic facts about the current rate of population increase and where the numbers are headed, then offers a selective country-by-country examination of the impact, especially on poverty and the natural environment, of current trends. Kenya, India, China, and the United States are the four countries featured. The interviews are skillfully conducted and consistently engaging. The film footage alternates between breathtaking and wrenching. (The most suitable audience would probably be college-level or adult.) Perhaps the greatest strength of the video is its avoidance of hackneyed ideas. It raises unusually interesting questions, such as: Will economic prosperity in China lead to reduced fertility or just the opposite? Why did the once-falling fertility rate in Kenya *stop* falling? And why does the government of that country, which officially supports family planning, not devote more resources to it? The answers are not simple—because the questions are so probing.

Contact Information for
Video Distributors and Vendors

Bullfrog Films
P.O. Box 149
Oley, PA 19547
(800) 543-3764
E-mail: info@bullfrogfilms.com
Website: www.bullfrogfilms.com

Filmakers Library
124 East 140th Street
New York, NY 10016
(212) 808-4980
Fax: 212-808-4983
E-mail: info@filmakers.com
Website: www.filmakers.com

Films for the Humanities and Sciences
P.O. Box 2053
Princeton, NJ 08543-2053
(800) 257-5126
Fax: 609-671-0266
E-mail: custserv@filmsmediagroup.com
Website: www.films.com

PBS Home Video
P.O. Box 279
Melbourne, FL 32902-0279
(800) 531-4727
Fax: 800-890-9043
Website: www.shoppbs.org

Population Communications International
777 United Nations Plaza—5th floor
44th Street at 1st Avenue
New York, NY 10017
(212) 687-3366
Fax: 212-661-4188
E-mail: info@population.org
Website: www.population.org

ShopWGBH.org
P.O. Box 2284
South Burlington, VT 05407
(888) 255-9231
Fax: 802-864-9846
E-mail: wgbh@ordering.com
Website: http://shop.wgbh.org

The Video Project
P.O. Box 411376
San Francisco, CA 94141-1376
(800) 475-2638
Fax: 415-241-2511
E-mail: video@videoproject.com
Website: http://www.videoproject.net

Glossary

age-specific rate   The rate of any type of demographic event (births, deaths, etc.) calculated for a particular age group; for example, the teen fertility rate is the rate of births to women aged 15–19.

Agricultural Revolution   The shift, first seen in the Middle East about 10,000 years ago, from a nomadic lifestyle to a more stable, settled way of life based on the cultivation of food crops, leading eventually to higher rates of population growth.

antinatalist policy   An effort or program to curb population growth by discouraging births.

baby boom   The extra-large generation of people born after World War II; in the United States within the baby boom years are generally considered to be 1946–1964.

balancing equation   A simple equation showing the change in population for a given year to be equal to the number of births and immigrants minus the number of deaths and emigrants; the population change can be either positive or negative.

birth control   Actions taken by a couple to reduce or eliminate the risk of conception from sexual intercourse.

birthrate   The number of births in a given year per 1,000 population (sometimes called the crude birthrate).

Cairo consensus   The acceptance by most parties interested in the population issue of the principle that the best way to lower population growth rates is through efforts to (1) equalize educational and other opportunities for girls and women as compared with men, and (2) make available safe, inexpensive family-planning services that allow for choice about family size. The consensus was reached at the United Nations population conference held at Cairo in 1994.

273

carrying capacity   The maximum population that could be sustained indefinitely, at a constant standard of living, in a given area.

census An official count of the population of a specified area (usually a nation), often including details on age, sex, income, and marital status.

childbearing years   The age span during which women may conceive and bear children; arbitrarily assumed, in the United States, to be 15 to 44.

cohort   A group within the population who share a common characteristic, usually year of birth; for example, the oldest baby boom cohort is the one born in 1946.

contraceptive prevalence   The proportion of women of childbearing age (or, sometimes, of couples) who are making use of contraception to space or limit births.

cornucopians   A term that refers to those who view population, even rapidly growing population, as a positive thing (opposite of neo-Malthusian).

death rate   The number of deaths in a given year per 1,000 population (sometimes called the crude death rate).

demographic transition   An influential notion that countries begin with high birth- and death rates, then make a transition, first in their death rates, then in their birthrates, to lower levels of both rates. Until birthrates decline and the transition is completed, population may grow very rapidly.

demography   The scientific study of population; often said to have started with Malthus.

dependency ratio   The ratio of people considered economically unproductive (under 15 and over 64) to those considered economically productive (ages 15 to 64); a rule-of-thumb concept with obvious arbitrary elements.

depopulation   Loss of population, typically from an excess of deaths over births; a prospect now faced (and feared) in a growing number of countries, especially in Europe and East Asia.

doubling time   The number of years it would take a population, growing at its current rate, to become twice as large. For example, it takes a population growing at 3 percent annually about twenty-four years to double. The analogous concept on the downside is "halving time," the number of years it would take for a country's population to be cut in half if it were experiencing a constant rate of depopulation.

emigration   An outflow of people from their native country, seeking permanent residence in a new country; one of the sources, along with death, of population decrease.

family planning   Deliberate efforts by couples to change (usually reduce) the number of births they will have or the spacing of those births.

famine   A situation of food deprivation leading to widespread hunger and starvation, with causes ranging from crop failure to political instability and military conflict.

fecundity   The physiological capacity of women (or couples, or men) to produce children.

fertility   Actual childbearing performance, as opposed to theoretical capability of bearing children; one of the basic demographic processes.

general fertility rate   The total number of births in a given year per 1,000 women of childbearing age.

Green Revolution   The development of high-yielding strains of wheat, rice, and other grains, beginning in the 1960s, which led to enormous increases in world food output.

HIV/AIDS   A deadly viral disease, spread mainly by sexual contact, occurring globally but with heaviest impact in sub-Saharan Africa. There life expectancies are falling sharply in the worst-affected countries due to rising AIDS-related death rates.

ICPD   The acronym for International Conference on Population and Development, the 1994 Cairo meeting, sponsored by the United Nations and attended by nearly 200 government delegations. The ICPD reaffirmed and clarified the international community's commitments regarding population and socioeconomic development.

immigration   The entry of foreign persons into a country with the aim of establishing permanent residence; one of the sources, along with births, of population increase.

infant mortality rate   The number of infants under 1 year old dying per 1,000 live births in a given year; a key indicator of socioeconomic well-being.

IPAT   An equation made famous by Paul Ehrlich that sees population (P) as one of the variables having a harmful impact (I) on the environment, the others being average level of affluence (A) or consumption, and technology (T); the actual equation is I = PAT.

life expectancy   The average number of years a population can expect to live beyond a given age (that age usually, but not necessarily, being zero or birth).

life span   The maximum age that humans can reach under optimal conditions.

life table   A tabular display of the probability of dying at any given age; from such a table, life expectancies can be computed.

Malthusian   Relating to the demographic or economic ideas of Thomas Malthus (1766–1834); generally taken to mean pessimistic about population trends; sometimes qualified by "neo-."

marriage rate   The number of marriages occurring in a given year per 1,000 people in a country.

maternal mortality rate The number of deaths among women either from pregnancy or childbirth complications per 100,000 live births in the year.

Mexico City policy The executive order issued by the Reagan administration in 1984 forbidding any U.S. aid to foreign nongovernmental agencies that performed, counseled on, or advocated for abortions, even in countries where abortion is legal. The policy was continued by George H.W. Bush, rescinded by Bill Clinton, and reinstated by George W. Bush.

migration   The movement of people across designated boundaries in search of permanent, new places of residence; one of the basic demographic processes.

mobility   Demographically speaking, the movement of people within or across borders.

morbidity   Illness or disease in a population; a contributor to mortality.

mortality   Deaths in a population; a key demographic process, along with births and migration.

neo-Malthusian   A policy or attitude favoring slower population growth through the use of various methods of birth control. (Ironically, Malthus himself opposed contraception on moral grounds.)

net migration rate   The difference between migration into and out of a country, expressed per 1,000 population. Currently, the United States has a net migration rate of about 2, meaning that it gains two persons per thousand, annually, when migration in both directions is taken into account.

nuptiality rate   The rate at which people get married; other things being equal, a higher nuptiality rate will mean faster population growth, and vice versa.

out-of-wedlock birth rate   The rate at which births are occurring to un-married women, usually expressed as live births per 1,000 women of childbearing age.

population bomb   The idea, popularized by Paul Ehrlich, that the world's population is growing at an explosive pace, with possibly cata-strophic consequences.

population implosion   A term that has been used to describe the ef-fects of declining fertility rates worldwide; a few, mainly European, na-tions are already seeing their populations begin to "implode," and many more will soon join them.

population momentum   The upward (or downward) pressure on pop-ulation resulting from a large (small) number of young people soon to enter their reproductive years; upward momentum can exist even if the TFR is below 2.1, and downward momentum can exist even if the TFR is above 2.1.

population policy   The set of explicit or implicit measures by which a government attempts to achieve certain population objectives (usually in terms of size or growth rate).

population projection   An estimation of the future size of a population based on assumptions about fertility, mortality, and migration; demog-raphers issue such projections periodically, but there are no guarantees they will prove correct.

population pyramid   A graph of the age and sex characteristics of a country's population, its shape giving clues to the future growth, stabil-ity, or decline of that population. A pyramidal shape, for example, indi-cates that there are few people in the upper age brackets and many in the lower (younger) brackets, suggesting that future population growth will be rapid.

prevalence rate   The number of people having a disease per 1,000 of population at risk; for example, the prevalence of AIDS in some African countries now exceeds 150 or 15 percent of the population.

pronatalist policy   An effort or program to increase population by en-couraging a high birthrate.

rate of natural increase   The rate at which a population increases solely due to the excess of births over deaths (thus ignoring migration); computed by subtracting the crude death rate from the crude birthrate.

replacement level fertility   The situation that exists when women are bearing just enough children to sustain the current population over the long run; in countries like the United States, this means a TFR of about 2.1.

sex ratio   The number of males per 100 females in the population.

total fertility rate (TFR)   An estimate of fertility based on the current age-specific birth rates of all women in a population; complicated to compute, it is basically the average number of children per woman.

United Nations Population Fund (UNFPA)   The main outreach arm of the United Nations in support of family-planning programs around the world; its initials derive from its original name (United Nations Fund for Population Activities).

vital statistics   Data relating to births, deaths, and sometimes marriage, divorce, and abortion.

zero population growth   A situation in which the births, deaths, and migration movements in and out of a country combine to keep its population constant from one year to the next.

Index

279

About the Author

Geoffrey Gilbert is professor of economics at Hobart and William Smith Colleges, Geneva, New York, where he teaches courses on population, poverty, and microeconomics. A former chairman of his department, Gilbert now holds an endowed chair at HWS. He is the author of *World Poverty: A Reference Handbook* (ABC-CLIO, 2004) and editor of the Oxford edition of Malthus's *Essay on Population*.